W9-BVU-478

MONEY BRAIN

How Your Subconscious Mind Can Hijack
Your Investment Decisions

**"Nothing may prove more disastrous
than pursuing a rational investment
policy in an irrational world."**

John Maynard Keynes, *economist*

Les Szarka, CFP®, ChFC®

@2013 Les Szarka, CFP®, ChFC®

Money Brain

How Your Subconscious Mind Can Hijack Your Investment Decisions

Published in the United States of America by
Magyar Publishing

First edition 2013

www.moneybrainbook.com

Set in Cambria text – used with permission from Microsoft.

Cover design by Alex Szarka
Image courtesy of Fotolia

ISBN: 9780615891262

Money Brain is available at a special quantity discount to use as premium gifts, sales promotions or for use in corporate training programs.

For information about having Les Szarka speak for your group, conference or event, special discounts for bulk purchases and customized copies for financial advisors, please contact:

Szarka Financial at 800-859-8095

DEDICATION

This book is dedicated to my son Matthew, who had one of the most inquisitive and insatiably curious minds I have ever known. May his new journeys take him to places even he couldn't imagine.

And to complete the circle of life, it is also dedicated to my two incredible grandsons, Gabriel and Emeric. I just hope the financial world comes to its senses before it's too late for them.

And last but not least, to my wonderful wife, whose patience over the past few years allowed me to pursue my passion of writing this book. Thanks honey, I owe you big time!

CONTENTS

PREFACE

In late 2007, as I celebrated my 25th year as a financial advisor, I had much for which to be thankful; a wonderful family, good health, and a gratifying career. I have had the good fortune to be able to spend my days doing precisely what I love and feel born to do. I have had the privilege of knowing and advising some wonderful people, salt-of-the-earth, Midwestern folks, the very exemplars of the hard-working American dream. Having been born and raised in Ohio, these are the people I can most easily relate to.

I am also blessed that I get to work with some of the brightest and most genuinely caring people I know. People who don't just understand the *how to*, but more importantly the *why*. It is an eclectic group of personalities that mesh together like a great musical band. I have repeatedly said that we could develop a TV sitcom of our office and never run out of material. Even on the most difficult days, we always seem to be able to have a good laugh. And even with all the typical trials and tribulations life likes to throw in our way, I was truly blessed. Life was good.

At that time, we couldn't even begin to imagine how our lives would be forever changed in the blink of an eye.

When the first signs of that catastrophic financial storm began to hit in 2007, most felt that it would likely be your typical recession and stock market correction—unpleasant, but manageable. Few accurately predicted the actual category 5+ hurricane that ended up decimating the world economies.

The first tremors of this frightening financial upheaval appeared in 2007, and by the spring of 2008 the global stock markets began acting erratically, unnerving even the most sophisticated veteran investors and market observers. That whole summer was full of fear driven, stomach-churning volatility. But that was merely the warm-up act; the worst was still to come.

By September of 2008, the markets were in free fall, venerable banks that had outlasted the Great Depression lay in ruin, and the governments of several major countries, including the U.S., moved to nationalize key parts of the financial sector, a previously unthinkable idea. Many knowledgeable experts insist to this day that the global economy was only days from a potentially disastrous meltdown—a financial "China Syndrome." On the other hand, many feel that the government's actions where nothing more than a massive bailout of the big New York banks and Wall Street, the very institutions that created the crisis, with little left over for those who suffered the consequences.

I vividly recall talking with people who were in outright panic, folks whose lives had been turned upside down by those churning waves. Watching the news only fed the panic, as they listened to government officials declaring that if Congress didn't immediately pass the bank bailout bill the entire world economy could go over the cliff. Day by day, it appeared that some of the biggest names on Wall Street were on the brink of bankruptcy. They were watching their life savings dwindle before their eyes, and it appeared to them that no one had a clue how to stop the bleeding. For most, this was the worst financial nightmare they had seen in their lifetimes. The world had turned completely irrational and no one knew what to do or who to believe.

But before I continue, first let me back up a few more years, to the middle of that same decade. My daughter was studying psychology at Otterbein College. As we had the opportunity to discuss her courses, I became increasingly curious about her chosen field of study. Until that time, I hadn't really given much thought to how the mind worked. Like most, I took the incredible power of our minds for granted. But I began to get very interested in the science behind how the brain processes information, especially how our behavior—with all its emotional baggage—influences our daily decisions, and especially about how it affects our finances.

As I read through her textbooks, the more I learned about the intersection of human behavior and finance, the more curious I became with the topic. It was like opening a door into a whole new world. This led me to read more and more books on this fascinating subject. My intense curiosity eventually led me to methodically research the fields known as Behavioral Finance and Neuro-economics. The more I researched the subject, the more I became aware of why the financial world can behave so irrationally at times.

In 2008, with the world economy seemingly spinning out of control and people desperately searching for answers about what they should do to preserve their hard-earned life's savings, the clashing subjects of emotions and finance took on a more urgent meaning.

For a time, I found myself researching almost uncontrollably, trying to find the reasons behind all the irrational behavior we were all witnessing in the financial markets. It was a world where all the normal rules didn't seem to apply. As I dug deeper into the subjects of psychology and behavioral finance, learning about heuristics, cognitive bias and the many other ways the human brain processes information about financial matters, things finally started to become clearer. After extensively researching the field, and learning how people's mental perspectives affect their views on money, investing and financial security, I had the first of my several *ah-ha* moments. It was as if someone had wiped the Vaseline from my glasses, and things started to appear clearer. The clarity wasn't necessarily in the form of making sense of the events, but rather why the world we were witnessing could behave so irrationally.

As I gradually incorporated the principals of behavioral finance into my work, a major disconnect started to emerge for me—for decades, I had worked in a profession that was seemingly dominated by logic and reason. Money and finance, or so I had always thought, followed straightforward and logical rules. They were supposed to conform to a set of principles that were consistent and relatively easy to understand. The fundamentals of the stock market, after all, are incredibly simple, despite the veneer of complication that many people like to surround it with. Simply put, if the economic and financial outlook is favorable, and there are more buyers than sellers at any particular time, stock prices should go up. If the outlook turns more negative, and sellers outnumber buyers, prices go down. Even a child can understand that.

As the events of late 2008 and early 2009 unfolded, that seemingly clean, logical, linear world began to implode, crashing in on itself. We were witnessing the pillars of that formerly orderly and logical world, led by the large Wall Street banks and the Federal Reserve, begin showing some disturbing actions. These institutions seemed to be grasping for answers to problems that seemed unimaginable at the time. Public confidence in these pillars was deteriorating by the day. Surveying this ever increasing financial carnage, I kept asking myself, "How can seemingly rational people, some of the brightest icons of the financial and industrial communities, do such irrational things?"

The book you're now holding in your hands represents my effort to answer that question. It's the culmination of years of careful research, combined with over 30 years of first-hand observations of the financial markets, and of dealing personally with investors, and at times their irrational behavior.

While I don't have formal training in psychology, there are times I feel that my role is more like that of a *financial psychologist*. My role tends to be much more than just advising people on their investments and financial issues. It has also become challenging trying to educate people on how not to become victims of their own mind's powerful subconscious forces. We can be our own worst enemy, because at times it seems that our brains may be hard-wired to make foolish and potentially devastating financial decisions.

For those familiar with the movie and hit TV series the "Odd Couple", this may prove to be a useful metaphor. As you may recall, the two main characters **"Felix"** and **"Oscar"** where two men with diametrically different personality types, who because of circumstances ended up having to share a single apartment. Felix was the calm, logical, tidy and precise character. Oscar, on the other hand, was the messy, loud, impulsive and emotional one that Felix had to try and keep in line at times. Observing the ongoing conflict between these two very different characters' trying to live in the same apartment made for good entertainment.

The same could be said about the daily conflict occurring in our own minds (without the entertainment aspect). And where once I might have thought of the financial world as akin to the logical Felix, I have come to realize that many times it behaves much more like the emotional Oscar.

Our financial decision-making process is like a dance between two parts of our brains: the more advanced, conscious, logical and analytical side (Felix), and its roommate, the more primitive, subconscious, impulsive, and emotional side (Oscar). For me, Felix and Oscar is a useful metaphor for the perpetually clashing perspectives that play out every day in our minds, and how it impacts the investment world, as well as the overall economy. When you have two diametrically opposing personalities trying to cohabitate under one roof, you are bound to have occasional fireworks.

As you begin to better understand human behavior, it is truly an enlightening experience. You start looking at the world, the people around you, and even your own decisions, in a very different light. Some researchers estimate that 90% of the daily decisions made by the average person are being made when their mind is in a *normal* operating status—meaning Oscar and Felix are cooperating with each other. The other 10% of the time may be more heavily influenced by the more impulsive and emotional Oscar. One could argue that we could break it down even further, and say that maybe 1% of those decisions are vital, ones that could potentially carry more serious longer-term benefits or consequences.

To a large extent, it's how we perform during that 10% of the time (especially that 1%), that can be the difference between our success and failure. Are we making those decisions in a cool and logical frame of mind or are we acting out of impulse and emotions? It's during those times that we may be more heavily influenced by our subconscious mind (Oscar's domain) because of stress or some other emotion. Therefore it would stand to reason that if we want to make better financial decisions, we should spend more time and effort to increase our mind's effectiveness during those vulnerable times.

Each of us has created our own elaborate *operating system* in our subconscious minds, to cope with the overwhelming number of decisions we have to make at any given time. Most of the decisions we make are very trivial. Take a drink of coffee (I need caffeine). Wear that shirt (I like blue). Quick, swerve the car (something's moving in the bushes). Call the broker to sell your stocks (I'm scared).

If you were to think back to many of the decisions you made today, you would be hard-pressed to come up with a reason as to why. As a matter of fact, we may not even remember making most of them. They were just instinctive, with very little conscious effort.

As a coping mechanism, each of our minds has set up its own elaborate *system of short cuts* that are based on our own past experiences, information we have learned, observations we have made, and our perception of these things. In addition, much of your system has also been influenced by *external* forces, such as advertisers, the media, and very effective public relation efforts. Just as our subconscious influences our decisions and behavior, those external forces exert influence our subconscious mind.

In this book we will explore the following assertions:

- No one is immune from the mind's powerful behavioral influences and subconscious bias.
- Don't be overly confident in your views, especially if they are based on complex forecasts.
- You probably don't know nearly as much as you think about a given situation.
- Gathering large amounts of information is not always helpful in making decisions.
- What you recall as a memory, may have actually occurred quite differently.
- Don't accept information at face value. Be aware of how and by whom it was presented.

- Humans love to forecast things. But, we're not very good at it.

- Investors should actively seek out opinions and views that they don't necessarily agree with.

- We should make decisions based on the most likely outcome, and not on initial reaction.

- Investors tend to find safety in a herd, even if they may feel it is wrong. Safety in numbers.

- The past outcome of a situation does not necessarily mean that it will repeat this time.

- We have a tendency to favor things that are simple to understand, or seem familiar to us.

- Investing is a long-term proposition. Short-term trading is more akin to gambling.

- Investors should focus on the facts, and not necessarily on someone else's conclusions.

I don't pretend to have mastered this fascinating and complicated subject. Like the experts in this field, my understanding of these issues remains a continuing learning process. My hope is that this book will advance your own understanding of how you approach money issues, including on subconscious levels you may not have ever glimpsed before. If it helps you to better grow and preserve your own wealth, I'll have achieved my goals for writing this book.

Les Szarka, CFP®, ChFC®

SECTION I

CHAPTER ONE

Some Unwelcome Surprises On The Road To Retirement Paradise

> *"I know enough of the world now to have almost lost the capacity of being much surprised by anything."*
>
> Charles Dickens, *author*

Before we get started, I would like to introduce you to two wonderful people, a couple whose personal financial saga over the last several years touches on some broader themes.[*]

Frank and Jane are both 72 years old. They have three grown children and six wonderful grandchildren. After serving his time in the military, Frank worked as an electrical engineer for 40 years at a Fortune 500 company. Jane was a stay-at-home mom when the kids were younger, and went back to work part-time in a dentist's office when the kids were all in school.

---

[*] Hypothetical examples are not intended to be indicative of any specific investment. Hypothetical results are for illustrative purposes only and are not intended to represent the past or future performance of any specific investment.

Most of the money she made went to help the three kids pay for college.

After 40 years of working hard and saving diligently, Frank decided to call it quits and retire. Frank and Jane wanted to have more time to travel and visit the kids, who were now spread all over the country. Frank was also looking forward to having more time to devote to his passion, fly fishing. Over the past 20 years Frank had become something of an expert in the field, and taught several classes throughout the year.

As retirement grew closer, Frank spent a considerable amount of time preparing for his "golden years." Their house was now completely paid for and they had no other debts. He took several classes at the local college on investing, and bought a software package to determine how much income they could expect to live on. Based on his thorough analysis, he and Jane should not have any problem retiring with enough money to live very comfortably for the rest of their lives. They should still have enough left over to make sure the kids and grandkids would inherit something to give them a financial jump start as well.

The year was now 2000, and Frank and Jane were eager to welcome in the new century as retirees. All those years planning for their "golden years" was finally going to pay off. They were truly living the American dream!

Having benefited from the huge stock market gains in the mid-to-late 1990's, Frank, using some popular investment allocation models, decided to take the $750,000 in his IRA, and invest 75% of it into several highly rated stock mutual funds, half of which were heavily invested in high-performing tech companies. Following the advice of the software programs, he reluctantly put the remaining 25% into bond funds, hoping that the bonds would not be too big of a drag on his investments' performance.

He then used his retirement-income software calculator to determine how much he could safely pull out of his investments each year, without jeopardizing his retirement income. Based on one of the widely used income optimization programs, he figured that with the allocation he selected, if he limited his withdrawals to 4% of the portfolio per year, he would have less than a 5% probability of outliving his income. He thought those are pretty good odds. Armed with this information, he set up a regular distribution of $2,500 a month from his IRA to supplement their Social Security income. He figured that this should provide them more than enough income for a comfortable retirement.

Based on Modern Portfolio Theory and the vast majority of sophisticated retirement-planning software programs, Frank and his wife should have been set for life. Unfortunately, a very unlikely thing happened on the way to their retirement paradise.

The Storm Begins

It all started with the tech bubble bursting in early 2000. Just when it looked like things were starting to get better, we had the terrorist attacks on September 11, 2001. Stock markets reeled. All along the way down, Frank kept trying to keep Jane calm by reminding her (and himself!), that it is normal for the stock market to experience an occasional severe pull back. But even this cool and calculating engineer was starting to show signs of panic.

By March of 2003, the U.S. stock market had plunged nearly 50%! The last time the market dropped that much was 27 years earlier, in 1973. Frank barely even remembered it since he was in his early thirties then, and didn't own any stocks at that point in his life.

So when Frank opened his IRA statement in March of 2003, and saw that his $750,000 IRA was now worth barely over $400,000, he slumped over and began to cry. Other than the tears of joy shed at his daughter's wedding, this tough, old, former Marine couldn't even remember the last time he had cried. He wasn't sure how he was going to be able to tell his bride of 40 years that he had lost almost half of their life savings.

After sitting down with his calculator, he figured that up to that point they had withdrawn about $97,500 in monthly distributions, and the market had taken away the rest. After beating himself up most of the day, Frank sat down with Jane later that evening and told her the bad news. Jane was almost in shock, and this time they both had a good cry.

During the day Frank had come up with a plan to try to salvage what they had left of their retirement dreams. To be able to sleep at night for the time being, he took the majority of the remaining portion of his portfolio that was in stocks, and moved them into his bond funds, which had performed fairly well during the crash. That 25% that he put into bonds so begrudgingly ultimately turned out to be a major blessing. Diversification * had worked.

He went back to his retirement software. Based on the recommended 4% maximum withdrawal rate, he calculated that they could now only withdraw approximately half of what they were currently taking out. So somehow they would have to cut approximately $1,200 from their monthly budget.

But Frank and his wife were troopers, and they had been through tough times before. They tightened their belts and somehow made do with their newly reduced income. Still, having to watch how they spent every single dollar took some getting used to. This was not how they had envisioned their golden years.

Over the next four years things steadily improved. The economy seemed to be doing better, and the stock market was recovering much of its earlier losses. Frank was feeling a little disappointed though, since most of his portfolio was still in bonds. He felt he had missed most of the recovery. He had, however, slowly moved about 35% of his portfolio back into stocks, but this time he stuck with large blue chip companies. His IRA was now worth about $475,000, and he was able to increase his monthly withdrawals by an additional $300 a month, which came as a welcome relief to Jane.

By late 2006, Frank was getting antsy. The economy and the stock market were in full bloom, and he had missed most of the

---

* Diversification does not guarantee a profit or protect against a loss in a declining market. It is a method used to help manage investment risk.

recovery. If only he would not have sold his stocks at the bottom, he would have been so much further ahead by now. He couldn't decide which was dumber—putting as much as he did in stocks in the first place, or selling them at the bottom!

So he started doing more research. As he did so, he came to a couple of conclusions. First, since the stock market had just recently dropped 50%, it was nearly impossible for that to happen again in his lifetime. Prior to 2000, drops of that magnitude had only occurred every 25 to 30 years.

Secondly, he felt his initial mistake was not diversifying his investments enough. While he did split them between stocks and bonds, he learned he left out some key asset classes. His research indicated that to properly diversify his IRA, he would also have to add exposure to international stocks, some corporate bonds and an asset class he had never really even considered before—real estate. His research revealed that real estate in the past few years had actually done much better than even stocks. How could he have missed that!

So after dozens of hours of research, armed with this new information, he set out to make up for lost time. But this time, he would do it the right way! His new portfolio was now completely diversified. It had all the critical elements. It had U.S. stocks, international stocks, U.S. government bonds, corporate bonds, high-yield bonds, and a healthy portion in real estate.

For the next year it had appeared that Frank had finally figured it all out. His new portfolio was behaving exactly as he had hoped. The IRA was up to nearly $550,000, and he was able to increase his monthly distributions by another $300. It was still $600 less than it had been at the beginning, but at this rate he should be able to exceed that easily within a few years. It appeared that things were finally starting to get back on track.

Then in the fall of 2007, things started to take a turn for the worse again. But the more Frank researched, the more he became convinced that with their newly diversified portfolio, they should be able to weather this temporary storm much better. Sadly, Frank's son became an early victim of the recession. He lost his job, and later almost lost his house. With his son needing to support a wife and two children, and having exhausted all their family savings, Frank and Jane decided to help them out with their mortgage until they got back on their feet.

By September of 2008 the global economy was in a free fall, with no end in sight. This time Frank was determined not to make the same mistake by selling his stocks at the bottom. Besides, this time he had all those other asset classes to help him minimize the drop in his portfolio.

By March of 2009, the stock market had plunged 50% again! But this time it was even worse. Unlike in 2000, the global meltdown led to panic selling of literally everything. Investors were selling even *safer* assets, just trying to raise enough cash to weather the storm.

At the end, when the dust settled, pretty much everything was left in shambles. Virtually nothing was spared—not corporate bonds, not high-yield bonds, not international stocks. And, of course, the hardest-hit was real estate. The only exception was the 10% of his portfolio that Frank had put into U.S. Treasuries. It was the only investment that investors felt safe with as the world economies moved ever closer to the cliff. This time, not even diversification would help.

By March of 2009, Frank's IRA was down to approximately $325,000. "How could this have happened AGAIN? It wasn't supposed to be this way. The experts said this couldn't happen again so soon. How could I have been so stupid?" He thought... "How am I ever going to tell Jane...will my son be able to keep his house...?"

The Limits of Playing By the Rules

Frank and Jane played by the rules all their lives. They worked hard, paid their taxes, raised their kids, paid their bills on time, never spent more than they could afford, and diligently saved for their retirement. After they retired, they diversified their portfolio, and didn't withdraw any more money than was commonly recommended by experts. They did everything they were told to do to ensure a wonderful retirement.

And this is how were they rewarded for playing by the rules and for their hard work?

Frank and Jane may be a fictional couple, but they are an accurate composite of real people whose retirement dreams were shattered by the 2008 financial crisis. This tragic scenario is still being lived out by MILLIONS of hard-working people all across America. And it's not merely limited to retirees, but also extends to younger families, like Frank and Jane's son, who have seen their lives turn into nightmares.

These are people who worked hard, saved their money, didn't run up excessive credit card balances, and played by the rules. Yet millions lost their jobs, lost their homes, and had their plans for retirement shattered. They saw their kids' college dreams get wiped out, and in many cases the financial pressures even led to divorce. All of us can probably think of several family members and people close to us who have been affected by this economic calamity.

This is the source of my anger and outrage. It didn't necessarily have to be this way.

How could this have happened? How could so many seemingly intelligent people, who are supposed to be experts in their field, be so wrong? The simple answer is greed, fear and human behavior.

Allan Greenspan (also known as the Maestro), who was the Federal Reserve chairman at the outset of this financial meltdown, made the following statement to financial reporter David Favre in 2009 on CNBC's documentary special, "House of Cards":

"I have a fairly heavy background in mathematics, but some of the complexities of some of the instruments that are going into CDO's (collateral debt obligations) bewilder me. I don't understand what they are doing. And I figured that if I didn't understand them, and I have access to a few hundred PhD's, how the rest of the world was going to understand them bewilders me. Even if they would have read the fine print, it wouldn't have mattered, since they wouldn't have understood it anyway."

He later went on to say that he and the Federal Reserve just didn't see this debt crisis coming.

Bear in mind, this is the chairman of the Federal Reserve Bank, who has access to every bit of banking and financial information in the entire country in real time, and hundreds of experts at his beck and call to analyze all this information. And even though there were several prominent people and institutions, including the Bank of International Settlements (BIS)[1], that had warned of the impending mortgage crisis—the Federal Reserve Bank didn't see it coming. Either this man was woefully unqualified to be in his position, or more likely, he was not being completely truthful with the American people.

The more complex answer is that to a certain extent, we have also been played like a violin by concert *maestros*. I am in no way placing the complete blame for the financial meltdown on Alan Greenspan and the Federal Reserve. Quite the contrary. While its easy money policy certainly played a significant role; there are many villains in this Greek tragedy that we will examine in this book, including Wall Street greed, political cronyism, unscrupulous bankers and mortgage brokers, real estate developers and salespeople, and inept rating services. But at the end of the day, let's not completely exonerate one of the main players in this tragedy— consumers.

Whether they were driven by greed, naivety or gullibility, without someone to buy those houses they really couldn't afford, and mortgages that in the end they couldn't pay, this mess couldn't have happened. As painful as it may be for some to admit, ultimately personal responsibility has its place in this mess as well. If there ever was a *perfect storm*, this was it. The question is, could it have been avoided, and more importantly, how do we avoid future meltdowns? I have observed many economic, financial and investment market conditions over the past 30 years, but more importantly, I have been able to observe firsthand how people reacted to them, especially in times of extreme fear, greed and anger.

As I mentioned earlier, I became a student of behavioral finance almost by accident. But the more I continue to research this field, the more I become convinced that for individuals to avoid becoming the victims of any likely future financial meltdowns, they will need to pay attention not only to their own financial decisions, but also to how OTHERS may react to a financial crisis.

Years ago, when I first thought of writing a book, I never imagined it would be this one. I always thought it would be a more uplifting *how-to* book, on the subject of how to plan for a fulfilling and financially successful life.

As the financial world changed, I instead felt compelled to write this book. The purpose of this book is to serve as your financial wake-up call. It's not a "go-build-a-bunker-and-buy-a-gun-and-some-bullets-because-the-world-is-ending" book. There are many of those out there, and while I may agree with much of their analysis and observations, I respectfully have to disagree with their extreme Armageddon conclusions.

The near-term looks very challenging to say the least. We are likely in a period of *new normal* that may last well into the foreseeable future. This *new normal* is not really new though; it's just not anything we've seen in quite a while. Periods of excessive government spending and enormous debts have been with us since the very beginning of money. Many empires and countries have gone through this boom/bust cycle. The United States has gone through it several times in its history, the most notable being the Great Depression. As seen throughout history, many will be negatively impacted, and some even devastated by this continuing financial storm. Those wise enough to recognize the warning signs, and act accordingly, will be able to ride it out with minimal damage.

One of the techniques governments use when faced with a debt crisis is called "financial repression." It is a set of government policies designed to keep interest rates low to help the government get out of debt. This technique calls for desperate measures, including:

- Keeping interest rates extremely low—the goal is to achieve a negative *real* interest rate. This means that the interest rate on *safe* investments is lower than the inflation rate, thereby producing a "negative real rate of return" for savers.

- Putting pressure on financial institutions and other entities over which the government has leverage to buy the low-yielding government bonds. These institutions may include banks, insurance companies and pension funds.

- Igniting inflation. Rising inflation allows the government to pay back its debt with cheaper dollars. It also allows for maintaining a "negative real rate of return" if interest rates were to rise.

Periods of financial repression tend to last for many years, frequently a decade or more. The consequences of this policy are typically borne by savers and retires, who will receive minimal interest on their investments while inflation eats away at their standard of living.

Eventually we will work our way through this financial mess. The American spirit and ingenuity have pulled us out before, but at times we can be our own worst enemy. As Winston Churchill once said, "America always makes the right decision—after it has exhausted all other options."

This book was written to not only explore what happened, but more importantly to examine why it may have happened, and most importantly of all, to address how to possibly recognize the danger signs in the future. It is based on the extensive research I have done over the past seven years, interpreted through the lens of thirty plus years of accumulated observations in the financial profession. I felt compelled to share my observations and conclusions with as many people as possible, in hopes that it may help them avoid future personal financial disasters, and that one day you will be one of those people who look back at this and say, "yes those were tough times, but thankfully we got through them". Consider this your own financial wake up call.

Chapter Footnotes

[1] – The Bank of International Settlements (BIS) is the "central bank of the world's central banks". They warned of a mortgage problem in their June 2007 Quarterly Review Report – "International Banking and Financial Market Developments"

CHAPTER TWO

Taking Control Of Your Mind

> *"If you do not conquer self,*
> *you will be conquered by self."*
>
> Napoleon Hill, *American author*

Buy low, sell high, and you'll make money with your investments. Don't take more risk than you can afford to lose. Spend less than you make, and save some money for a rainy day. We all know the rules. They are not that complicated.

Yet, at times, most investors insist on doing exactly the opposite. They may get sucked in and buy when the market is high, and bail out at the bottom right before it starts to rebound. The majority of investors can't seem to follow these simple rules. And this includes many professional money managers, whose job it is to oversee the vast sums that are in mutual funds, pensions and endowments.

It's similar to the dynamics that are at work with dieting. We all know the rules: Eat less and exercise a little each day, and you'll lose weight and be healthier. It's not even that hard to do. But do most of us do that? Of course not.

My first grade teacher, Mrs. Brandt, had more success getting her class of 25, six-year-olds to follow her rules while on a field trip. So why would seemingly intelligent adults have a harder time following simple financial and investing rules than six-year-olds?

It's All in Our Brains

Much of the answer lies in a modest three-pound piece of gray matter that sits inside our skulls. I'm not talking about intelligence or IQ. Instead, I'm focusing on the brain's hard wiring, the result of eons of human evolution, which have had the result of channeling our emotions in ways we may not even be aware of.

Why do so many otherwise smart people make such horrible decisions with their investments and general finances? For most people, investing is a necessary evil. They don't particularly enjoy doing it. They get frustrated, and at times they get downright scared. They get angry at how the rules always seem to be changing in the middle of the game. But at the end of the day, most people realize that they have to do it to meet their financial goals. There is no *opt-out* box they can simply check.

Some approach investing as if it's a chess match, hoping they can outmaneuver the markets. Others view it as a Las Vegas-like experience, where investing is simply the result of blind luck. The pessimists, meanwhile, may see it simply as a form of Russian roulette, "sooner or later I'm going to get the bullet!"

Many people view investing as a blood sport, like contests waged by the Gladiators of Rome, where there were only winners and losers. What they need to consider is that there were many other jobs in the Coliseum besides being a gladiator. Those other jobs didn't have the same glamour or rewards, but neither did they carry the same level of risk. And when it comes to investing, you don't have to work in the Coliseum as a gladiator. You can occasionally choose to get out of the ring and simply be a spectator.

None of this should suggest that investing isn't often frustrating. It is. You make some nice gains for a few years, only to give it back in an afternoon. The key is to know when to get in and when to get out. As investing guru Warren Buffet says, "Investing is simple, but not easy!"

All too often, investors find themselves plagued by indecisiveness because of a lack of experience or not having enough time to devote to sifting through the thousands of bits of information required to make an informed decision. So instead, they turn to magazines and talking heads on television. The problem is that for every screaming pundit like Jim Cramer who may be saying "buy, baby, buy" there is another one warning you to sell all your stocks and buy gold before the financial world implodes.

This information overload makes for a very fertile environment for our emotions and biases to take control. Unfortunately, when you allow your emotions (especially fear and greed) to drive your financial decisions, it often can lead to disastrous outcomes.

Our problem is hardly a lack of financial information. To the contrary, most of us have access to way too much information. What we need is a huge filter in which we can dump all this information, so that all we have left are a few actionable nuggets with which to guide our investment decision-making. But of course, this is much easier said than done. The emotions we have to fight through to get there are very powerful.

Traditional economic and investment theories base their assumptions on a "rational investor"—that is, someone who is driven by logic and the instinct to maximize their own gains. Behavioral finance, on the other hand examines the emotional factors that guide investors in their financial decisions. Experience has shown that the cold, calculating rational investor mostly exists only in the theoretical realm, not necessarily in the real world of investing. Investment decisions are often driven by neurological and emotional elements. They include fear, greed, the thrill-seeking instinct, the desire to conform to others, and a host of human instincts. As a result, we have to accept that there are both *rational* and *emotional* investors. And we can be either one depending on the circumstances.

Animal Spirits

Noted economist John Maynard Keynes (of Keynesian economics fame) coined the phrase "Animal Spirits" in 1936, in an attempt to describe the possible psychological and behavioral forces acting on the economy. His theory tried to explain why the economy doesn't always behave in a logical, predictable manner. In classical economics, people are expected to act and react in a rational and non-emotional manner. It assumes that after examining all the facts, people will act in their own logical best interest.

What history has taught us though is that the economy at times seems to march to a drum beat all its own. Sometimes the economy simply seems to get ahead of itself, apparently encouraged by an optimistic public, who choose to ignore obvious warning signs. At other times the economy seems to be stuck in the mud, again influenced by that very same public, but this time feeling that the end of the financial world is just around the corner.

It was this human effect, at times emotionally driven, that led Keynes to suspect animal spirits may influence the economy. Sometimes these animal spirits may be a minor influence, while other times they can be the driving force.

The premise behind animal spirits can be summed up as follows: if people generally feel good, and are optimistic about their futures, they are more likely to increase their consumer spending. This increased consumer spending tends to lead to economic growth and higher business profits, which in turn can lead to higher stock prices. This economic growth may encourage businesses to be more optimistic and confident to further expand and invest in their business, and to hire new employees.

Overall business expansion may lead to lower unemployment and higher wages for workers, which may further increase consumer confidence and spending, which could further feed the positive animal spirits. It tends to create what is called a "positive reinforcement loop." Good news leading to more good news.

Economic growth and optimism may also have a positive effect on investments. As the economy expands, people have more money to save and invest. As confidence in the economy continues to grow, people may be more willing to invest in more aggressive investments like stocks, small businesses and real estate. As more money flows into these investments, the prices tend to go even higher, further feeding the confidence. The one thing that every strong investment environment needs is optimism. Rarely do people invest or take risks when they are pessimistic or afraid. As we'll discuss later in this book, there is a risk of this "infectious optimism" getting out of hand in every economic expansion, and in extreme cases, it can lead to an "investment bubble."

At this point, it would probably be helpful to differentiate between my discussion of investments and that of the economy in general. While the economy can certainly be prone to overheating and growing too fast, it does have some built in "speed bumps" that investments in general do not.

For the economy to keep growing at a brisk pace new businesses have to be created and/or existing ones must expand. In most situations, business creations and expansions are held in check by the need to build additional production facilities, open new retail spaces or hire new workers. Additionally, there may be government compliance requirements that need to be met, such as licensing,

2030. The dates typically refer to the date when an investor may possibly need the money, such as for retirement. (*.)

The basic strategy would be to pick an account that would most closely match a person's specific investment goals, such as "I would like to retire sometime near the year 2025." The investment manager would then allocate the assets in the portfolio based on that time horizon. Typically, the closer the date that the money may be needed, the more conservative the allocation should be. The more distant the date, the more aggressive it could be.

Over the past 10 to 15 years, many 401(k) plans have added these types of options to assist their employees who do not wish to, or are uncomfortable allocating their own accounts. In many 401(k) plans, the majority of assets are in one of those types of accounts. As a matter of fact, in many plans they are the *default* option to which employees are assigned when they do not pick a specific option on their own. For many years, the arrangement seemed to work as planned. Then things changed.

The shock for many people came in 2008, when numerous of these asset allocation accounts did not perform as investors had hoped, and asset value dropped much more than they had anticipated. The S & P 500 Index was down approximately 37% that year. A review of three of the largest providers of these types of accounts shows that on average, the three were down as follows:[1]

Target date 2030: - 37%

Target date 2020: - 31%

Target date 2010: - 25%

([1] – Fidelity "Freedom Funds", Vanguard "Target Retirement" and Principal "LifeTime")

*Indices are unmanaged and investors cannot invest directly in an index. The Standard & Poor's 500 (S&P 500) is an unmanaged group of securities considered to be representative of the stock market in general. It is a market value weighted index with each stock's weight in the index proportionate to its market value.

In fairness, 2008 was an extraordinarily horrible year, when most asset classes (with the exception of U.S. Treasuries) decreased in value. It didn't much matter where you had your money, it probably went down. But the burning question still remained in the minds of many investors: Why did my account go down SO much? Why didn't the age old theory of asset diversification help cushion the drop this time?

To help answer that question you have to dig a bit deeper into the theory itself, and it's underlying basis. The next section will discuss the predominant theory of asset allocation, what it is based on, how it became so widely accepted, and it's potentially inherent flaws.

A (Mercifully) Short History of Modern Portfolio Theory

The father of Modern Portfolio Theory (MPT) is a man named Harry Markowitz. He introduced his theory in 1952, which subsequently provided the basis upon which most current investment portfolios are constructed. He originally simply called it "Portfolio Theory", since he didn't think there was anything modern about it. At its core it is rooted in the belief that all investors are *rational* and that they have access to all the information they need to make an intelligent investment decision. The theory was designed to maximize an investor's return based on the amount of risk an investor was willing to take. His theory proposed that by properly diversifying a portfolio with assets that had a low correlation to each other, an investor could expect a higher portfolio return without taking on additional risk. Investments that have a low correlation to each other simply mean that they don't tend to move in the same direction. So when one is going down, hopefully the other one is going up to offset it.

Then, 38 years later, in 1990, Markowitz again reshaped the investment world when he shared the Nobel Prize in Economics with Merton Miller and William Sharpe for their work that has become arguably the most widely used theory for investment portfolio selection. Markowitz's theory of diversification requires one to believe that most investors will act in a *rational* manner, and base their investment decisions on the best available current data and facts, unimpeded by their emotions.

Ignoring the impact of human behavior can take its toll on your investment results. As Ronald Reagan once quipped, "Economists are people who look at reality, and wonder whether it would work in theory."

Irrational Markets

The problem with Modern Portfolio Theory is this: even the average person can regularly observe utterly irrational behavior at work in the global investment markets. Stock market bubbles are a good example of this irrational behavior. In an investment bubble, millions of investors continue to buy an investment, even though they may feel that it may already be significantly overvalued. This behavior, by the way, is certainly not limited to stocks. It can apply to any commodity or other items that are bought, sold or traded.

You may have already heard of the "tulip mania" that occurred in the Netherlands in the 17th century. It is often referred to when discussing the origins of investment bubbles. During that time, tulip bulbs became increasingly popular and their prices increased dramatically over a few short years. The value of these bulbs was determined by the ultimate color of tulips. People went to great lengths to cross-breed various types to come up with even more exotic colors. It became a huge and profitable business.

Unfortunately, you couldn't determine the tulip's ultimate color simply by examining the bulb. So you were betting that the bulb would bloom into one of the rare colors cherished by everyone else, thus making it more valuable. If it did, you made a lot of money, if not, you lost money. As tulip mania spread, the colors that were deemed valuable would change depending on their rarity. Incredibly, the price of the bulbs eventually increased to the point where people were speculating their houses and entire life savings on buying tulip bulbs. So much for the rational investor!

In hindsight, it seems absurd to bet your life savings on something as silly as tulip bulbs. You would think that only someone very gullible or naïve would become enticed to invest in such an absurd venture. However, it is reported that some of the most sophisticated bankers, merchants and even royalty got caught up in this mania. Some very wealthy merchants and nobility were completely wiped out. And before we get too smug and simply dismiss that anything this ludicrous could happen in modern times, let me remind you of our own more recent tulip mania—the tech bubble! This was yet another example of smart money chasing some dumb ideas.

A Brief Historical Perspective of the U.S. Stock Market

Modern Portfolio Theory has been the guiding light of asset allocation for well over 30 years. Of course it didn't hurt that during that time the S&P 500 went from approximately 100 points to 1550, an astounding 1,400% increase in 20 years, averaging gains of more than 16% per year (from 1980 to 2000). It was one of the largest increases in the U.S. stock market's history. You didn't need to be a genius to make money in stocks during those years. Ah, the good old days! (See chart below) Interestingly though, most individual investors only made a fraction of what the market returned during those same years. More about that later.

S & P 500 Stock Market Index
from January 1, 1980 – March 15, 2000

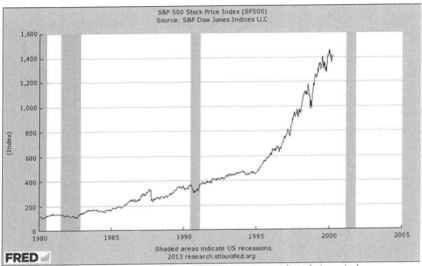

Indices are unmanaged and investors cannot invest directly in an index.

Of course, we did have some major hiccups along the way as well. There was Black Monday on October 19, 1987. I remember that one well. In four trading days the market dropped more than 30%. It fell 23% on Black Monday alone. It was the biggest single-day drop in the history of the stock market. I vividly recall how we were sitting in our offices watching the television on that Monday, hoping that there was really a bottom. I was only about five years into my chosen profession back then. I remember seriously thinking I had made a career mistake, and that I should have gone into accounting like I had originally planned. It was not a good day to be an investment advisor!

Then there was the drop in October 1996. The S&P 500 dropped over 10% in three days when the Russian economy imploded. It happened again in the fall of 1998, when it dropped nearly 20%. That time, one of the major contributors was the fall of the hedge fund Long-Term Capital (LTC). LTC took risky bets on U.S. government bonds. When their bets went bad, LTC was forced to liquidate, throwing the world financial markets into turmoil. Interestingly, two of the three founders of LTC were Myron Sholes and Robert Merton, who shared the 1997 Nobel Prize for Economic Sciences. (I wonder if they were ever asked to give back their prizes, considering they helped to almost drive the economy over the cliff!)

In all three of these major stock market drops, the fall was quick and violent, and the recoveries were swift. In all three drops, the markets fully recovered within a few months to one year of the drop. So the impression that many investors may have been left with was—yes, the stock market occasionally drops, but it quickly rebounds. This may have led some investors to inaccurately interpret the true risks involved in stock investing.

Then we hit the new century mark of 2000 and all hell broke loose. We had two near 50% drops in the S&P 500 in the first nine years of the new century. To put a 50% drop in the stock market into perspective, the last one before 2000 was in 1973-1974. The one before that was in the 1930's! So for many investors the risk of such a large drop was extremely rare, since the spacing between them was 26 to 40 years apart. This again may have led some investors to inaccurately evaluate the true risks involved in stock investing.

That is why the two 50% drops in the stock market within 8 years of each other (2000-2009) came as such a shock to many investors. History may not have properly prepared investors for such an extreme possibility.

S & P 500 Index from January 1, 2000 to March 15, 2009

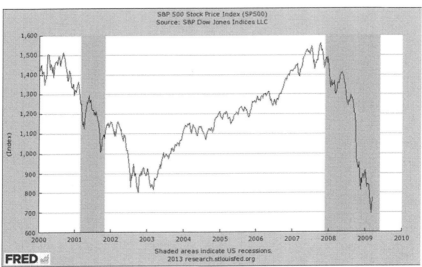

Indices are unmanaged and investors cannot invest directly in an index.

The significance of this discussion about Modern Portfolio Theory is that it relies heavily on the data accumulated between the wonder years between 1980 and 2000. In addition, prior to 2000, you had at least one whole generation of new investors come into the stock market between those major 50% drops. This allowed for new investors, who didn't experience the pain of the previous significant drop, to provide the new assets to drive the next exuberant *bull* market.

The question remains—what psychological impact will the two 50% drops over an eight-year period have on investors' psyche in the future?

It's similar to a shark sighting at a beach. Once a shark is sighted, everyone runs out of the water. Over time, a few brave souls will go back into the water. And if they don't get eaten, a few more may be willing to risk it. Over a longer period of time, many more may be willing to tempt fate for the pleasure of swimming in the ocean once again. But there may be some who will never go back in, or if they do, it may only be in the shallow areas. Any additional sightings may significantly increase the number of those who may never go back in, or if they do, it would be in a much more measured way.

How willing will investors be to jump back into the risk pool after experiencing two 50% drops? Or has this more recent pattern left a longer-term psychological scar on investors' view of risk?

How Modern Portfolio Theory Works

This next section is designed for those readers who wish to have a more in-depth understanding of MPT. It delves more deeply into its history, its underlying principals and some of its shortcoming. Those readers, who may not be as interested in this subject matter, may choose to skip over this section and go directly to the "Investor Lessons" section (even though I did put a lot of effort into writing it for you!).

MPT's roots can be traced way back to 1932, when Benjamin Graham first published his paper on "security analysis." He was one of the first to provide a formula to identify the *value* of a security. This was revolutionary, since for the first time, it allowed investors to mathematically calculate whether a particular security was over or under priced. Graham was a true pioneer in modern portfolio construction, and his ideas are still widely used and taught today in various forms.

As mentioned earlier, the recognized father of Modern Portfolio Theory is Harry Markowitz. His work on Portfolio Selection, laid the foundation for how investing is still performed today. His work was truly groundbreaking because it incorporated risk into investment portfolio construction. Prior to that, most portfolio construction centered on maximizing the investment returns, with little consideration of risk.

Today, it's hard to imagine constructing a portfolio without paying considerable attention to risk and volatility. Back then it was revolutionary. No one had ever attempted to define or measure risk, let alone try to manage it inside an investment portfolio.

For those that are interested (or gluttons for punishment), the following are some of the highlights of Markowitz theory on portfolio construction:

- He theorized that investors should be equally concerned about risk and return.
- He introduced the standard deviation of expected returns as a useful measure of risk.
- He was one of the first to use the theory that there is a direct relationship between risk and reward.
- Risk was something that could be measured, and should be monitored and controlled in a portfolio.
- You should only add an additional investment into a portfolio after measuring the effect it will have on the

overall portfolio. In other words, even if an investment looks good on its own, you should only add it if it enhances the entire portfolio.

- Adding or having investments in a portfolio that all moved in the same direction would not properly diversify a portfolio.

- The goal of portfolio construction is to assemble a number of investments that move inversely or independently of each other. Optimally constructed, this could virtually eliminate risk. This part of his theory has proven to be too lofty! In reality, it has been proven that the right combination of investments with low correlation to each other can significantly reduce risk in a portfolio, but it has its limitations.

- He also introduced the concept of the "efficient frontier." It proposes that various combinations of investments can produce better returns at various levels of risk. Theoretically any point along this line could be an optimal mix of investments, at any given level of risk. (See chart)

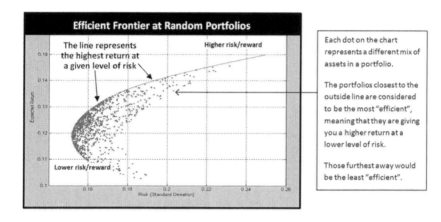

The appeal of this approach was that the individual investor theoretically could choose what was more important to them. If possible, would they rather:

1. Attempt to increase their potential investments returns, while maintaining the same level of risk, or

2. Decrease their investment risk, while trying to maintain the same potential for gain.

Markowitz's theory didn't gain widespread acceptance until many years after his thesis was first introduced. First off, the investment world was not ready for such radical changes, since measuring or managing risk in an investment portfolio was not a major consideration back then. It wasn't until the big crash in 1987 that investors and Wall Street seriously attempted to formally manage the risk in their portfolios.

In addition, much of Markowitz's work required considerable computing power to run a complete portfolio optimization calculation, which wasn't readily available until the late 70's and early 80's.

After the stock market crash of 1987, with the aid of modern computing, the genius of Markowitz was finally realized. With MPT widely accepted as an investment risk management tool, Markowitz shared the 1990 Nobel Prize for Economics, 38 years after his thesis was first published.

Modern Portfolio Theory Dissected

(_Warning:_ This is for the true financial masochist!)

While MPT was a major breakthrough in investment allocation theory, it does have some practical limitations, and its share of critics. In May of 2011, in a speech to investment advisors at the Investment Management Consultants Association annual meeting, Arun Muralidhar made the following opening statement in an attempt to dig the grave for MPT: "If I can't kill it today, I'm going to stab it enough times that it stumbles out the room." Mr. Muralidhar is a Massachusetts Institute of Technology trained economist and served as head of investment research at the World Bank, and as managing director of JP Morgan Investment Management.

Outlined below are some the fundamental assumptions upon which MPT is built. After each of the assumptions are some of the issues and limitations that critics have voiced.

<u>THEORY</u>:   **All investors have equal access to all the information they need to make an informed decision.**

Critics Response: Some investors, especially large institutions, are privy to information that other investors may not have. There is also the issue of insider trading and paid-for information. In reality, many investment decisions are based on inadequate or misleading information, while some are simply "hot tips" or hunches.

<u>THEORY</u>:   **All Investors are rational at all times and risk averse.**

Critics Response: History has proven repeatedly that investors can be anything but rational at times. This theory does not take into account "herd behavior", "panic behavior", and a whole host of other human behaviors. It also does not account for those investors that are not risk averse, either by choice (thrill-seeking or "gamblers' fallacy"), or because they are unaware of the risks involved.

<u>THEORY</u>:   **Correlations between assets are fixed and constant.**

Critics Response: The correlation between two assets (how they behave relative to each other) is based on past variables and conditions. When the variables change, the correlation may change as well. For example, new technology regularly renders old technology obsolete. This could dramatically change any previous correlation that may have existed. Also, during large market crashes or times of severe economic crisis (such as 2008) many assets tend to become positively correlated, as they move down together. So at the very time you would most want to control risk, MPT may be temporarily rendered useless as assets that in the past may have been negatively correlated, now drop together.

THEORY: **Security prices accurately reflect their true values. Any mispricing will be immediately corrected when other investors realize it, and they jump in to buy or sell it.**

Critics Response: Any investment can be mispriced for a considerable period of time. This can occur when investors continue to buy or sell the asset well after the asset has reached its fair market value. Many times this continued buying or selling can be attributed to the behavioral tendencies that we discuss throughout this book.

THEORY: **All investors have access to all investments at any time.**

Critics Response: Some investments are not available to all investors. For example, many hedge funds are not available to many individual investors because of their minimum investment requirement (frequently $1 million or more) or suitability requirements. Some investments may be limited by geographic reasons (real estate), while some large institutional investors may not buy into a smaller investment, since it could have a large impact on the price of the security when they bought or sold it.

<u>THEORY</u>:   **Taxes and transaction costs are ignored in the evaluation.**

Critics Response: In the real world, taxes and transaction costs play a significant role in the net return of a portfolio, and therefore in its construction. Including these costs could dramatically alter the composition of the portfolio.

More recently, Modern Portfolio Theory has come under much criticism for its poor performance during extremely volatile economic conditions. When you would likely need it the most, it appears to be the most vulnerable. How could something that received so many accolades have failed so dramatically when it was most needed? If you examine the economic and market conditions of the two decades during which MPT gained its wide spread acceptance, we begin to see why it may have performed as well or as poorly as it has.

First, the stock markets were pretty much moving in a consistent upward direction. As discussed earlier, the few corrections that did occur were swift, and the recoveries were almost immediate. This meant that the "optimal portfolio" constructed by MPT also recovered quickly. So while the theory's shortcomings might have ordinarily been revealed during a prolonged market correction, investors may have tended to ignore them, due to their own portfolio's quick recovery. What many investors didn't ask was: how would the theory hold up under severe and/or prolonged corrections?

Second, the theory may have performed well since longer-term interest rates during that time were on a steady course downward. (See chart). This is significant because interest rates and the value of bonds move in opposite directions. Bond prices tend to benefit as interest rates drop. This is important since MPT combines investments that tend to move in opposite directions to control risk. Consequently, for much of that time, certain bonds tended to be an efficient way to reduce the risk and volatility of stocks in a portfolio at times of high uncertainty.

Interest Rates on the 10 year U.S. Government Bond

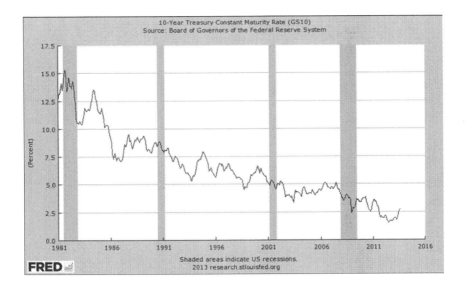

Modern Portfolio Theory uses historical data to calculate the correlation (relationship) between assets. What happens if those correlations change? What if interest rates are close to the bottom (as of 5/8/13 the current yield on a 10 year U.S. treasury was near a historic low of 1.7%)? What if interest rates changed direction and started on a longer-term trend upwards? If so, the relationship between stocks and bonds may also change, but it may take many years for that new trend to have a significant impact on the new relationship. In the meantime, the relationship may still suggest continuing to use certain types of bonds (long-term U.S. government bonds) to reduce the risk in a portfolio. These types of bonds may perform very differently in a rising interest rate environment, than they did over the past 30 years, when interest rates were dropping.

One of the major problems of traditional MPT is that it is designed on mathematical models and probabilities based on past data. It does not attempt to answer *why* a drop or surge in prices occurred, and under what conditions. It simply records the data and calculates the probability of it occurring again based on how often it happened in the past.

This would be similar to calculating the probability of a hit occurring in a specific game situation, without taking into consideration *who* the batter is, his current physical condition, or his mental state (e.g. he may have just found out that his wife was filing for divorce). All of these could have an effect on a hit occurring, regardless of what the past statistics say.

Even if you created an ideal investment model that not only took into account what happened in the past, but also under the conditions at that time, it would ignore one other critical element—human behavior. How much of past stock market outcomes have been due to human behavior, such as greed or panic? This is critical, because the next time an event occurs, even if it is very similar, there is no certainty that investors will react to it again in the same manner.

For example, when 9/11 happened, people in the U.S. reacted by being shocked. Consumers and investors alike responded by climbing into a shell for a prolonged period, and simply sat on the sidelines. The consequence was that the economy slowed and the stock market dropped. The question is, if there was another terrorist attack of that magnitude, would we react differently? It is possible that we could have a very different reaction, which could produce a very different outcome. MPT only looks at the outcome, and not the reasons behind it, or how they may be different next time.

INVESTOR LESSONS:

While Modern Portfolio Theory can be a useful tool, it is not a solution unto itself. MPT seems to work best under more *normal*, less stressful market and economic conditions. It seems to break down during times of extreme economic stress. MPT gained much of its acceptance and popularity in the 1980's and 1990's, during one of the stock market's biggest bull markets, with relatively few significant drops. Many investment professionals have become very vocal in questioning the reliability of Modern Portfolio Theory in general.

Hunting for the Elusive "Black Swans"

The hardest part of planning for something is trying to anticipate the unknown. In his excellent book, "The Black Swan" (no, not the one about the ballerina!), Nassim Nicholas Taleb discusses the concept of black swan events or unforeseeable events.

The term "black swan" can be traced back to 16th-century London, and was a commonly used term to describe something that seemed impossible, or nearly impossible. The term black swan was used because until then, only white swans had ever been seen. Black swans were then only a myth.

But, in 1697, a Dutch expedition led by William de Vlamingh discovered black swans in Western Australia. The term then morphed from describing something that was impossible, to describing something that "was once thought to be impossible, but later proved incorrect."

In his book, Taleb uses the term black swan to describe events that would have been nearly impossible to predict ahead of time, but which when they occurred left lasting and profound effects in their wake.

Some examples of black swan events would be large-scale epidemic outbreaks, magnitude 9 earthquakes, and world wars. The common characteristics of these types of events are that while they are *possible* events, they happen so infrequently that it is nearly impossible to calculate when and where the next one may occur. And while black swans are rare, they may leave a large and lasting effect.

They are also not limited to natural occurrences. There have been many technology black swan breakthroughs as well. Examples include the radio, telephone, oil, combustion engines, computers, and the atomic bomb. For each of these, it was nearly impossible to predict in advance their eventual long-term effect on society.

Some examples of black swan events in the financial world were the Great Depression, the U.S. going off the gold standard in the mid 1970's, and the 2008 financial crisis. While recessions and large drops in the stock market happen fairly regularly, those of such magnitude happen so infrequently that you really can't develop any type of usable model to predict them ahead of time. Since they happen rarely, it is impractical to incorporate their occurrences into investment modeling tools, consequently they are typically ignored. The rationale being, that as "once-in-a-generation-events", they are not likely to happen during your investing lifetime. But simply ignoring them doesn't mean they can't happen. And when they do, look out!

A good example of a recent classic black swan event was the sub-prime mortgage catastrophe that contributed to the 2008 financial meltdown. In the years leading up to the crisis, some very smart mathematicians and Wall Street gurus developed very sophisticated financial modeling programs that helped create and dramatically expand the mortgage derivative markets.

These very sophisticated mortgage models were predicated on the belief that real estate prices in the United States would continue to increase. So long as they did, everyone made a lot of money. Of course they knew that it was *possible* that real estate prices in the U.S. *could* fall, but historically it happened on so few occasions that it was difficult to calculate. So it was easier to simply ignore the possibility.

When real estate prices did start to fall, the whole house of cards began to crumble. Most sophisticated investors and financial people were unable to understand these complicated and risky instruments, and by the time they began to suspect the risks, the ensuing economic meltdown was well on its way. Welcome to the world of the black swan!

To better understand potential future black swans, Taleb outlined some of the characteristics that they tend to share:

- The event tends to catch people by total surprise (at least initially).

- The repercussions of the event may have a major and lasting impact.

- In hindsight, people start to feel that the event should or could have been anticipated. This is typically referred to as "hindsight bias," which we will discuss later.

Taleb also contends that the event is typically viewed from the perspective of the person suffering or witnessing the event. For example, "what was a shocking event for the turkey at Thanksgiving was not a surprise to the butcher."

The basic lesson of black swan events is that you shouldn't focus only on the probability of an event occurring, without closely examining all the potential consequences as well. Therefore you should not ignore something, simply because it has a low probability of occurring, if the consequences could prove potentially catastrophic. For example, let's suppose the odds of buying a defective lighter are 1 in 100. You would not necessarily be concerned about the odds because, even if you were unlucky enough to have bought the one defective lighter, your consequence would probably be minimal. (I wouldn't want to tell that to a smoker!)

In contrast, what were the odds that the U.S. residential real estate market would suffer a large enough decline, so as to collapse the entire mortgage market? It could have been as probable as buying that one defective lighter. But the consequences of this real estate crash brought the entire world economy to its knees!

The lesson is that you cannot ignore something simply because it has a low probability of occurring, if it has a potentially high consequence. These potentially *low probability–high consequence* outcomes are called "Fat Tails", and should play a significant role in constructing an investment portfolio.

While there are always potential "fat tail" events out there that we can choose to worry about, there are times that we should be on a high alert. I feel very strongly that we are in one of those periods. Below are some longer term potential fat tail events that may merit closer scrutiny:

- **The massive global build-up of both public and private debt.** Historically, excessively high levels of national debt have often led to dramatic economic upheavals and social unrest. It also typically leads to governments employing a technique called "financial repression", which can result in prolonged periods of artificially low interest rates for savers and high inflation for consumers. We may be witnessing such a period now in the United States, Europe and Japan. Financial repression may help governments out of their debt problems, but it tends to penalize citizens by decreasing their income (lower interest income) and the value of their savings by excessively inflating the cost of the products they need to purchase (inflation). As we will discuss later in the book, debt is a modern day form of slavery.

- **The future survival of the Euro Zone.** Collectively, the Euro Zone is the largest economic engine in the world. There is great concern about the potential global consequences if the Euro Zone were to suffer even a partial collapse.

- **Middle East unrest. The Middle Eas**t has been a hot spot for decades (some would argue even centuries). However, with the expansion of the "Arab Spring", and the heightening tensions between Israel and Iran, the threat of a milit.ry conflict is increasing. The risk is that a major conflict could cause oil prices to soar, thereby throwing the current delicate global recovery back into a serious recession.

The real potential risk is that any one of these fat tail events (along with those we are not yet aware of) is that any one of them may lead to another global "financial contagion." The term financial contagion refers to an event where a relatively small financial shock occurs, which may initially only affect a few financial institutions or a particular region of the world economy, but then quickly spreads to other financial sectors or other countries whose economies were previously healthy. It is analogous to the manner in which a contagious medical disease can be transmitted exponentially.

The potential danger exists that an event, however seemingly benign at the time, may have a significant and *immediate global impact.* In these instances, the consequences may be *fast and furious* and may evolve over a matter days, or even hours. Over the past few decades we have seen several examples of financial contagions, including several Mexican debt defaults, the 1998 Russian default, the 2000 tech bubble collapse, the 2008 U.S. mortgage default crisis, and most recently the European debt crisis.

Evidence suggests that over the past few decades, the world has become even more susceptible to these financial contagions. This may be due in part to three major factors.

First, world economies and markets continue to become even more interconnected and interdependent. It is now virtually impossible for a country to be an economic island unto itself, or to isolate a financial problem to a specific region. This is often referred to as "complexity risk"[1].

Second, the substantial use of leveraging (debt) has dramatically increased the risks to the overall system (too big to fail). Borrowing money to make an investment can potentially increase your profits, but it will dramatically increase your risk if the investment fails to perform as expected.

And third, technology has allowed for instantaneous news dissemination, whether accurate or not. With the ability to trade globally, in real time, it is even easier to trade on that information. But, at times this ability to respond immediately has its dark side, as it may lend itself to overreacting to a situation. We'll discuss the potential consequences of this later in the book.

Taleb further contends that modern day computer-driven mathematical risk management tools, that were initially designed to reduce risk exposure, have actually increased it, and dangerously so in some cases. He points to the mortgage market collapse as evidence. Ironically, the very models created to reduce risk in these investments, contributed heavily to their implosion.

The reason for this, he contends, is that sophisticated quantitative models (math and computer driven models) can mistakenly lead people to believe that they have greater control over the risks involved, lending a false sense of security. Over reliance on these computer driven models may lead some people to take on inordinate amounts of risk that they may not have otherwise considered.

As stated earlier, the Achilles heel of the study of economics is that in many cases, there are only a very limited number of similar past events to examine; and reliance on outcomes only, fails to address underlying causes. Therefore, Taleb argues that the conclusions of many of these "quant" programs should be viewed with skepticism. Because many of these models are extremely sophisticated, they tend to give an impression that their conclusions are much more definitive than the facts would merit.

Attempting to control risks by simply looking at their probabilities can lead to illogical and tragic financial and investment decisions. It is important to understand how those probabilities were determined, and what the potential magnitude of the consequences may be.

For example, let's suppose that you are very nervous about skydiving for the very first time. Logically, you would want to know what the probability is that your parachute will open successfully. So after doing your own Google research, let's suppose you find that based on all the jumps in the United States over the past 10 years, the odds that both of your chutes (primary and backup) fail to open is only 1 out of a million. Armed with this very reassuring statistical information, you confidently put on your parachute and climb into the airplane. Part of your confidence may stem from the fact that the probability was *overwhelmingly* reassuring. This may have given you a much skewed view of the *real* odds of a mishap.

In reality, a very important bit of information was ignored— knowing who the guy is who packed YOUR parachute. The fact that parachuting mishaps are so rare is totally irrelevant to your outcome, if the guy who packed your parachute just got off a three day drinking binge, and could barely tie his own shoelaces this morning. Your outcome will be determined by who packed your chute, and not the overall probability statistic.

Humans don't like uncertainty, so we look for things that may make us feel more secure and comfortable. Statistics can have a tendency to do that, even if they may be misleading or irrelevant!

While measuring probabilities can be a very useful tool, it has to be viewed in context. How useful a past probability is to the current situation, is dependent on how much influence the current variable may have on the outcome. As in the case of the parachute, the more a current outcome can be affected by the current variables, the less you can depend on the overall probability.

That is why I feel that economics and investing is much more of an art than a science. The widespread use and reliance on statistics and probabilities in these fields may delude some people into feeling that things are more scientifically predictable than they really are. This false sense of security may lead some people to take on much more risk than they should, or in some cases, more than they thought they actually were. This is exactly what happened with the mortgage debacle in 2008.

How the Use of "Fuzzy" Statistics Contributed to the 2008 Mortgage Meltdown

By using long-term statistical analysis, many on Wall Street thought that they could control the risk of defaults in a mortgage portfolio by hedging their bets using "derivatives". Simply put, a derivative is a financial contract whose final value is determined by the performance of an underlying asset or market factors, such as interest rates, currency exchange rates, commodities, bonds, and stock prices.

Derivatives can be used either for managing risk in a portfolio, or in an attempt to enhance returns. When used for defensive purposes, a derivative contract can act as a "hedge" or "insurance" by providing compensation in the event an unexpected or undesired event occurs. When used for speculative purposes, derivatives can offer investors an opportunity to increase profit, but at the cost of additional risk. At times, this additional risk can be substantial.

Buying insurance on these mortgages meant that even if some of the mortgages did default, losses could be limited. Buying that insurance cut into their profits. Fed by greed and over confidence, some firms decided to leverage their bets, by borrowing massive amounts of money. This allowed them to exponentially increase the number of mortgages they could buy, thereby offsetting the cost of the insurance and dramatically increasing their profits. Thanks to the Federal Reserve's low interest rate policies, borrowing money was cheap which further encouraged this risky behavior. In fact, these deals looked so attractive that some firms abandoned some of their other traditional, less lucrative lines of business, and focused much more heavily on mortgages and their derivatives.

At the height of the real estate bubble, one problem that some Wall Street firms encountered was the ability to buy *enough* mortgages. This mortgage shortage encouraged some firms to buy even riskier mortgages. In these cases home buyers may have had very little or no down payment, their houses may have been over appraised, or their incomes may not have been properly verified. But the insurance that firms bought on those mortgages, allowed them to believe that their risk was under control.

The companies that were offering the mortgage insurance assumed that their risk was limited, since over the long run, a very small percentage of mortgages had ever defaulted in the United States. Since the probability of a large number of mortgages defaulting was so low, or so they believed, they priced the insurance accordingly. Many of these companies erroneously concluded that this could be a very profitable business since they would be able to collect premiums to insure against events that rarely occurred in the past. They failed to recognize the fact that traditionally mortgage lenders required 20% down, and mortgages were generally permitted to account for at most 30% of a buyer's income. But the new system encouraged little or no down payment, optimistic appraisals, and little or no income verification.

All the parties involved assumed that the current upward trend in real estate prices would continue. And why shouldn't they, all the statistics and probabilities pointed in that direction. So long as real estate prices continued to appreciate there should be relatively few mortgage defaults, and everyone would be profitable and happy.

We now know better. The real estate bubble burst, and home prices fell. At the same time, as the economy weakened and unemployment rose, many people couldn't make their mortgage payments. In numerous instances homes were worth less than their mortgages, and since they had no or little down payment at risk, some people simply chose to walk away from the property.

Initially, as the defaults began to mount, Wall Street was not overly concerned, since they had insured these mortgage pools. For as long as the mortgage insurers could make good on the insurance, they were protected. As it turns out, that was a huge miscalculation. The companies insuring these mortgages were so convinced by the low probability of defaults that they miscalculated the true odds, and the potential impact of defaults. In the end, some insurers could not make good on their claims, and ended up defaulting, while others teetered at the cliff's edge.

This meant that Wall Street firms lost insurance on the defaulting mortgages. Without insurance, many of these firms were unable to absorb the massive losses they were incurring.

The first victims were Bear Sterns and Lehman Brothers. As additional firms continued to be crushed by the weight of their losses, the entire financial system came to a screeching halt. This in turn led to one of the most painful economic disasters since the Great Depression.

Even as people like Nassim Taleb, Peter Schiff and Nouriel Roubini emphatically warned people of this impending disaster, Wall Street ignored them. Why? Could their overconfidence have been in large part caused by their perception that the *data* was on their side?

According to Taleb, and based on estimates by the International Monetary Fund (IMF), *the entire global banking system lost more money in the 2008 subprime crisis, than the TOTAL of every penny of profit they had EVER earned!* (You may want to read that sentence again!)

In the end, much of this can be traced back to the failure of quantitative risk management. It appears that this overconfidence in statistical modeling led many firms to assume much more risk than they could actually afford. It is possible that if the banks had limited their risk to a manageable amount, they may have been able to handle their losses and survive, and we could have averted the whole economic collapse.

Overconfidence in statistical modeling could help answer the question, "How can otherwise intelligent people do such stupid things?" The 2008 economic implosion was a very painful reminder of what can happen when people rely too heavily on statistics and probability, and lose track of the ultimate potential consequences. This is the most recent example of the ultimate black swan.

Conclusion: Even if you have the odds on your side, you still need to know who is packing your parachute!

The Continuing Global Economic Paradigm Shift

The purpose of discussing black swan events is to illustrate the importance of incorporating unexpected events into investment portfolio risk management.

This may be especially important in the years to come, as financial markets appear to be in the midst of a major global paradigm shift, as well as a shift in overall global economic power. It appears that the stage is set on a major collision course between the traditional economic and political powers of the United States, Japan and Western Europe, and emerging economic powers of China, India, Indonesia, Brazil, Russia and the Middle East. In the past, when these types of global paradigm shifts occurred, they have typically been characterized by unusual, and at times, severe economic upheavals lasting for extended periods.

To see an example of this shift in power, one only has to look at the passing of the global economic torch from England to the United States in the 1940s. "The sun never set on the British Empire" prior to England's economic demise. But, by the 1970's, Britain's economy was completely dysfunctional. While the United States may not yet be at the point of having to hand over the economic torch, we certainly have to share the world economic stage with some very large and formidable economies.

History is littered with examples of once great economies that became victims of reckless and excessive spending which led to unsustainable levels of government debt. Sound familiar? The consequence of this crushing debt is that it typically forces governments into a corner, compelling them to make some very tough decisions. Often, they revert to the financial repression option. As discussed earlier, this technique typically includes keeping interest rates artificially low and forcing institutions to hold more government debt.

While financial repression may help a government deal with its debt crisis, it is often at the expense of savers and investors, especially the middle class and poor families, and the elderly who are on fixed incomes. This policy punishes savers and investors on two fronts.

First, the income from their savings is slashed. For example, in 2007 if a retiree had accumulated $1 million in retirement accounts, a 6% one year CD would have provided them approximately $60,000 in annual income. In 2013, because of financial repression, the same CD would have provided less than $8,000 per year!

Second, because of inflation, the purchasing power of their money dramatically erodes. So not only do they receive less income, but it costs more to buy the same amount of goods and services.

The significance of this unfolding economic paradigm shift is that the magnitude and frequency of black swan events may be even greater in the future. If that proves to be the case, the use of traditional Modern Portfolio Theory to allocate investments may prove less effective and even dangerous.

The scope of this book doesn't allow me the luxury of going into great detail regarding this paradigm shift (that's the topic of a future book). For those who are interested in learning more, I would highly recommend the following books: "When Markets Collide" by Mohammed Al-Erian (Co-Chief Investment Officer for PIMCO); and "Currency Wars" by James Rickards. Both of these books do an excellent job explaining the potential consequences of the current fiscal and monetary policies being employed by the United States, Europe and Japan.

Chapter Footnotes

[1] – "The Misbehavior of Markets: A Fractal View of Financial Turbulence" Benoit Mandelbrot and Richard L. Hudson, 2004

CHAPTER FOUR

Economics 101

One of my college economics professors once said in a class, "The one good thing about being an economist is that if you consistently predict the same thing, you will always be proven right—eventually."

To the casual observer, economics can sound very impressive and downright scientific. For all its use of mathematical formulas, "inverted yield curves," "fungible prices," "the producer price index" and "Gross Domestic Product" one would be tempted to think that it was some sort of "real" science. In reality, I feel economics is much more of an art than a science. Because at the end of the day, after all the formulas are run, and every scenario is exhausted, it's human behavior that will determine the final outcome.

A dear friend of mine, Chuck Sarka, shared this very simple but profound *psychological equation* with me. Simply put, an *event* happens, and eventually there is a final *outcome* from it. But the event doesn't always determine the final outcome. Rather, it may be our own individual *response* to the event that will determine our own personal final outcome. Therefore, not everyone's outcome will be the same. In other words, E+R=O (Event + your Response = Outcome).

Throughout history, time and time again you can see how differently people fared through common traumatic experiences. Individual outcomes were very different. After the Great Depression, some people looked back and saw that it had devastated their families' lives. Many wealthy families lost everything and ended up in poverty. Middle class families barely survived by working on government work programs. Businesses supporting multiple generations were wiped out. Tens of millions of lives were devastated.

Yet at the same time, others not only survived but thrived. Many great businesses were started during that period of time. Some saw an incredible opportunity, scraped together a few dollars, and seized upon it. Some made their fortunes while others were losing theirs. Same event but very different outcomes. What some saw as a potential disaster, others saw as an opportunity.

You can observe the same phenomenon today. Two people get laid off on the same day by the same company. One may choose to view it as a devastating blow, while the other chooses to see it as an opportunity to do something new. While the event may be similar, how each chose to view it is up to the individual. Obviously, there will be situations where a person is simply dealt a rotten hand, and regardless of their outlook, they will have a difficult outcome. But in many cases, our outlook and perception of an event will have a lot to do with our final outcome.

When it comes to the macro economy, however, it's not just our own individual reactions that matter. It is also important to assess how others may react to the same event. I frequently remind people, "It doesn't matter if you are the only calm person in a rowboat full of panicking people. If enough of the others panic, you're going to get wet!" And there is little consolation in saying "I told you so", as you swim with all the others in the shark-infested waters.

For example, if you knew in advance that enough people were going to panic and sell their stocks in the near future, you would be better off selling now, even though you weren't necessarily panicking. You could then wait until the panic subsided, and buy back the stocks after the market had bottomed out. Sounds great in theory, but how can you know in *advance* how investors may react in a stressful situation? The one predictable thing about humans is that we can be very unpredictable.

E+R=O is a simple but critical concept to grasp. Much of this book will build off of this concept. While we may have little or no control over many events that shape our lives, we do have some control over how we choose to respond to them. Because our responses are heavily influenced by our subconscious, at times, it can be very difficult to make logical decisions. This book will help you identify some of these subconscious influences, and explain how you can better deal with them in stressful financial situations. Much of my personal philosophy and outlook on life can be attributed to my wonderful parents,

Sandor and Ilona. Both lived very hard lives, but always made the most of their situation. My mom especially had a gift for seeing life as a glass half full. She always reminded us not to get too discouraged if something didn't work out as we had hoped. She would say that someday you may look back at this *terrible setback* and, in hindsight, find that it was one of the best things that could have happened to you.

My parents were forced to leave Hungary in 1944 during World War II, and lived in several resettlement camps in Germany until 1951. As it was for the millions of other refugees, those were very terrifying and difficult years. They ultimately immigrated to the United States with nothing but a few suitcases and the clothes on their backs. Despite their ordeal, they would tell my sisters and me that if it hadn't been for that terrible experience, they never would have had the OPPORTUNITY to raise their children in the United States of America. For them, their chosen response to a terrifying event was to view it as an OPPORTUNITY. Now, that's looking at a glass half full. If more people took that attitude, there would be a lot less rowboats tipping over in the world!

I'm one of those very fortunate people who came from a very close and loving family. I look back on my childhood with great fondness, full of wonderful memories. And it certainly wasn't because my parents were wealthy. Based on their income, to this day I am in awe of how they were able to put five kids through private schools, and support my grandparents. Rather, it was the basic moral and financial principles they instilled in us that proved to be so invaluable.

Outcomes are Influenced by Our Responses

Before every Super Bowl championship game, we are subjected to hours of mind-numbing statistics and trends, micro-analyzed by dozens of "experts" who viewed hundreds of hours of films of past games. No big name player is spared this scrutiny, and no inane fact is left out. Then, after all this information is fed into a NASA sized super computer, they come up with their predictions on who will win the game (mind you, they could flip a coin and probably be as accurate!)

Once the game starts all the statistics and analysis becomes irrelevant. In many championship games, a lesser known player can have a bigger effect on the outcome of the game than the superstars. No amount of statistical analysis can accurately predict how an individual player will perform on any given day, especially under pressure. Some players can channel the pressure to their advantage, while others fold under it, like a cheap lawn chair. In other situations, an athlete's performance may be affected by their health or some other personal or family issue. In any case, it's that human element that makes it so difficult to predict sporting outcomes. The statistics can only take you so far.

It's the same when trying to predict the economy or the stock market. At the end of the day, all the statistical modeling and trend analysis can't accurately predict how we humans may collectively decide to react to any given situation. It's this fickle, at times irrational human element that economists can't factor into their forecasts.

Now, don't get me wrong. I have great respect for many economists and the valuable information and service they provide. Most money managers will incorporate economic outlooks when making our own investment decisions. And there is a great need for the study of economics. But experience tells me that much of what happens in the *real* world cannot be easily explained or predicted in advance by statistical modeling and quantitative analysis.

Economic forecasting is not like building a bridge. Engineers who design bridges have the advantage of "true" science aiding them. They have reliable, consistent data and formulas that can produce a near 99.9% predictability rate. You can only achieve this level of predictability if you can repeat an experiment or observation thousands of times. The more outcomes you observe the more reliable and accurate the results will be. For example, because engineers have run thousands of stress tests on a certain material, they can be much more confident about how much weight a specific steel beam can hold.

This is why I feel that economics is much more an art than a science. Unlike engineers, economists don't have the luxury of examining thousands of past observations when trying to predict the odds of an economic outcome. To further complicate matters, it is almost impossible to isolate any one single variable to assess its true impact on a situation. For example, if the stock market takes a big drop—was it the news that the Fed raised interest rates that caused it, or was it that some key corporate earnings came in weak, or possibly because there was a rumor that China would announce slower than expected growth for next year? It is virtually impossible to isolate all the different variables and see their true impact on the outcome.

In the midst of the 2008 economic collapse, economists were trying to determine what the odds were that we could fall into another Great Depression. And if so, what strategies could potentially be implemented to help avoid it, or at least minimize its effects. A major obstacle was that they didn't have the ability to examine hundreds of previous U.S. depressions, in order to see what did or didn't work in the past. Actions that were taken during the Great Depression may not have been helpful in 2008. As a matter of fact, much of what was done back then still remains a great source of debate. Did it help or prolong the depression?

This may also help explain why so many economists have such a bad track record when trying to predict even simple things, such as next quarter's GDP or the unemployment rate. Many times the results may be influenced by non-quantifiable, human behavior variables, that can't be easily quantified or explained.

SECTION II

CHAPTER FIVE

A Glimpse At How The Brain Is Wired

> *"The newest research is showing that many properties of the brain are genetically organized, and don't depend on information coming in from the senses."*
>
> Steven Pinker, *author and cognitive psychologist*

To better understand how our minds process financial and investment decisions, we first need to delve into how this incredibly complex organ, called the human brain, operates. It is important to understand that the vast majority of the decisions we make are made in our subconscious mind, without the aid of any conscious thought. In addition, many of our decisions may be the result of the hard wiring in our brains that was formed by thousands of years of evolution. So before I move forward, let me cover some of the basics of our brain's anatomy.

Allow me apologize in advance to anyone who might be offended by my oversimplifications of a very complicated and highly debated topic. My intention is not to fully explain the inner workings of the human brain, or prep you for an anatomy exam, but rather to put the discussion into layman's terms; and demonstrate how it may impact your financial and investment decisions.

I assume that when you started reading this book you were hoping to find some sound financial and investing insights, and not necessarily a primer on how the brain is wired, or a bunch of psycho mumbo jumbo. I get that, I really do. But after many years of observation and research, I have come to the conclusion that many of the mistakes we make with our money, especially the really big ones, have more to do more with the inner workings of our own minds, than from our failure to interpret key financial or economic data, or picking the wrong mutual fund.

My hope is that you don't skip or glance too quickly over this section. The rest of the book will build off the important principles and ideas that we cover here. Who knows, you may even find this as fascinating of a subject as I do; and it may open up a whole new world of perspective for you as well! So here we go on our journey into the fascinating inner workings of your mind!

When I first became interested in psychology and started researching human behavior, and more specifically behavioral finance, what struck me was how little we really know about the human mind. The more I researched, the more I realized that we are still in the early stages of truly understanding exactly how our incredibly complex human brains work. Our conscious mind, the part we are aware of, is truly only the tip of this vast iceberg that is our mind. In his wonderful book "Incognito", neuroscientist David Eagleman compares our brain to a newspaper that is reporting on the vast activities inside an entire country.

In his example, our *subconscious* mind represents the entire country, buzzing with billions of bits of daily activity. Our *conscious* mind, the portion that we are aware of, represents the newspaper. Just as in real life, newspapers only report a summary of the most critical or interesting pieces of information, or things that have caught their attention. The country goes about its daily tasks—factories making products, telephone lines transmitting information, power plants producing energy, police making arrests, teachers grading papers, doctors healing patients, construction crews building new roads, pipes carrying water to your faucets, farmers growing food, planes flying passengers, and trucks delivering products to stores.

While you may desire to know everything that is happening in the country, you simply couldn't process the billions and billions of bits of information. In fact, it probably wouldn't be to your advantage to know all the individual details. It would be useful to have a "newspaper" that could inform you of the important events. You could quickly scan the headlines for critical topics, and determine if any of it was important enough to read the whole article.

For instance, if you were buying a bar of soap at Wal-Mart, it would not be necessary to know when the truck delivered it to the store, or what warehouse it was shipped from, or when it was made in the factory. All you really need to know is that you are out of soap and where you can buy it.

And, so it is with our conscious minds. At any given time we are consciously only scanning the "headlines". Some make it into our conscious minds, some don't. Typically we are oblivious to our subconscious world, and the tens of thousands of *autopilot* decisions it is making on the *local* level. All we typically *see* is the decision that we subconsciously made, and not necessarily why we made it. How many times a day do you stop and wonder, "why did I just do that?"

According to David Eagleman's analogy, there are also many types of *newspapers* where people can get their headlines based on their interests. It would be like comparing the headlines of local vs. national newspapers, business vs. general topics, or in-depth vs. superficial reporting. While you would expect them to have different headlines because of their varying focuses, you might even find variances among similar newspapers due to editorial staffs interests.

Each of our minds has also developed its own unique *editorial* process to determine what makes it to our conscious *headlines*. This *editorial process* is unique to each of us, and has been developed over our lifetimes through the knowledge and personal experiences we have accumulated. This may help explain why you can have two people look at the same situation or information, and come to very different conclusions. Examining your own editorial process (and those of others) can be an especially enlightening experience indeed!

The Study of Behavioral Finance

The study of human behavior has been with us for thousands of years, and goes back to our ancient ties to Plato and

Socrates. While the past century has given us some tremendous insights into our behavior, the past few decades have been truly remarkable. Many recent insights can be attributed to the breakthroughs in the field of neuroscience, a greater understanding of the "hard-wiring" of the brain, and how it can affect our behavior and decisions.

Within the larger context of human behavior, there are two very interesting fields of study—behavioral finance and neuro-economics. These two areas attempt to explain how human behavior and our brain's hard wiring may affect our financial decisions, and influence the overall economy.

Most behavioral finance and neuro-economics research has been approached from the psychological, rather than the financial perspective. The majority of experiments and observations in the early days were in controlled environments, typically in university settings. The vast amount of data that came from these studies helped explain why we may behave in certain ways when confronted with various financial situations—but they also have their limitations. Many researchers agree that the limitations in these studies may stem from the following issues.

First, experiments are typically conducted in a controlled setting, examining a small number of variables at a time. In such a controlled setting, you simply cannot replicate the *real world* with its myriad of ever-changing variables. It is nearly impossible to conduct this type of research on a large scale under real-world conditions and achieve repeatable results. In addition, people tend to act differently when they know they are being observed. For example, our *herding instinct* may tend to make participants want to answer questions the way they think the researchers would expect, thereby potentially affecting the outcome.

The second issue is that the subjects being tested were typically college students. For the experiments that were examining more general psychological tendencies, that may not have presented a serious problem. But when you narrow the focus to the study of investments or finance, many college participants lacked the real world knowledge or experience of real risk and its consequences to be useful subjects. Some more recent studies have used real world investors and investment professionals as subjects. These studies continue to unearth some very interesting insights into investor psychology.

Third, it is nearly impossible to replicate the two most critical situations that affect people's finances, namely the times when the brain is acting out of sheer greed or extreme fear. These two primal emotions cause, by far, the most financial damage. These are the emotions that create investment bubbles and then panic selling. It would be very helpful to be able to identify in advance the behaviors and trends that may predispose one to these emotions. But, it is also quite difficult to recreate a situation that can even closely mimic these conditions in order to provoke these extreme emotions.

In addition, over the past decade significant advances in the neurosciences have been made. Neuroscience is the study of the physiology or functioning of the human brain and the nervous system. Some findings have validated many of the behavioral finance theories that were first pioneered by people

such as Richard Thaler, Amos Tversky and Daniel Kahneman, decades earlier.

This has led to a newer, specialized field called neuro-economics which combines the fields of neuroscience with psychology (human behavior) and economic theory. The goal of this new field of study is to better understand how and why people make financial decisions.

Growing evidence suggests that many of the financial decisions we make are made impulsively deep inside the more primitive portions of our brains, areas that are still driven by our survival instincts. While this instinctive part of our brain is critical for survival, it may not be best suited to make more sophisticated financial decisions.

With recent technological advances, such as functional magnetic resonance imaging (fMRI), it is becoming possible to advance our understanding of how the brain works, and enables the ability to evaluate our mental processes to determine what we're thinking and feeling. This technology works by detecting changes in blood oxygenation and flow that occur in response to neural activity—when a brain area is more active it consumes more oxygen. To meet the increased demand for oxygen, blood flow increases in the active area. The imaging can show which parts of the brain are involved in different mental processes. It provides an opportunity to gain new insights into how memories are formed, how we learn, and how we make decisions.

The research suggests that if we can pin point which parts of the brain are involved in making a decision, we can examine the role of emotions and risk taking predilections in decision-making. We now know that emotions can change risk-taking preferences and confidence in our beliefs.

While this research is in its early stages, psychologists as well as economists are encouraged by these findings. As you'll see, how someone's emotional response to a situation affects their decisions, is deeply influenced by which portions of the brain are involved. With fMRI we can see this brain activation. That response can be even more critical during periods of high stress or heightened emotions. Soon we may be able to predict an individual's response to changes in financial policies, markets and environments.

The Triune Brain

In this section we will briefly examine some of the inner workings of the human brain. The goal is to give you a simplified overview of how the different parts of the brain interact, and how they may affect some of the daily financial and investment decisions we make.

For our purposes, (since we are not prepping you for a neurology exam) it makes sense to classify the brain into three basic areas, delineated by the general functions they provide, and not by their actual physical locations. The theory and term "triune brain" was developed by American physician and neuroscientist Paul D. MacLean, and can be broken down into three sections—the brainstem, the "reflexive" (impulsive) brain, and the "reflective" (logical) brain.

The Brainstem

This is the oldest portion of the brain, also known as the "reptilian brain." The brainstem controls key involuntary body functions such as breathing, heartbeat, body temperature and metabolism, swallowing, blinking of the eyes and other basic body functions. The majority of the time this part of the brain is on auto pilot. While very interesting in its own right, this portion of the brain has little to do with behavioral finance, so we won't spend any more time on it. (You're welcome!)

Our "Impulsive" Brain (Oscar)

The term "reflexive brain" is not a biological term, but rather attempts to explain its general function [1]. This portion of the brain is called the amygdale. It is the emotional center of the brain. It is known as the reflexive part of the brain, since it controls our more instinctive reflexes that don't require conscious thought. Since the terms reflexive and reflective are so similar, they may cause some confusion. To help avoid this, going forward I will refer to them as your "impulsive-**Oscar**" brain, and your "logical-**Felix**" brain.

It's the home to powerful emotions and unconscious emotional memory. It is associated with emotions involved in survival, fear, immediate gratification, pleasure and lust. Evidence suggests that it may also influence how vividly and accurately we recall memories and past experiences.

This part of the brain operates mainly in the subconscious. It is instinctive, emotional, intuitive, operates lighting fast, and can process hundreds of tasks very quickly and efficiently. It demands instant action and desires immediate gratification. It also tends to be stubborn, so once it has formed an *opinion*; it may take quite a bit of behavior modification to change its influence. In addition, it doesn't require *attention* from our conscious mind, because it operates in auto pilot mode. Interestingly, it is inclined to learn things more easily when narratives, examples and analogies are used.

This portion of our brain provided our primitive ancestors the instinctive tools necessary for daily survival. It increases the odds of survival by intuitively doing whatever would improve the odds, such as fattening up in the fall to help survive a long winter; and avoids that which could threaten survival odds, such as avoiding face-offs with saber-tooth tigers.

This part of the brain controls our *fight or flight* instincts that were so crucial to the very survival of early man. It is this *impulsive* part of our brain that immediately and instinctively determines whether or not we stand and fight or run to live another day. Even today it plays a critical role in our daily survival. For example, most drivers have had this type of experience. You are driving in the rain, or on a dimly lit road. For a split second, you think you see something in the corner of your eye. You are already turning your steering wheel and hitting your brakes before you actually see the ball rolling into the street. This *reflexive* part of your brain has already hijacked your body and demanded action, before the logical part of your brain has even had a chance to fully analyze the situation.

It's this automatic and immediate response system that causes you to flinch unnecessarily at times, but that's favorable for survival. We have survived because we adapted, we don't adapt in order to survive. After all, it's better to flinch and look like a fool a hundred times than to be sorry just once.

This part of the brain fields the thousands of impulses that are continually fed into our brain from our senses—our eyes, nose, ears, and sense of touch. It sorts through all the information it gathers and instantly decides what is relevant and what can be ignored. To help it sort through the thousands of bits of information, our brain uses "heuristics," or a series of self-developed shortcuts. These shortcuts are based on our own unique personal experiences. Depending upon how an intense earlier life experience might have been felt, may influence how a similar occurrence will be intuitively viewed in the future.

For example, if you were mauled by a dog as a young child, the impulsive part of your brain will instinctively indicate danger whenever you see or hear a dog. In many cases it may even evoke a physical reaction, such as being startled. Contrast that with a child who grew up in a home with three wonderfully friendly dogs. That person's *reflexive* message will be pleasure. Your past experiences help determine the *shortcut* response your brain will provide in a given situation. These shortcuts also help develop our personal psychological biases that we carry with us, often throughout our entire lives. Later in this section, we'll discuss how some of these biases may dramatically affect our financial decisions.

This part of the brain is also home to our *pleasure zone*, which instinctively drives us to do what makes us happy and gives us pleasure. When we experience pleasure, the brain produces a chemical called dopamine which gives us that euphoric feeling. Once the *reflexive* brain detects something that causes the release of dopamine, it will aggressively seek to repeat that sensation again whether by eating chocolate, taking drugs, looking for romance, or finding the next hot stock. And it will do so without necessarily considering the long-term consequences it may carry. This part of the brain is looking strictly for immediate gratification.

This addictive response may also be involved in the thrill of winning. In fact, some studies have suggested that the anticipation of winning may be greater than the actual win itself. This may help explain why gambling can be so addictive. Most gamblers lose money, yet they continue to gamble. They may be addicted to the feeling and anticipation of winning.

Our impulsive brain is also continually trying to detect patterns, whether they actually exist or not. It is in our human nature to look for patterns everywhere. Our observations tell this part of our brain that just as nature makes the sun rise and set every day, and the seasons change on a predictable schedule, there must be other patterns to find. Again, it was crucial to early man's survival to notice things such as weather patterns and animal migrations, since it could mean the difference between life and death.

These pattern-seeking instincts still exist in our modern brains. For example, a gambler may notice that the last three winning horses had names associated with flowers, so his next bet is on *Magnolia,* assuming that the trend is likely to continue.

Pattern-seeking also applies to our investment experiences. An investor may notice a pattern in the way a certain investment moves. For example, she may notice that for a certain period of time large cap stocks tend to perform better than small cap stocks, and then the pattern reverses. Based on this pattern, she may decide to makes changes to her portfolio to take advantage of the trend. If the pattern continues a few more times, a feeling of *winning* may surface. This would lead to an increased confidence in that pattern, thus encouraging her to make even larger bets on it in the future.

Eric Kandel, a neuroscientist at Columbia University, suggests that this part of the brain may also influence the actual intensity of some of our memories. Events that involve more intense emotions at the time they occur, tend to generate more vivid memories when later recalled. The more vivid the memory, the more influence it is likely to have on our present decisions.

For instance, the intensity of recalling a 50% drop in the stock market ten years ago could be very different for a 35-year-old who had *lost* $2,500 in his 401(k), than it would be to a 65-year-old, who had to delay his retirement because he *lost* $500,000. A vivid memory, especially a negative one, can have a significant impact on a decision that an investor may be currently facing.

If our 65-year old detected a current *pattern* that may lead him to conclude that another dramatic drop in the stock market was possible, his intense, painful memory may encourage him to quickly sell his stocks to avoid another painful experience. At the same time, our 35-year-old, not having suffered the same painful experience, may be more willing to hold his positions.

The "Logical" Brain (Felix)

I'll refer to the third part of the brain, which is called the prefrontal cortex, as the "logical" brain. This is the most advanced part of the brain, and is responsible for analytical thinking, learning, calculating and planning ahead. Its advanced development is what differentiates humans from primates.

This portion of the brain enables us to learn, remember, reason, and assemble seemingly unrelated data into a logical conclusion. This ability to reason, think and plan is what has allowed humans to advance beyond living in a constant survival mode.

Unlike the reflexive portion, this part of the brain is slower and more methodical. It is logical, rational and controlled. It tends to handle tasks one at a time. It's inquisitive and flexible, more open to change as new evidence is gathered. It drives the desire to seek out additional data before reaching a conclusion or initiating a course of action. Unlike the emotional brain, that is impatient and demands immediate gratification, the logical brain is willing to defer action or gratification, if there is a potential for greater reward in the future.

Why Two Brains are Better than One

To survive, our brains must process tens of thousands of stimuli and data simultaneously. To be capable of handling this massive amount of information, our brains have evolved into our current "two-brain" system, one that acts on reflex, the other on reflection.

All of our senses of sight, smell, sound, and touch; and external stimuli feed into the brain which must somehow manage all this information in an orderly fashion. As I noted earlier, to handle the massive amounts of data, it has developed its own short cuts and rules of thumb, called "heuristics" (we'll cover this in more detail a bit later). Part of heuristics is to simplify most things into general categories or patterns that can be quickly recognized and acted upon without need of analysis.

After filtering all the data from the senses and the environment, the impulsive brain (instinctive) discards all the information it deems currently irrelevant. The remaining data is then filtered through additional heuristics and biases, and then acted upon instinctively. All this is done in microseconds, most of it without the aid of any conscience thought. As you read this book, your brain is continually being bombarded by inputs from your senses. Somehow your brain is unconsciously deciding which of all the sounds, sights, smells and other distractions to ignore; and which are important enough to pay attention to. Without the ability to filter all the distractions, you would never be able to read this book.

The logical brain handles higher functions, such as memory recall, rational and comparative thought, calculation, and the ability to *connect the dots*. Under normal conditions, these two systems operate effortlessly and in harmony, taking turns performing their respective tasks.

But under stress, the two systems can come into conflict. Being a bully, the impulsive brain tends to revert to survival mode. If it feels threatened, or when a pleasurable opportunity is available, it will demand immediate action. As the logical brain tries to weigh out the options and potential consequences, the impulsive brain will continue to push for a quick decision, even if there could potentially be negative consequences.

All this brain power requires a lot of energy as well. Even though the brain typically comprises only 2% of our total body weight, it consumes more than 20% of our total energy. And when the brain is in overdrive, it consumes even more [2]. Thus when you are in an intense or emotional situation, or working on a mentally demanding task, you can literally become physically tired, and mentally exhausted.

Self-Control can be a Draining Experience

Interestingly, research suggests that the ability to exercise self-control to override or control a strong emotional reaction may actually be a limited resource. The more we engage our self-control in a situation, the less self-control we may have in reserve for the next incident [3]. This could help explain why people may feel so exhausted or overwhelmed during extreme emotional situations, such as a dramatic stock market decline, or when facing potentially dire economic prospects. As the waves of emotions continue to pound away, the reserves for dealing with them become depleted.

The research also suggests the following interesting findings:

1. When people are under emotional distress, they tend to favor higher risk and higher payoff options; even if it may be something they would not typically choose. Emotional distress can short circuit our ability to carefully think through a situation and consider all options. This may

help explain why at times some investors are willing to take even larger risks, right after suffering a loss.

2. If one's self-esteem is threatened, they may become upset and find it difficult to control their emotions. This may prove to be particularly troublesome for someone who holds a high opinion of themselves. A blow to the ego can instigate the feeling that I must do something *big* to prove myself. Again, this may lead some investors to assume greater risks than normal, after suffering a big loss.

3. When people are unable to control their emotions, the result is often self-defeating behavior. One of the potential consequences may be to seek immediate pleasures over delayed rewards. The ability to control our emotions appears to depend on the limited resources of our strength or energy. Since these resources are limited, people can only regulate themselves up to a certain point. After that, they may become more susceptible to emotional decisions.

4. Research suggests that making a series of critical decisions can deplete these same resources. As a result, the person may become fatigued and subsequent decisions may become more irrational.

5. The desire to belong or be accepted by a group is one of the strongest human needs. If a person feels rejected by the group, that person may begin to feel desperate to conform, even against his or her own wishes and desires. We'll discuss each of these findings in much more detail in following chapters.

These vulnerabilities are not unique to individual investors. They also apply to professional investment managers. For example, a pension manager who has been substantially underperforming his targeted rate of return over the past few years may feel the pressure to *catch up*. This could be strong enough to encourage him to take more investment risks than would otherwise be warranted or wise. This kind of thinking could become narrower and focused only on the short-term. In addition, injury to his pride and self-confidence may also become an obstacle to making long-term logical decisions.

Impulsive vs. Logical Brains

A fascinating part of this topic is how the two very different parts of the brain continually interact with each other. Since the impulsive brain is effortless, automatic, fast and impatient, it can lend itself to errors. The logical brain requires more effort. Since it is slower, more logical and patient, it is less prone to impulsive mistakes.

One way to consider our brain's partnership is to think about it as the two main characters on old TV series "Wild, Wild West." Recently it was remade as a movie with Will Smith and Kevin Kline.

The show was about two Secret Service agents fighting crime in the 1800's. The impulsive part of the brain is similar to the James West character. He was a tough, emotional, quick-to-act character, who relied on his instincts and fists for survival. The logical brain is more like Artemus Gordon, the intelligent, cunning, master-of-disguises character, who relied on his cunning and careful planning for survival.

As a team, they were very successful. Neither was clearly the dominant partner. When there was imminent danger (or a beautiful lady!) at hand, West would take the lead. At other times it was Arty who would take the lead, creating a carefully thought out plan to foil the enemy. While fans of the show may have had their own favorite character, one could not have survived without the other. It took the cooperation of both of to succeed.

The same could be said for the two parts of our brain. Survival would be much more difficult without the cooperation of the two regions. Unfortunately, the two characters in our brain are not as carefully scripted as equals! In real life, the two brains don't tend to be co-equals. As stated earlier, the more primitive emotional brain can be a bully. If it perceives a threat or an opportunity for immediate gratification, it goes on high alert. If it feels that the logical side is reacting too slowly, it may become impatient and hijack the situation, acting on pure impulse.

This hijacking tends to occur during periods of heightened emotions, such as fear, anger, and lust. To accomplish the hijacking and drown out the slower side, the reflexive brain releases a chemical called Cortisol. This chemical serves to dampen the effectiveness of the more conscious brain, allowing the reflexive side to operate more easily. This is why at times you will hear people who are under a lot of stress say "I can't think straight." It's the impulsive, emotional brain trying to drown out the slower, logical side [4]. As the perilous situation abates, Cortisol is reabsorbed fairly quickly, and the system goes back to normal operating status. This can help explain why people may later scratch their heads and wonder, "What in the world was I thinking when I did that?" The impulsive mind was in control, and the person was not likely to have even been fully aware of it.

One way to combat this hijacking is to attempt to keep stress and emotions in check. That's why your mom always told you to take a deep breath and count to ten when you were upset. This actually works! Slow, deep breathing can actually slow your heart rate and may decrease your heightened emotional state (I learned that in my one-and-only yoga class!). This temporary reprieve may allow your logical brain an opportunity to have some say into your decision.

While the instinctive brain may have been critical for survival for our primitive ancestors, and still is in our daily lives, it can wreak havoc with our financial decisions. Most financial decisions tend to be more complex and require some calculation and forward thinking, making these decisions better suited to logical thinking. Sometimes under stressful situations, fed by both fear and greed, and possibly time limits, the bully impulsive brain may demand immediate action, before a situation can be thoroughly analyzed. That may also help explain why seemingly intelligent people can make disastrous financial decisions.

How the Two Brains Work Together

The following is a simple example of how your impulsive, emotional brain works with the more logical side. See if you can identify with this example.

Imagine you're alone in your car on a scenic country road. The sun's shining, you have the car's top down and your iPod is playing some of your favorite songs. Your impulsive brain is processing the nice breeze and the warmth of the sun on your skin. It's also starting to want to take a sip of the fresh cup of coffee that it smells in your cup holder. Just then, a song by the Moody Blues starts to play. You immediately recognize it. It was the song that was playing at your school dance the first time you kissed your high school sweetheart, Barbara.

Now your logical brain brings up additional pleasant memories. As the logical side begins to recall those memories, it starts to calculate just how many years ago that was, and then starts to wonder if she ever got married and had any kids. With all these pleasant senses and memories around you, you can't help but feel very comfortable.

Then suddenly, your impulsive brain picks up a loud sound that is very disturbing. It sounds out of place. You hear several more sounds, and you immediately recognize them as gunshots. Your impulsive brain instantly goes on high alert and shuts off all the other senses. No more warm sun, no Moody Blues or thoughts of Barbara at the dance. All are wiped out in an instant by your impulsive brain.

Still in control, your impulsive brain realizes that the sound was louder in the left ear, so you conclude that the danger must be on the left side. The impulsive brain instantaneously orders you to hit your brakes and turn to the right, away from the danger. Your body is tense as you firmly grip the steering wheel waiting for further instructions.

A few moments of quiet go by, and your heart rate begins to slow down. You see a deer limping across the road, obviously hurt. Your logical brain is now fighting to get some input into the situation. Seeing the injured deer, it figures that since you are in the country, the shots more than likely have come from hunters. Even though it's not a direct threat, you still decide to be cautious, since you don't want to get caught in the cross fire. So your impulsive brain then instructs you get away from potential danger.

This example illustrates how your impulsive brain may intuitively interpret data and act on it before the logical side even has a chance to process it. The impulsive brain is "on" at all times, looking for patterns and potential threats. In a way, you could say the impulsive side of your brain acts like a street cop on his beat, alert and ready to guard against potential threats, ready to leap into action when necessary.

Comparing the Duel Systems of Your Brain

Impulsive Brain "Oscar"	Logical Brain "Felix"
Emotional	Rational
Automatic	Analytical
Effortless	Effortful
Lightning fast	Slower thinking
Passive	Controlled
Subconscious	Conscious thinking
Intuitive	Focus
Resistant to change	Willing to change
Immediate action	Forward thinking
Immediate gratification	Will defer gratification

INVESTOR LESSONS:

- When facing an important financial or investment decision, be aware of influences that past experiences may be have, especially negative ones. Each situation is unique, and past experiences may be helpful in evaluating the current situation, but you don't want it to be the overriding factor.

- Avoid making important financial decisions when you feel under pressure, or are in an emotional state. If a decision must be made immediately, take time to write out the pros and cons of all your options. This will force you to engage the logical side of your brain in making the decision.

Chapter Footnotes

[1] - The terms "reflective" and "reflexive" brain are credited to UCLA psychology professor Matthew Lieberman, who in turn attributes them to John-Paul Sartre in his essay, The Transcendence of the Ego.

[2] - "The Brain Explained" Daniel Drubachl, 2000

[3] - "Self-regulation and depletion of limited resources: Does self-control resemble a muscle?" Mark Muraven; Roy Baumeister, Psychological Bulletin, Vol 126(2), March 2000

[4] - "Under Pressure: Your Brain on Conflict" Joshua Gowin, PhD, April 2011

CHAPTER SIX

How the Mind Processes Information

> *"Perception is reality."*
>
> Lee Atwater, *political consultant*

We've all heard the saying "perception is reality." But most people don't realize just *how* accurate that statement is. Our minds don't *see* the world, they *interpret* it. At any given time our minds are interpreting the millions of bits of information our brains are gathering and processing. That interpretation is subject to an emotional filter that can alter our perception.

Picture for a moment a beam of light being directed into a prism. On the other side of the prism different —colored light rays shoot out. That single light beam has now transformed into a series of colored rays.

Similarly, at any given moment, what we perceive as reality is being viewed through our own prism of emotions. Imagine that single beam of light represents some information that has just entered your brain. That information could be a sensory input, such as something you just saw, heard, smelled or touched. Or it can be information you just learned, some news about an event, the death of a friend, or something you just read. This information, that single beam of light, is now shot into your brain's prism.

Picture those colored rays on the other side of the prism as your emotions. Each color represents a different emotion, such as happiness, sadness, fear, greed, confidence, pessimism, anger or generosity. At any given time, typically we will have one or more of those emotions influencing our overall mood or state of mind. Therefore, how we receive that single beam of information will be positively or negatively influenced by the emotion (colored rays) through which we view it.

Let me give you an example. Let's pretend you are at work and your boss calls you into his office and informs you that due to dropping sales, your services will no longer be needed. As Donald Trump would say, "You're fired"!

As you pack up your desk you can feel all your co-workers' uneasy eyes on you. As you walk out of the building, you trip down the last step and twist your ankle. While driving home, you get a flat tire, just as it starts to rain.

As you walk into your home dripping wet, before you even have a chance to tell your wife what happened, she informs you, "I just want to let you know that I caught Jimmy (your 13-year-old son) smoking a cigarette and drinking a beer in the garage with his friend today."

How do you react? You march into little Jimmy's room, and take him to task!

Now let's change the scenario. Your boss calls you in his office and tells you that due to your sales production, he is promoting you to manager. He informs you that along with a nice pay increase, you also get a new company car. On the way home, you stop to get a bottle of wine to celebrate. You buy an instant lottery ticket and win $500!

As you walk into your house anxious to tell your wife the great news, she stops you and says "I just want to let you know that I caught Jimmy smoking a cigarette and drinking a beer in the garage today with his friend today."

How might you react? This time you hug your wife and say, "Honey, I did the same thing when I was his age. I'll have a talk with him after dinner about how disappointed we are in him. By the way, you won't believe what happened today..."

You received the same news from your wife, but had very different reactions. What was the difference? The information about little Jimmy was being filtered through a set of very different emotions. In the first scenario, the dominant emotions may have been anger, fear and pessimism. In the second scenario, the emotions may have been joy, pride and optimism. The emotions present at that time helped influence your reaction to the news about little Jimmy. As we discussed earlier, E+R=O (Event + your Reaction = Outcome).

The strength of those emotions will also contribute to how we may interpret and react. The stronger the emotion, the more influence it may have. That is why at times you may get a more violent reaction from someone who is already angry or agitated, than you would have if they had been in a good mood.

The same can be said when dealing with your investments. How you perceive some new bit of information may be colored by your emotions. Depending on your mood, you may react very differently to your quarterly 401(k) statement's decline of 15%. A fearful outlook may invoke a very different reaction (the world is coming to an end!) than if you feel very positive (don't worry, it always bounces back).

The same is true when interpreting financial or economic news, such as the release of new unemployment rates, GDP or some other geopolitical event. You may process the information very differently, depending on your mood. You may also be increasing that emotion by your "confirmation bias," which selectively focuses on information that confirms your already established beliefs. This "confirmation loop" only goes to further strengthen your view, whether it's accurate or not.

Investors must be keenly aware of how they may be processing information, and how their emotions may be influencing their outlooks and opinions. As I work with people, I try to be cognizant of what potential emotions may be driving their opinion or outlook at that given time. There may be a more deep-rooted reason for their pessimism or optimism. They may be dealing with the loss of a loved one, are worried about being unemployed, or are concerned for a friend or spouse who is sick. All these things could affect their overall outlook, and influence their decisions. By bringing these subconscious feelings to the surface, it may allow you to be more objective when assessing your situation and actions.

To some, this may initially sound like a bunch of touchy feely, psycho mumbo jumbo, but let me assure you it's very real. My observation after many years of watching and working closely with investors is this: being unable to control your emotions can be the single biggest contributor to making big financial and investment mistakes. Fear and greed are the most destructive emotions. Many times I have told people that if I could go back in time, I would trade my degree in finance for one in psychology, in a heartbeat. While having accurate financial data is critical, understanding how and why people may react to them is just as important.

The Battle for Your Mind

While we struggle with our own internal battle between the conscious and subconscious minds, there is another whole external war being waged for your mind, and chances are you are not even fully aware of it. This war is being waged on several fronts, with the opposing combatants trying to influence your opinions and behavior. Believe me when I use the war analogy, it's not just hyperbole. It is a war with a lot at stake.

Most of us are probably aware of the obvious attempts by advertisers and marketers to influence our thinking and behavior. They try to win us over by convincing us that we simply can't live without their product or service. And over the past 100 years or so, they have gotten very good at influencing our purchasing behavior. Madison Avenue has perfected the art of emotional manipulation.

They can get us to laugh, cry, and even get angry by showing just the right images, or writing an effective script. They know that if they can evoke the right emotion strongly enough, they stand a much better chance of getting us to remember their product or message. At times, they can even get us to buy products or services we don't need or want. If you don't believe me, walk through your house and look at all the things and gadgets you own. Then ask yourself, did I really need that? In many cases the honest answer may be "no," since you rarely, if ever use this stuff.

The question then is, why did you buy it? More than likely, the answer is that the advertiser influenced you. The reality is that if you didn't know the product existed, you probably would not have sought it out on your own. Seriously, did you really need to be able to scramble an egg while it's still in the shell? But hey, at least you got the free toothpick organizer that came with it!

Advertisers have perfected behavioral manipulation to an art form. With the use of focus groups, psychological testing, surveys and feedback analysis, they know what motivates consumers better than we even know ourselves. If it didn't work, they wouldn't be spending billions of dollars on advertising and research every year.

In many cases, they can influence our behavior by appealing to our more primitive instincts and desires, such as pleasure, fear, greed and lust. Since many of these emotions operate in our subconscious, we may not even be fully aware of the manipulation.

How many times have you watched a commercial and felt an emotional reaction? Whether it's an ad showing a loving wife beaming over her new diamond ring, images of starving and abused pets, or a burglar breaking into a home while a frightened young mother holds her young child. The most effective ads will get you to feel some strong emotion and influence your behavior.

The key to not falling victim to this war is to be cognizant of these attempts, and understand that you are being manipulated. The good news is, once you bring it to your conscious mind, these attempts become very obvious, and easier to control.

Think about this the next time you are watching a commercial. When you start looking for the manipulation you will be surprised how obvious it is. I actually enjoy watching some commercials just to see which techniques they use, and how effective they are in stirring an emotion. As a consequence, my wife hates watching TV with me now!

While this attempt by advertisers is obviously manipulative, we can at least justify it since they have a very upfront and simple objective in mind—they want you to buy their product. At the end of the day, we have the ability to say no, if we tamp down the desire for some immediate gratification driven by the reflective brain.

This battle for your mind is not limited only to advertisers. There are other groups battling to influence your subconscious as well. These other battles can be much more subtle, and in some cases more devious and nefarious.

Political Propaganda

> *"These various remedies, eugenic, educational, ethical, populist and socialist, all assume that either the voters are inherently competent to direct the course of affairs or that they are making progress towards such an ideal. I think [democracy] is a false ideal."*
>
> Walter Lippmann, *journalist and author*
> *"The Phantom Public"*

Propaganda in politics is nothing new. It has been used as long as politicians have been around. The father of modern American propaganda was President Woodrow Wilson. He knew that for the United States to enter into WWI, he had to have the backing of the people. In an effort to rally support from an unwilling public, in 1917 Wilson created the Committee on Public Information (CPI). Its purpose was to use propaganda as a tool to convince Americans that it was necessary to enter the war. Members of the committee included the legendary advertising pioneer Walter Lippman, George Creel and hundreds of PR and advertising executives, along with scores of journalists.

In his book, *Public Opinion*, Lippman describes how in short order, the committee used effective propaganda techniques to convince a very anti-war American public to wholeheartedly support the war effort, both emotionally and financially. Up to that point, it was one of the most effective efforts to socially manipulate the feelings and behavior of a large number of unsuspecting citizens. Since then, propaganda has been used extensively by our government to rally support from the American people on various fronts, from supporting unpopular wars, confronting social issues, to fighting inflation. Remember Gerald Ford's WIN buttons (Whip Inflation Now). These are but a few examples of social propaganda.

Routinely, we see the use of economic propaganda all around us. As we discussed earlier in the "Animal Spirits" section, how people feel, can play a large role in how markets and economies behave. If people generally feel good about their own situation and future prospects, they tend to spend and invest more freely. Consequently the markets and the economy perform better. The opposite is true if people are more pessimistic or negative about their futures. Markets tend to drop, and the economy tends to slow.

It stands to reason then that if you could somehow influence people's moods, you may also be able to influence the markets and the overall economy. Today, we see evidence of this almost daily, whether it's Wall Street, the government or the Federal Reserve, spinning the most recent economic data in a more positive light. By putting a positive spin on things, the hope is that people may become a bit more optimistic about the future which can help to boost us out of the current economic malaise. Is this deception or reality?

Putting a positive spin on economic data is certainly not a new development. Data such as Gross Domestic Production (GDP), inflation (CPI) and the unemployment rate are often reported with a positive spin. Most voters tend to vote their pocketbooks. Therefore they tend to grade politicians by how well the economy is growing, whether or not they have a job, and whether they can continue to afford their current standard of living. If the answer is no, a politician may be out looking for a new job. I would venture to guess that the average person would be outraged if they knew how creatively these numbers can be "massaged."

So it behooves everyone involved to keep the public as content as possible. As the Romans said "Give them bread and circuses and they will never revolt." But in times of financial hardship, this becomes increasingly difficult, since the desired message may be in direct conflict with what can be easily observed firsthand. It's hard to convince the public that unemployment is getting better when you, a family member or a close friend is out of work. Or that inflation is only 3%, when it becomes increasingly difficult to pay your bills on time because gas is $4 a gallon and you had to take out a home equity loan to get your car repaired. How can the economy be recovering, when factories and the stores in my neighborhood are continuing to close?

In financially difficult times, investors must be aware of attempts to prop up the public's animal spirits. At times, it may become difficult to distinguish between the real facts, and wishful thinking.

It may be beneficial for investors to focus more closely on the raw data that is being reported, and less on the opinions of others, especially of those who may have their own agenda to promote. For example, a stock fund manager may soften his negative outlook on the stock market, in fear that people may sell his fund. A gold analyst may take a more optimistic view of the precious metal, since it might persuade more people to buy it. A commentator may take a more extreme outlook, to hype the sales of their new book or newsletter. The difficult task for an investor is to find data and opinions that don't come with a vested interest attached. We'll discuss how to find reliable information later.

Media Mania and Hype

A source of frustration, for many, is the role the general media plays in disseminating economic, financial and investment information. My disappointment lies with the general media outlets, and not necessarily the channels dedicated to business topics, such as Bloomberg and CNBC, and publications like the *Wall Street Journal Business Week*, *The Financial Times* and *Kiplinger*. In general these types of outlets tend to do a good job.

In contrast, I feel the general media frequently fails to adequately and accurately inform the general public about important financial and economic information and events. While the general media should play a critical role in informing people about financial issues, at times it appears the facts get blurred by the hype and sensational headlines. In this brave new world of 24/7 news, people have broad access to much of the same news, so if you want to stand out in the news business, you may have to say something provocative or controversial.

At times investors may be exposed to views and opinions that may not be widely accepted. But because of its extensive coverage, it could be easily perceived as being so. The additional coverage may further fuel any existing concerns or panic. For example, extensive coverage about the possibility of a severe market drop could actually help fuel such a drop. We saw many examples of this in 2008, as the financial crisis continued to unfold. At the very time we could have used the calm, rational voice of someone like a Louis Rukeyser, we instead got a screaming Jim Cramer.

At other times, the media can further fuel unrealistic expectations, which in return may lead to "irrational exuberance." In the late 1990's we were being bombarded by stories of ordinary people who had made incredible returns on their investments buying tech stocks. Highlighting a few examples of extreme profits gives people the impression that it is easy to make money in the stock market. Remember the stories about ordinary people quitting their jobs to become day traders? Or how the exponential growth in the economy was rationalized because the "old economy" was being replaced by the "new economy?" Well, I guess the economy didn't get the memo!

A big disappointment is that many "non-financial" reporters are simply uninformed or misinformed about finance issues. This can make them ill-equipped to effectively question or challenge some of the information or claims that their guests make. Without this challenge, the viewer or reader is often left with the impression that the information must be accurate. Useful and accurate financial information is out there, but you must make an effort to check the facts.

At times the media itself can become a tool of those pushing their own agenda, whether that is Wall Street, corporate America, our government, or some other group. It is not difficult to influence opinions and behavior by using the techniques that have been perfected over the years. Some of them may include carefully placed and repeated "expert opinions," anecdotal stories, paid-for advertising, and the selective release of financial data. As Madison Avenue learned, if you can influence people's opinions and perceptions, you can also influence their behavior. While certainly not easy, it has proven to be very effective.

Framing—How We *Choose* to See Things

At times we can be our own worst enemy, simply because we may choose to see what we *want* to see. As we discussed in the previous section, at any given time, much of what we *perceive* is being filtered through our emotions, which can influence our frame of mind. This "framing" is not only affected by what we currently encounter, but also the "frame" that may have been set by some past experience. And the strength of the previous emotion, will determine how much it may influence the current situation.

Take for example someone who as a child had the traumatic experience of almost drowning in a large wave while vacationing with their family in the Gulf of Mexico. That feeling of not being able to breathe and almost dying would certainly leave a very vivid, powerful and lasting impression on that person. Now contrast that with someone who grew up in Hawaii, and as a young adult surfed the huge waves of the

North Shore. All that time spent in the water, experiencing the thrill of riding those large waves, would probably leave some very pleasant memories.

If you took both of these people out to the beach and showed them some large waves crashing on the shore, and asked them to describe their feelings, you're likely to get very different answers. For the first person, it might conjure up negative feelings of fear, risk and maybe even panic. He would probably have very little desire to go into the water. The surfer, on the other hand, would probably have very positive feelings of excitement, joy and a longing to jump in the water with a surf board.

Both of these people are looking at the same thing, but come to very different conclusions. The difference is their *perception* of what they are seeing. Their *perception* was formed by their own unique past experiences, which are now being viewed through very different frames. Each of them has valid reason for their own particular viewpoint. Neither one is right or wrong. Their perception is their own reality; their frame of reference. And both would have a difficult time convincing the other to change their perception.

This does not mean, of course, that someone's perceptions cannot change, but it may not be easy. Emotions are under the influence of the impulsive brain, which is more difficult to change. As time goes on, if the near-drowning victim allows himself to have positive experiences with water, his perception may be more likely to mellow.

However, some perceptions will be more difficult to change than others, since the intensity of the emotion at the time of the original event directly impacts any future recollections of it. And fear is one of the hardest emotions to overcome. It resides in the inner, more primal part of our brain, so it is typically more difficult to modify.

Perceptions can be one of the biggest obstacles we face when dealing with our investments. We all carry around a certain amount of *baggage* regarding our investments, both positive and negative. These preconceived notions about certain investments, or about investing in general, can heavily influence our decisions. This baggage, to a large extent, can be developed from three basic sources:

- *Our first-hand experiences.* These are based on our personal investment experiences. Personal experiences carry the most weight when forming our opinions, since they have directly affected us. They also tend to be the most difficult to dislodge, especially if they were particularly painful. For instance, if someone suffered a tremendous loss in the 2008 stock market drop, their perception of stocks now may be that they are too risky. Therefore, going forward, they may be less inclined to invest in them, or more willing to sell them at the first sign of trouble.

- *Observed experiences.* These are events that we have observed others experience. They may not tend to carry as much weight as personal experiences, but they can be very, strong especially if the person observed was particularly close, such as a family member, and/or the experience was very traumatic. Many people who lived through the Great Depression as children, still carry the scars with them today. In some cases, witnessing their parents lose everything, and having to rely on relatives or strangers for their very survival, may have taught them some very bitter, vivid life lessons. I know people who have a very difficult time spending their money, because of these past experiences. For them, the pain of doing without something, even if most would view it as a necessity, is less painful than the possibility of running out of money, regardless of how unlikely.

- *Learned experiences.* These are beliefs that we have *learned* from an outside source, but have not experienced or observed firsthand. This acquired knowledge plays a significantly smaller role in forming our beliefs, and can be more easily changed when new evidence is presented. This information can come from a wide range of sources including formal education, books and periodicals, the news, or opinions we have heard from "experts" or influential or successful others.

IMPORTANT CONCEPT: Throughout our lives we accumulate "knowledge", process much of it subconsciously, and then develop these beliefs into something that is perceived to be based in facts. In essence, we are converting what many times is simply an opinion (our own or others) into "facts." Out of these *facts* we develop our beliefs. Therefore, in our minds, much of what we "believe" is grounded in fact. We tend to further cement these beliefs by actively seeking out additional information that will further reinforce them, and discount any that may contradict them.

This is referred to as our "confirmation bias." We'll discuss that in more detail later.

Some of the "knowledge" we gather may be erroneous. The information may be incorrect, facts may be misleading, and some opinions be just plain wrong. Our brain's attempt to quickly and efficiently process information, can lead it to get sloppy and fail to filter out errors. As a consequence, some of the things we may currently *believe* to be true may simply be wrong, because they were formed on faulty information. As the old computer adage goes, "garbage in—garbage out."

How much conviction we have in our *beliefs* will be largely dependent on the source of the knowledge, first-hand, observed or learned. This in turn will determine how difficult it may be to change your mind sometime in the future. For example, you may intellectually know that the odds of finding a mouse tail in a can of XYZ cola are astronomical, but if you were one of the unlucky people to do so, it is highly unlikely you will ever want to drink another can!

As a consequence, our view of the true probability of something occurring may become skewed, even if the odds of it happening again are highly unlikely. Because of our firsthand experience, we may overestimate the probability of the same experience re-occurring. For instance, if someone's first experience with buying real estate resulted in a large loss, they may erroneously conclude that buying real estate in the future is very risky.

The same can be said for underestimating risk. A large gain made on an initial investment may also lead an investor to miscalculate the real risk involved. This may have been the case with many investors who got caught up in the euphoria of the late 90's tech bubble. Some of the initial gains investors experienced as the tech bubble grew may have led them to miscalculate the true risks that were involved in these types of stocks.

Our Perception of Risk

> *"Everyone is a long-term investor,*
> *or at least until the market drops."*
>
> Sir John Templeton, *legendary money manager*

How investors perceive or interpret risk can vary by situation. Investors can categorize risk by different standards, depending on the potential effect on their lives. We tend to pay more attention to those things we perceive as having the greatest potential consequences, while possibly choosing to ignore others. Therefore, investors tend to have their own unique definitions of what they consider risky and safe. At times these definitions can be downright baffling.

I have a friend who is a big Harley-Davidson motorcycle guy. He has several classic bikes, and makes the most of them. In a typical year he probably rides several thousand miles throughout the country, in all kinds of conditions. He has shared with me stories about driving through horizontal rain storms at night, where he had to guess where the road was. Or the time he had a blow-out going 65 mph. When he gets home from Sturgis or Daytona, one of the first things he tells me is that year's "body count." He doesn't even wince when telling these stories. He's your typical, tough Harley guy. To him riding a motorcycle is not a risky proposition.

His view of the investment world is another story. He has trouble stomaching the volatility that the investment world churns out, and at times even small fluctuations can cause him concern. To him, the world of investing is chaotic and downright illogical. He perceives that investing is a very risky proposition.

His view of risk is curious, to say the least. The man, who doesn't think twice about riding his motorcycle on the highway through the pouring rain, perceives investing as a very risky proposition. I have discussed this odd dichotomy with him on several occasions. I've pointed out to him that a *mistake* with his investments won't put him in the hospital or worse yet, the morgue. A motorcycle crash on a highway can be much less forgiving than a plunge in the S&P 500. But his perception is his reality.

While most people don't ride motorcycles, we do take calculated and potentially life-threatening risks every day. Every time we get into a car, we run the risk that an 18-wheel truck will cross over the white line and hit us head on. How about when we run across a busy street, or agree to a medical procedure? Doesn't getting on a rollercoaster or climbing up a high ladder to put up Christmas lights entail potentially catastrophic risks? Sure they do, but we are willing to assume the risk to have some sort of quality of life. It wouldn't make sense never to leave your house just because it may rain. We take calculated risks all the time and don't even think twice about them. As the old saying goes, "a ship is safest when it's in harbor, but that's not what it was designed to do."

Investors use different standards when assessing and accepting investment risk, than they do in their other daily activities. Some people have trouble dealing with their investments simply because of how they choose to define and view risk.

There are two basic forms of investment risk:

- *Risk of Loss* – This risk is the actual loss of your investment. You invest $10,000 in a stock or a small company, and it goes bankrupt. In this scenario you lost all of your investment.

- *Volatility Risk* – This second type of risk deals with the volatility and price fluctuations of the investment. For example, you invest $10,000 in stocks, and during the time that you own them, the price fluctuates daily, at times dramatically.

It is easier to manage the risk of loss than the risk of volatility. You can reduce the risk of loss by diversifying your investment over a larger number of similar investments. For example, instead of buying a single stock, you could reduce your risk by owning 50 or 100 different ones.

Volatility risk, on the other hand, is much more difficult to manage. To effectively reduce the volatility in your portfolio, you not only have to diversify over a larger number of investments, but you also need to find investments that have a "low-correlation" to each other. Generally, investments that have a low-correlation to each other don't tend to move in the same direction or with the same severity, at the same time. Basically, the goal is to pair up investments that may move in opposite directions. The goal of incorporating low-correlation investments into a portfolio is to hopefully reduce the portfolio's overall volatility.

Investments don't always behave in the real world as they do in theory. Over time how you would expect two investments to behave (their correlation to each other) may change dramatically. They may tend to move in different directions (have a low-correlation) for a period of time, only to become more correlated at a later date. The concept of utilizing low-correlated investments to reduce volatility in a portfolio may work better in *normal* economic conditions, than in stressful economic times. To a large extent, how an investor decides to construct their portfolio may be determined by their perception of risks at that time. For most people, their perception of investment risk will vary over time. This variation typically reflects changes in age, personal circumstances, and prior investment experiences and even by how certain risks may be presented to them.

For example, younger investors tend to have a greater willingness to assume more risk than older investors. When investing their IRA or 401(k) funds, a 35-year-old person may be willing to take on more risk since they may not need the money for 25 or 30 years. A 55-year-old doesn't have the luxury of time and may opt to be more cautious. As a person gets older, the natural tendency is to become more cautious. We tend to see the biggest change in investors attitude when they cross over from their working career into their retirement years.

I have witnessed otherwise perfectly normal people enter retirement, and slowly transform into business news junkies, staring at the business channel for hours, glued to every slight movement of the stock market, obsessing about how it may affect their accounts. Sometimes this can even inhibit their ability to enjoy their retirement. I doubt this is how they envisioned their *golden years*.

An investor's risk perception may change after they retire. Some retirees mistakenly assume that they no longer should, or need to take any risks with their investments. They figure they have reached their ultimate goal—retirement. What they forget is that the ultimate goal is not to simply reach retirement, but rather to provide a steady stream of income for the next 20-30 years to maintain their pre-retirement lifestyles. For many people retirement is simply the 6th inning of a 9 inning game that may even go into extra innings.

While an investor *should* be more cautious with their investments in retirement, most people simply can't afford to avoid *some* investment risk. This has become increasingly important as people live longer and healthier lives. Without sufficient growth in their post-retirement investments, many people may be in for a rude awakening.

By trying to completely eliminate volatility risk in their investments, many retirees may be inadvertently introducing a whole new risk—the risk of outliving their money! Most people need to ask themselves one simple question: What is my greater risk—that I wake up one morning and my portfolio is down 20%, or that I wake up one morning and I realize I spent it all, and I have nothing left? The sad truth is that for some people the real risk in their retirement won't be dying too soon, but rather living too long.

Situational Risk Perception

A person's perception of investment risk may also vary from situation to situation. At the beginning of this chapter I used a quote from the legendary mutual fund manager John Templeton: "Everyone is a long-term investor, or at least until the market drops." Meaning most people tend to have a much higher risk tolerance when the market is doing well. It's easier to tolerate short-term drops, even significant ones, if the market quickly recovers and then continues to move up.

An investor may become unnerved if a substantial market drop does not recover quickly, or if it continues on a longer-term downward trend. In a severe or prolonged down market, an investor's fear may have an opportunity to creep in and take control. That's when your emotional **Oscar** brain may try to push you into self-preservation mode. Fear can de-rail even the most disciplined investment strategies. Even the most battle-tested investors are susceptible to this potential mid-stream change in risk assessment. In the past decade, many disciplined investors panicked, and threw in the towel.

This does not mean that at times midstream adjustments may not be required. It simply means that you should be cognizant of the reasons behind the change in your strategy. Are they based on a change in the facts and circumstances, are they being driven by your emotions or both?

This is why you can observe people morph from ultra-confident, aggressive investors into a deer caught in the headlights. I had the opportunity to observe this phenomenon with someone in the late 90's. At the time, the market was soaring and the tech bubble was in full bloom. Alan Greenspan had recently made his infamous quote about the stock market's "irrational exuberance."

This person was in his mid-50s, and had virtually all his investments in stocks, most of them in tech-related industries. Because of the tremendous growth in his portfolio over the previous three years, he was actually contemplating retiring early. His comment to me was, "If the market continues this way for the next few years, my investments should easily double."

As we discussed, most people who are nearing retirement have a tendency to become somewhat more cautious with their investments. But this particular person was fighting the classic "overconfidence bias". He didn't want to do anything that might "inhibit the growth of my investments", so he decided to leave well enough alone, stay the course.

I didn't hear back from him until a few years after the tech bubble crashed. By this time he had capitulated and had sold most of his stocks and invested the proceeds into bonds. To illustrate how dramatically an investor's attitude can change, in 2011, he moved half of his investments into a money market account that was paying nearly 0% interest. He did this because his short-term bonds had declined slightly from the previous quarter. He made the change even though his annual dividend income dropped from nearly $35,000 to under $1,000! He said that at that point he simply needed to be able to sleep at night. I guess "inhibiting the growth of his investments" was no longer an issue—same person, very different attitudes.

This is an example of a classic "situational aggressive investor." Some people are aggressive by nature, while others get sucked in because of the situation. An investor who is aggressive by nature may have an easier time coping with dramatic and sometimes horrific drops in the market, because it is built into their DNA. This is not to say they are immune to panic, but they may typically stay the course longer, and make more incremental changes.

Others, who view themselves as *aggressive* investors, may feel aggressive when their investments are doing very well. It's easier to be more optimistic when things are going well. These may be the same people who are also more susceptible to selling when the market sharply declines. It is during market declines that a person's true tolerance for risk may emerge. As the saying goes, "you can always tell who's been swimming naked when the tide goes out.

INVESTOR LESSONS:

It is very difficult to objectively assess yourself. It's human nature to feel that we are at least a little bit braver, smarter, faster and more talented than we really are. The brutal truth is that most of us have a higher opinion of ourselves than we merit. This can be a dangerous combination for investors. Not everyone has the stomach for excessive investment volatility. Knowing your true tolerance for risk is critical to your investing success.

Presentational Risk Perception

A person's perception of assessing a risk may also vary dramatically depending on how the risk is represented to them. As we discussed earlier, our nature is to focus more on avoiding pain or risk, than it is to gain pleasure or reward. While pleasure and reward are tremendous subconscious motivators, pain and loss are even stronger. Studies suggest that a dollar of loss is twice as painful as a dollar of gain is pleasurable [1].

Here is an example of how someone may perceive a risk, depending on how it is presented. Let's say a particular life-saving surgery was recommended to you. You interview two surgeons. They tell you the following:

- Surgeon A: "If I perform the surgery, you have a 10% chance of dying."

- Surgeon B: "If I perform the surgery, you have a 90% chance of survival."

While both are statistically equal, most people would respond better to surgeon B's statement. This is because subconsciously surgeon A's statement is focusing on the negative outcome and is stirring up your fear. Surgeon B's statement, on the other hand, is focusing on the positive outcome—living. This appeals to your pleasure emotions—or in this case, the odds of your survival. Although both options have the same potential outcome, your perception of the risk will be influenced by how it was presented to you.

This may also hold true when you are being presented with the potential risks associated with an investment. Most investment marketing materials focus primarily on the positive aspects of an investment to the extent permitted by the law. Investors should be wary of investment marketing materials that only seem to emphasize potential gains, and downplay potential risks.

Investors should spend an equal amount of time reviewing the potential risks of any investment, and not just on the potential gains. It is important to fully understand the potential consequences, and whether, if they were to occur, you could handle them both financially and emotionally. We'll cover this later in the book

As we discussed in the "Black Swan" section, avoid only focusing on the probability of a negative outcome, and examine the potential consequences. Sometimes, if the consequences are grave enough, it doesn't matter how unlikely the odds of it happening might be. In that case, you may want to avoid the investment altogether or at least try to minimize the potential damage by limiting your exposure.

Only commit to an investment when you fully understand all the potential risks and consequences. Keep in mind that all investments entail some sort of risk. There is no such thing as a truly "risk-free" investment. This includes U.S. Treasuries and money market accounts.

Some risks are obvious, such as volatility or even the risk of losing your entire investment. But some risks are more subtle, and therefore easier to overlook. For example, the risk of rising prices (inflation) decreasing your standard of living over time, or even possibly causing you to outlive your money, is a real risk that investors tend to ignore. This risk is more easily ignored since it is difficult to predict the likelihood that this *potential future risk will occur and bring with it the unforeseen consequences.*

The risk of an investment account dropping is much more immediate, and therefore may seem more real. Investors need to learn how to balance between short, intermediate and long-term risks; and better understand their potential ramifications.

INVESTOR LESSONS:

When analyzing the risk of any investment, be cognizant of the emotions that you may be feeling at that time, including any subconscious ones. Keep in mind that any similar, past experiences you may have had with a similar investment, or the efforts of a salesperson, may be influencing your perception. You may also need to assess which risks are more likely to occur, and what their consequence may be to your situation. No investment decisions should be made until you fully understand all the risks involved.

Chapter Footnotes

[1] -Daniel Kahneman and Amos Tversky, 1979

CHAPTER SEVEN

I Want it, And I Want it Now!

> *"Instant gratification is not soon enough."*
>
> Meryl Streep, *actress*

One of the strongest characteristics of the impulsive **Oscar** brain is its intense desire for immediate gratification. This stems back to its original drive for daily survival. For early man, survival was dependent on doing whatever was necessary right then and there, since there may not be a tomorrow. As a matter of fact, the very concept of *tomorrow* may not even exist for this part of the brain. The very ability to conceptualize the thought of there being a *tomorrow* lives in the more advanced cortex, which developed much later. The reflexive brain lives in the here and now, that's all that matters since it's all it knows. So if I'm hungry, I want food. If I'm thirsty, I want a drink. If I want to mate, I need to find one. If I'm scared, I run, or do whatever it takes to make me feel safe [1].

This is an important concept, since it explains why people sometimes do seemingly stupid and/or dangerous things. The impulsive part of the brain doesn't grasp the concept of long-term consequences. Thus, there are no long-term consequences to consider, so why shouldn't I do what feels good and gives me immediate comfort, relief or pleasure. Problems can arise though, when there is an imbalance of power between the impulsive and the logical parts of the brain. When the impulsive part starts to dominate the decision-making process, your decisions may become quite illogical.

Many times when you observe a person who is under considerable emotional stress, you can intuitively sense which part of their brain is controlling the decision-making process. That is why we may tend to instinctively look for the composed person in a time of crisis, hoping that their calmer outlook will lead to good decisions.

An example of this is the leadership of Mayor Rudi Giuliani and Dick Grasso (who was the president of the New York Stock Exchange) during the 9/11 attacks in 2001. Their seemingly calm and steady demeanor gave people confidence in their leadership. While I'm sure inside they were volcanoes of emotions, their outward appearance gave many people the hope they needed at a time of crisis. They took a horrible situation and helped keep it from turning into total chaos.

Testing the Theory

In the field of behavioral psychology, there have been numerous studies and experiments involving the impulsive brain and immediate gratification. One key study examining this issue, conducted by researchers D. Read and B. van Leeuwen in 1998, showed that when we are asked to plan ahead we are more likely to make the right choice because the logical part of the brain is involved [2]. In this study, participants were asked to choose between something delicious (immediate gratification) and something that was good for them (future benefit). They asked one group of people to pick what they preferred to have with their lunch *next week*: a nice fruit salad or a piece of delicious chocolate cake. The participants overwhelmingly (74%) chose the healthy fruit salad.

They then asked another group what they preferred with their lunch, but this time they asked them right before they were to eat. So which did they choose the healthy fruit or the delicious chocolate cake? The results were nearly reversed, with 70% wanting the cake!

Evidence suggests that when we are asked to *plan ahead*, we are more willing to choose the *right* thing (fruit salad) since the logical part of the brain is involved in making the decision. But if we have to make an immediate choice, we run the risk that impulsive **Oscar** will be making the decision for us. He wants his cake NOW!

Our logical brain helps us understand that well-considered plans can produce superior outcomes. But when the future arrives, our natural instinct may cause us to abandon our plans. We want to feel good now. We can worry about tomorrow, tomorrow!

One might conclude from this that we may be better served making important financial decisions that have long-term consequences, well in advance, allowing for input from our logical brain. Waiting until the last minute to make important decisions (not that we ever do that!) runs the risk of relying solely on our impulsive brain's judgment.

How the Brain Reacts Under Stress

> *"The greatest weapon against stress is our ability to choose one thought over another."*
>
> William James, *American philosopher and psychologist*

Evidence shows that our brain reacts very differently under stress. In 1999, Shiv and Fedorikhan set out to study the effects of stress on the decision-making process. In their experiments, one group was given a two-digit number to remember. Then they asked the subjects to go into a room down the hall and write the number on the chalkboard. On the way to the room, an assistant asked the participants if they would like a healthy fruit salad or a piece of chocolate cake (here we go again with the fruit vs. the cake!)

A second group of people was asked to remember a much longer seven-digit number, and asked to write it on the chalkboard in the room down the hall. Once again the friendly assistant was there to ask them if they would like a fruit salad or a piece of chocolate cake.

The results were very interesting. A significantly larger number of the participants that had to remember the more stressful seven-digit number chose the chocolate cake (22 %

more). Similar types of experiments have been done hundreds of times, with similar results. Shiv and Fedorikhan's concluded that when put under stress, it appears that an individual's choice is even more likely to be made by its impulsive brain.

These observations have implications for our daily financial decisions as well. Imagine that you are called into your company's human resources office. The manager explains to you that a few weeks ago you were mailed an information packet explaining the company's new 401(k) plan, and that today is the last day to sign up for it. If you don't sign up for it now, you will have to wait a year. She hands you a form and asks you if you would like to sign up today for the retirement plan. Let's examine a few different scenarios that could play out here.

Scenario #1 – You received a packet from the 401(k) provider last week. The packet outlined the rules and the plan options along with all the available investment options. It also had a handy calculator that helped you figure out how much you need to save for retirement. It also illustrated how much you would need to save if you started today, instead of waiting ten years. You noticed that if you wait, you would have to save almost twice as much as if you started saving today. You figured that there is no way you could save that much in ten years, so you decided that you better start now. The packet also outlined several portfolios you could choose from, based on your age and risk tolerance. Based on the information in the packet, you determined that you should save $150/ month and use the *moderate* investment allocation.

As you stand there in the human resources office today, you recall reading the information a few days earlier, and the decision you made. So you tell the manager that "yes", you would like to sign up for the retirement plan, and you proceed to fill out the forms.

Scenario #2 – You received a packet from the 401(k) provider last week. You threw it on the kitchen table along with the brochure you had just picked up at the new car dealership. You just bought a car two years ago, but it's nothing like this new hot, sporty model! You never looked at the relevant 401(k) information.

Now as you stand in the human resource offices with the form in hand, all you're thinking is that if you sign up for the 401(k), how are you supposed to get your new car? Besides, you're too young to be thinking about retirement anyway. You decide you are not interested. The impulsive brain wins.

Scenario #3 – As you stand in front of the human resources manager with your form, you can feel yourself tensing up because you don't have any idea what she is talking about. Frantically, you search your memory. You, only vaguely, remember seeing something in the mail about a retirement plan. As your mind continues to desperately try to remember, you suddenly recall some people at work were talking about the 401(k), but you can't remember any specifics. You now recall reading somewhere that everyone should sign up, so maybe you should too. But lately you've also heard people complaining about how much they have lost in their 401(k)'s, and you certainly don't want to lose your money! You know you should be putting some money aside for your retirement, but you have so many bills to pay right now. And, what on earth are all these options on the back side of this form? It looks like a Chinese menu with no English translation!

As she continues to stare at you, waiting for your answer, with all these random thoughts running through your head, the only thing on your mind is how quickly you can get out of there! So you blurt out, "no, not at this time, thank you." As you turn to head towards the door, you can't help but wonder if you made the right decision. The impulsive brain wins again!

This drive for immediate gratification can also influence your investment decisions. If the markets are going through a period of heightened emotions, either fear or greed, you can become even more susceptible to poor decision-making. For example, if the stock market is in a steep decline, you may run the risk of abandoning your long-term plan, *if* you let your emotions get the best of you.

One of our strongest psychological drives is to feel safe. Interestingly, several studies suggest that the financial "pain of loss" is processed in the same portion of the brain as is actual physical pain [3].

Consequently, if you felt your investments were under an imminent threat, you might allow your impulsive brain to take control, and seek out immediate safety. With your investments, this feeling of *safety* may mean you sell now and ask questions later.

The actual decision may not take into account the long-term consequences, or the wisdom of selling now. You simply want to feel safe. Sometimes this can backfire, because what may appear *safe* when in a highly charged emotional state may not, in reality, be safe at all. It's not unlike the golfer who seeks *safety* under a large tree during a thunderstorm. While he may stay dry and feel safe, he is also greatly increase the chances of being struck by lightning.

It reminds me of a conversation I once had with someone who was recalling their experience during the 2008 stock market plunge. He described in detail the physical pain he experienced as he watched the market continue its dramatic plunge day after day. I remember him still being confused that he could have suffered such great losses, even though "I sold all my risky investments before the big drops occurred, and I bought all safe, blue chip stocks, but they still continued to go down." Sometimes, safety is a relative term that can turn out to be a mirage.

INVESTOR LESSONS:

When you know you will be faced with an important decision or choice that may have long-term ramifications, be sure to think through all your options and their possible outcomes WELL BEFORE you have to make the decision. Write down all your options along with all the possible pro's and con's associated with each option, regardless of how inconsequential they may seem at the time. If applicable, try to use timelines and future calculations. This process will force you to involve your logical- thinking brain, since it involves future planning. Make sure you write down your best option on paper, and take it along with you for reference when you have to make the decision. This will reduce the pressure you feel when you make the final decision.

<u>Chapter Footnotes</u>

[1] - "Evolution of the neo-cortex: A perspective from developmental biology" Pasko Rakic, Yale University School of Medicine, 2009

[2] - "Predicting Hunger: The Effects of Appetite and Delay on Choice. Organizational Behavior and Human Decision Processes" D. Read, & B. van Leeuwen, 1998

[3] - "Emotional and Physical Pain Activate Similar Brain Regions: Where does emotion hurt in the body?" Alan Fogel, 2012

CHAPTER EIGHT

How the Brain Recalls Memories

> *"Memory is deceptive, because it is colored by today's events."*
>
> Albert Einstein, *physicist*

One of the more interesting aspects of researching this book has been discovering the way researchers believe the brain stores and recalls memories. I always imagined that when I wanted to recall a memory, it was like watching a specific scene in a movie. Some device goes on in my brain's library where all my memories are stored. It finds the specific scene, plugs it in, and suddenly my memory comes to life.

Well, as it turns out, that may not be how it happens at all. Evidence suggests that the brain doesn't recall memories in a complete sequence of events. So it's not like a scene from a movie being replayed at all. It's more like looking through an old photo album, where the pictures are not necessarily in order. In fact, in some cases they may not even be in the same book, or even in the same room.

When you are trying to recall a memory, you may actually be looking at a series of *still pictures*, not a continuous tape. When you find these *pictures*, you fill in the blanks to complete the sequence of the memory. At times, the pictures may not be in the right order. And that's where it can get complicated.

Memory fragments are believed to be stored in many different locations throughout the brain, not in one specific location. In addition, any senses that were in the memory, such as sound, smell, taste or touch, are stored in other areas. Any one of these senses can potentially trigger a memory. Walking into a bakery and smelling some fresh baked cookies can conjure up distant memories of grandma's house during the holidays. This initial smell can trigger additional memories, like the sights and sounds of her house. How the brain actually accomplishes this intricate retrieval task continues to baffle researchers[1].

As our brain begins filling in the *blanks* in our memory, our current mood and perception of the event will influence what we CHOOSE to remember them. As Einstein said, "Memory is deceptive, because it is colored by today's events."

Here's an example. Let's suppose its Bill's 25th wedding anniversary. He is reminiscing about his wedding day with great fondness. This is how he may remember it today. It was a beautiful, crisp, sunny fall day. All his close friends and family were there. The church service was beautiful, and his soon-to-be wife looked beautiful. The wedding reception was joyous. The hall was beautifully decorated. The food and music were incredible, and everyone had a great time.

Unfortunately, this is what actually happened. It was fall, but it was partly cloudy, with some light, scattered rain. Two of Bill's groomsmen, his brother and one of his best friends from college, got so drunk the night before that they missed half of the wedding. Though not very disruptive, he could at times hear his cousin's newborn crying during the service. His bride's mascara was slightly running down her cheeks from her tears, which were caused by the flower girl stepping on and tearing the back of her dress. After the service, the photographer took the bridal party to a park for over two hours, to take pictures in the light drizzle. At the reception, Bill's mom was frantic because the wrong flowers were delivered. The band was okay, but not quite as contemporary as he had hoped for.

Now let's change the current scenario a bit. Let's suppose Bill is currently going through a bitter divorce. He now recalls his wedding day as being a cold, bitter, rainy day. His college buddy and brother were the only smart ones, since they didn't have to sit through the whole God-awful long church service, with that kid screaming in the background. His bride looked like a raccoon with all that makeup running down her face. She yelled at that poor little kid who stepped on her dress. The whole church probably heard her screaming. And that damn photographer must have thought he was doing a Hollywood photo shoot. Two hours in the pouring rain. Everybody was soaked by the time they got to the reception. When he got there, the first thing he saw was his mother running around like a fool, yelling at some poor flower delivery guy. It still galls him that he had to pay extra to get that lousy band to play an hour longer.

This is an example of how the mind can play tricks on you. It's recalling the same *snapshots* of the wedding, but it's filling in the blanks based on your current mood and perception. These current feelings affect your recollection of that memory. Basically, if you are in a positive frame of mind, your recollection of the past may be more positive. If you are in a foul or pessimistic mood, it may be more negative. Be aware that when recalling a memory, it may be tainted and distorted by your current mood or outlook.

The next section will focus on some of the mechanics involved in recalling memories, and then I promise we'll discuss how this psych mumbo jumbo relates to your investments!

Types of Memories

Researchers typically divide memories into two basic types, short and long-term. Short-term is also known as your *working* memory. Your memory system can be loosely compared to how most computers work. Your short-term memory can be compared to a computer processor, while your long-term memories are similar to the hard drive. While this is not an accurate description since our minds are hundreds of times more complicated, it can serve as a good analogy about how our minds store and recall memories.

Short-Term Memory

Short-term memory (STM) is the brain's way of remembering information that it is currently using. It works something like this. The brain receives a message from our senses. This stimulus from the senses will only be held for a fraction of a second in the sensory memory. This *memory* will be lost shortly unless the brain deems it important enough to pay *attention* to the sense and register it. This takes about six to eight uninterrupted seconds. Because of this, the vast majority of the sensory inputs we receive do not even get *registered*. Our brains simply cannot devote that much time to each of the millions of inputs we continually receive. Even if we do decide to register the input, it will only remain in your short-term memory for about 30 seconds, unless there are additional reasons to remember it for a longer period of time.

That is why *eye witnesses* can be very unreliable. They may have been at the scene of the incident, but unless they were actively focusing on the actual *event* for at least six to eight seconds, they don't know for a fact what really happened. What they may remember is only the *snapshots* in their memory, and most of these memories may have been of the after-effects. From these snapshots our eyewitness will attempt to *fill in the blanks* to recreate the memory.

Here's an example of how this may work. Let's suppose you are sitting in your car at a red light. You hear several gunshots. You look over and see someone in a hat running out of a store across the street.

You pull your car over to see what happened. People are running out of the store. You can hear them talking about how a young, tall, thin man with long hair, wearing a New York Yankees baseball cap, came in and shot the cashier three times.

When the police question you about the incident an hour later, you tell them that you were sitting at a red light when you heard three gun shots (at the time you weren't sure how many were fired). You then saw a young, tall, thin man with long hair run out of the store. (At the time you weren't sure it was even a man). And you *think* he was wearing what appeared to be a New York Yankees cap (which at that distance and angle would have been nearly impossible to tell).

In reality, as you were sitting at the red light, the events happened so quickly that your brain had very little opportunity to register most of the information it was processing. Later, when you think back on the events, your memories of the event became tainted by information that you over heard or later learned. Your brain is looking at those snapshots, and merely filling in the blanks. The problem is that this reconstruction process is being done with input from your current mood and perceptions, as well as from other people's speculation about what happened. If you repeat the story several times, before you know it, you may convince yourself that this is what actually happened, whether it's accurate or not. That is why law enforcement officers and attorneys are usually dubious about eyewitness accounts. It is also why you can end up with multiple versions of the same event.

Earlier research estimated that most people could only hold five to nine items in their short-term memory at one time. Some of the early memory research was conducted by George Miller in the mid '50s when he was at AT&T. The design of our current phone number system is the result of his extensive research.

More recent studies, however, have estimated that at any one time, we only have the capacity to hold four or five items in our short-memory. The exact number is not as important as the realization that we can juggle only a finite amount of information in our short-term memory. We also have a tendency to remember things that are at the beginning or the end of a list. Typically we forget the middle. That's why when someone tells you to pick up ten items from the grocery store, you will likely forget some of them. And they will probably be the ones in the middle of the list. (Hint: make a list!)

There are several methods that can increase the capacity of your STM. One of them is the process of "chunking," or grouping things together. For example, your phone number is made of ten numbers, so we "chunk" them by using the three area code numbers, then the first three digits, and then finally the last four digits. It is easier to remember three sets of numbers than ten individual ones. Say your phone number out loud, and you'll see how the cadence changes between these groupings.

Let's return to our grocery list for a moment. To help you remember all the items on your list, you can mentally break them down into logical groups, such as three in the dairy department, three meats, two cereals and two cleaning supplies. "Rehearsing" them, either silently or out loud, also adds additional auditory cues. Now you stand a better chance of remembering all of them (but you're still better off writing them down!).

Just because a "memory" makes the first hurdle and is retained in the STM, this does not mean that information automatically makes it into your long-term memory. Quite the contrary. In fact, it remains a mystery even to experts as to why certain memories make it into long-term memory, while others don't.

Long-Term Memory

Our STM has a strictly limited capacity and duration. It is only available for a short period of time. By contrast, our long-term memory (LTM) can store an immeasurable quantity of information, potentially for our entire lives.

For example, someone may give you a seven-digit account number that you may remember for only a few seconds. This suggests that it was stored in your short-term memory. On the other hand, you may still remember your childhood seven-digit phone number after 20 or 30 years. Through years of repetition it has become stored in your long-term memory.

 It appears that only information that we feel may be needed or beneficial in the future tends to make it into long-term memory. For example, registering and recalling the sight, smell or sound of a predator would have greatly enhanced the survival chances of our ancient ancestors. Similarly, when you hear a car horn, or someone yelling "fore", you are conditioned to be alert.

Keeping it very simple, our long-term memory potentially involves four stages: encoding, storage, retrieval and forgetting. (Remember, I'm not trying to prep you for a psychology exam, but rather trying to help you become more aware of how psychology influences your financial and investment decisions!)

- **Encoding:** In creating a new memory or concept we must attach some meaning to it. This is done by building *context* around it as we continue to learn the new concept or experience. Building context around a thought, called "pointers" provides the mind with multiple ways to recall something in the future. For example, you may be researching small cap stocks. You may "encode" small cap stocks with the phrase "a type of stock" along with some key descriptive "pointers", which help describe the term small cap stock; such as "small companies," "long-term growth," "aggressive" and "volatile." Attaching these descriptive words helps your mind put the new concept into context.

- **Storage:** As we store the new concept, we attach it to other existing related memories, such as "small cap stocks are similar to mid-cap stocks, but more volatile", thereby connecting the new concept with older, more familiar ones, for easier recall. By attaching this new information to other things with which you are already familiar, you give the new thought more context and cement it in your long-term memory for future use. As stated earlier, research suggests that memories are stored throughout the brain, not in one central location. Some are stored in visual files, some in auditory files, while others may be stored as a smell or touch. So having these *connectors* is vital when trying to recall complete memories.

- **Retrieval:** This is truly the remarkable part of the brain's memory. When needed, we can recall a stored concept by following some of the "pointers" that were originally attached to it. If you can't remember exactly what "small cap stocks" are, you could look to any of the attached descriptive "pointers", such as "small companies," "long-term growth," etc. These descriptive terms connect with other terms, so one hint may lead to another, and another, and ultimately lead you to the desired overall concept. Basically, your brain is looking for fragments of information to put together like a giant jigsaw puzzle. Many times one thought or memory leads to several more that may even involve several senses such as a smell, taste or touch. As these puzzle pieces are being assembled in your mind the picture may not immediately be evident. But at times, as you struggle to recall a memory, you may experience a "eureka" moment, as an additional single bit of information suddenly allows you to see the whole picture. When that happens, you experience a sudden rush of additional memories, like a floodgate opening, to complete the whole picture. All of us have experienced times when we have gone from complete confusion to complete clarity in a moment's time.

How does our brain consolidate a new short-term memory such as "small cap stocks" and convert it into our long-term memory?

It is believed that the hippocampus, an ancient part of the cortex, is critical in consolidating new memories into long-term memory. Without it, new memories could not be stored in long-term memory. When you remember a new fact, say "small cap stocks," the new memory data converges on the hippocampus, which sends this data along a path several times, each time strengthening the various descriptive terms it is linked to. According to neuroscientist Bruno Dubuc, of the Canadian Institute of Neuroscience, making the information flow around the circuit many times strengthens the links enough that they *stabilize.* The hippocampus has done its job and is no longer needed to recall the data at a later date. The strengthened memory paths now become part of long-term memory.

Consciously repeating or speaking aloud any new thoughts or ideas also strengthens these new memories. Utilizing several different senses, such as visual, hearing smell or touch, increases the probability that a memory will be remembered. That is why writing things down dramatically increases the vividness of the new memory, since you are using multiple senses.

It is also thought that one of the primary functions of sleep is to improve consolidation of newly acquired information during the day. Several studies have shown that having a good memory may depend on getting sufficient sleep. So after spending several hours researching your investments, make sure you get a good night's sleep!

Your Emotions and Memory

Research suggests that emotions may also have a powerful impact on how we may remember something. The more vivid a memory, the more easily it may be recalled. Vivid memories are thought to be more easily *seeded* when there is a lot of emotion attached to it. The more powerful the emotion, the easier it is to recall the memory. Any elevated excitement and emotion, fear, hate, greed, passion or joy, can help create a vivid memory. This is especially true if the chemical Cortisol is present. Cortisol is the chemical the impulsive brain releases when it feels threatened or gets excited. The presence of Cortisol may help assure that a memory is properly *seeded*.

This process may have played a critical role in our ancient ancestors' survival. By properly seeding critical information in highly emotional times (like being mauled by a tiger or remembering where that abundant fruit patch was), may have helped them survive their next similar encounter.

This can be quite relevant to your investing. You are more likely to have vivid recall of negative experiences associated with your investments, than more neutral ones as when the markets may have been calmer. Why? These memories may have been *seeded* at a time when the market was in a free fall and you were very nervous (such as April 2000 and October 2008). This could have created some very vivid and painful memories, which then would be more likely to be recalled during subsequent market declines. These more vivid negative experiences can taint your view of the stock market during tumultuous times, and possibly make you more prone to panic selling.

Case Study

It is always useful to know if someone has had a previous bad experience with any investments. If so, you would want to know what the circumstances where at the time of the experience. Often these past bad experiences can leave a negative recollection which may have been based on incorrect or skewed information. By talking about it in a calm and logical manner, there is a chance that the past situation may be seen in a whole new light.

I once had an interesting discussion with someone, let's call him Monte. The interesting thing about Monte was how he absolutely hated bonds. We're not talking about simply disliking them, he HATED them. That's a strong emotion for an inanimate object! When we first met he was nearing retirement and he had his entire 401(k) in various stock funds. Typically, people nearing retirement tend to have their assets in a combination of stocks and bonds in an attempt to be more cautious with their investments. They usually start to move at least a portion of their investments off the roller coaster ride of the stock market.

With Monte though, the very mention of bonds sent him into a rant about the dangers of bonds, and how he hated them. It was obvious that we had hit a raw nerve, like a dentist with his drill. Even an amateur psychologist would have picked up on the fact that he must have had a very negative experience to cause such a vehement and painful reaction.

As we explored his reaction to bonds (at this point the drill was moving VERY carefully!), he exclaimed that that bonds were WAY too risky for him. His statement surprised me, since most people don't tend to think bonds are riskier investments than stocks (*Note: While certain bonds may prove to be riskier than certain stocks, in general, bonds have tended to be less volatile than stocks.*)

He proceeded to tell me a story about how he was talked into buying a substantial amount of high-yielding bonds of a large local company back in the early 80's, when interest rates were very high. To do this, he had sold a large portion of his stock funds. These company's bonds were yielding over 16%!

Everything went fine for the first few years, and he was very happy as he collected his 16% interest rate. Life was great. But, a few years later, the company fell on hard times, and was forced to file for bankruptcy. He went on to explain (in visible agony) how he only got back about 20% of his original investment, and it took over two years in court to get even that much back. At that point he was both emotionally and financially devastated. He and his wife had to dramatically cut back their living expenses, which has affected their relationship ever since.

To make matters worse, Monte is an engineer (just as there is no such thing as an ex-marine, there is no such thing as an ex-engineer!). He calculated that if he had just kept his money in the original funds, he would have been up over 50%! Talk about pouring salt into an open wound!

Based on Monte's own personal experience, his perception was that investing in bonds was very risky and had negative consequences. Otherwise, how could he have lost 80% of his money? Given the strong emotions that must have been present at that time (anger, fear, regret, uncertainty) is it any surprise that he had such an immediate, vivid and negative impression of bonds?

This is an example of the emotional baggage that many investors may be carrying around with them, in many cases, unknowingly.*

Are You a Victim of Selective Amnesia?

When recalling memories, one of the most important lessons to learn is that your mind can play tricks on you. What you remember about an event may not necessarily be how it actually played out. Occasionally we all fall victim to "selective amnesia". To avoid the pain of negative experiences we conveniently re-write history so that it fits more comfortably with how we currently feel or think. Most of the time this is accomplished subconsciously, without any awareness of the process. At times, our mind seems to have a mind of its own!

For instance, let's suppose its October of 2008. The market is in total free-fall. You call your broker and tell him you are worried that the market will continue to fall. He replies that if you are that concerned, you have three options.

---

* Hypothetical examples are not intended to be indicative of any specific investment. Hypothetical results are for illustrative purposes only and are not intended to represent the past or future performance of any specific investment.

- **First**, you can do nothing and hope the market recovers soon, but you run the risk of it continuing to drop further, thereby increasing your losses.

- **Second**, you can sell everything, making it easier to sleep at night and preventing further damage. But, locking in your losses creates the risk that when the market recovers you will have lost the chance to gain back some of your losses.

- **Or third**, you can sell some of your riskier stocks, and keep others. This way, you are hedging your bets both ways.

After discussing the options, you decide to sell some of your stocks but keep some of the others. As it turns out, the market drops another 25% over the next few weeks, and you panic. Now, you sell the remaining stocks. You are upset with your broker because all you remember is telling him a few weeks ago to sell everything. This is an example of *selective amnesia*, or outcome-based recollection. Because of the actual outcome (the market dropped another 25%), your memory may be strongly influenced by what you WISHED would have happened (sell everything). Since this WAS one of the options discussed at the time, it's easier to confuse what you actually did with what really happened. We'll discuss this phenomenon further when we cover "hindsight bias." At times *selective amnesia* can be a major response to making devastating financial decisions.

INVESTOR LESSONS:

When you must make major financial decisions, go through the following exercise. Remind yourself of negative past experiences associated with these decisions. Evaluate how your present thinking is being influenced by your past. Reflect on the emotions attached to this past event. Think through how the past is playing out in your decision- making now. This process allows your brain to more completely scan through all the descriptive markers that were set in place when the negative event occurred. By separating what actually happened from the emotions that may have been connected to it, this exercise will help you formulate more logical conclusions and create better outcomes.

Chapter Footnotes

[1] -"Brain Rules" Dr. John Medina, 2009

CHAPTER NINE

The Brain Takes Shortcuts

> *"Don't bother me with the facts, son;*
> *I've already made up my mind."*
>
> Foghorn Leghorn, *Warner Brother's cartoons*

As we examined in the previous section, our brains have to continually process tens of thousands of bits of sensory data simultaneously. Even as fast as the human brain can process, the only way it can manage this incredible volume of information is to set up some shortcuts to filter through the data.

The process by which our brains filter through all this information is called "heuristics." It is the process of arriving at an instantaneous intuitive conclusion, based on our past experiences. While very fast and efficient, there are times when these *conclusions* are based on limited, inaccurate, and often incomplete information.

Before I get into details, let me give you a quick example of how our brain takes shortcuts. When we read, for example, we don't typically read every letter in a word, or even every word in a sentence. Instead, we tend to simply scan the whole word or sentence. If you don't believe me, see if you can read the following paragraph.

> *I cnat blveiee taht I cna aulaclty uesdnatnrd waht Im rdanieg. The pahonmneal pweor fo the hmuan mnid! Aoccdrnig ot rscheearch at Cmabirgde Uinrevtisy, it deons't mttaer in waht oerdr the ltteers in a wrod aer, the olny iprmoatnt tihng is taht the fsrit and lsat ltteer be in the rghit pclae. The rset can be a taotl mses and you can still raed it wouthit a porbelm. Tihs is bcuseae the hmuan mnid dsoen't raed ervey lteter by istlef, but the wrod as a wlohe. Azmanig!*

How did you do? Most people don't have too much trouble reading this gibberish because your brain has set up a shortcut process that allows it to scan words it recognizes and not take the time to read every letter. This is just one very simple example of how our brain processes the massive amounts of information it receives. That's why you should always have someone else proof read your work. It's too easy to miss your own mistakes. Just ask my editor!

Explaining Heuristics (Your Brain is in a Hurry)

The process of heuristic shortcuts is accomplished by the impulsive brain—**Oscar**. To speed things along, all the data the brain receives is *filtered* through an elaborate series of shortcuts, so it can instantly discard any information it deems irrelevant. Of course the process is not fool proof. But it lets the brain focus on the important tasks at hand. This shortcut process is automatic, involuntary, lightning fast and is done at the subconscious level. We are not even aware that the process is occurring.

These *shortcut* filters are unique to each person, and are constructed and refined throughout our lives. They are shaped and developed by our own first-hand experiences, lessons we have learned from others, and our own perceptions.

When building our internal *filters*, our first-hand experiences, things we learned with our own senses, are given much more weight than those we may have learned from others. For example, we have all been told not to touch a bare electrical wire. But a person who has actually touched one will have a much more vivid and lasting recollection of it, than a person who was simply told about how much it hurts. It is also why "seeing is believing."

The same can be said for investing. Personally experiencing half of your 401(k) disappear in a stock market plunge is very different from reading stories about other people who are struggling because of their losses. Recollect the importance that vividness plays in recalling our memories. Living through the drop first-hand will make the recall much more intense.

Once established, these subconscious shortcuts or opinions, developed in the *impulsive* part of the brain, are difficult to change. With repetition, these shortcuts become thinking patterns or habits but don't always produce the desired results. **Oscar** doesn't like change. These *filtering* rules become rigid, inflexible and concrete. Unlike the logical brain–**Felix**, which is more open to compelling new facts.

The constant need to develop new and more efficient *shortcuts* drives our brain to continually search for new "patterns." Pattern-seeking appears to be hard-wired. When you think you've found one, it creates a new, potentially useful shortcut. This gives our brain a powerful incentive to detect patterns, even where they don't exist. To **Oscar**, even two consecutive occurrences may constitute a pattern, while three must be a rule!

This instinctive drive to jump to a quick conclusion, even if based on limited information, is what allowed our ancient ancestors to survive. If you see, hear or smell a predator— RUN! Even today, it can save us from many potentially dangerous situations. But jumping to a quick conclusion, based on incomplete or inaccurate information, can also lead to disastrous outcomes.

Here's an example of someone jumping to a conclusion too quickly. See if you have ever been guilty of something like this.

You're watching the Super Bowl with your friends at your house. Its halftime and you've already run out of beer. So you make a quick trip to the supermarket to pick up another case. You should be back in plenty of time for the second half kickoff.

You're standing in line to pay for the beer, but there are five people in front of you. You keep looking at your watch (as if it will make time slow down!). Its 15 minutes to the kick-off. It seems that everything is moving in slow motion. You can feel your blood pressure rising. Finally, there is only one more person in front of you, and they only have three items! You're silently thinking, *yes, there is a God, and he must love football!*

Just then, an elderly lady appears out of nowhere, holding a baby. The checkout girl immediately goes to her and starts playing with the baby. You can feel your anger rising with your blood pressure. How rude! Doesn't this stupid girl know the second half is starting in five minutes! You are ready to strangle the young checkout girl. You have jumped to a conclusion, and made assumptions based on the facts as you believe them to be.

You later learn that the young checkout girl's husband was a fireman. He was killed a year ago while rushing back into a burning house trying to save a child's life. The young checkout girl now works two jobs trying to support herself and her baby. The older woman is the check-out girl's mother. She brings the child to her daughter at work every evening. This is her daughter's only opportunity to see her child before he goes to bed.

If you had known ALL the facts, you probably would have felt quite differently about waiting in line for an extra few minutes. Yet, how many times in a day do we jump to conclusions before we know all the facts? We honk at the guy who just cut us off on the road, not knowing that he is rushing to the hospital. We yell at our child for something that we later find out they didn't do. We get angry at a co-worker for not pulling their own weight, not knowing that his wife was recently diagnosed with cancer. Regardless of how little we know about a situation, our reptilian brain jumps to a conclusion and demands action—now!

This rush to judgment is just as prevalent in the investment world. Millions of decisions are made on incomplete information, often causing unintended long-term consequences. In addition, this incomplete information is then quickly processed through potentially flawed filters and shortcuts. Now imagine this process taking place during times of high emotional stress, such as 9/11, or those dark days in 2008. It starts to make sense how seemingly intelligent people can make so many regrettable decisions.

It can also shed light on how two equally qualified and informed "experts" can arrive at diametrically opposing viewpoints. They may be viewing similar data (unemployment rate, GDP growth rate, etc.), but are filtering it through their own distinct filters. Thus, each interprets the data differently, leading to very different conclusions.

So where does this leave the average investor? How are we supposed to trust the experts when they can't even agree? One is yelling *"buy-buy-buy"*, while the other urges you to sell everything, buy gold and build a bunker! This conflicting advice can lead to even more confusion. If already in an emotional state, an investor may subconsciously turn to their impulsive brain for a quick decision. **Oscar** is only more than happy to jump to a conclusion for you.

The encouraging news is that it is possible to break your brain of bad habits. Given the opportunity, good habits (shortcuts) are just as easy to establish as bad ones. You just have to convince your brain into seeing it your way.

INVESTOR LESSONS:

- To tame your impulsive brain, you must be aware of it and its influence on your decisions. It operates on the subconscious level, leaving you unaware of how you may have reached a particular conclusion. The only way to combat its influence is to examine the feelings and facts that became your habitual thinking.

- The goal is it to make certain you bring important decision to your conscious mind, giving your logical brain the opportunity to provide input into your decision-making. Avoid making important long-term financial decisions based solely on your emotions at the moment. By introducing reason, logic and longer-term thinking, you can improve the ability to reach rational decision. At times you may come to the same conclusion (e.g. sell your stocks), but it will based upon rational thinking, not pure emotion.

In the next section we will focus on how your impulsive **Oscar** brain develops shortcuts and biases. We'll identify some of the more interesting instincts and biases that may challenge us when making financial and investment decisions. Research suggests that some of them may even be hard-wired into our brains, making them that much more influential. But remember, we are not pre-destined to live by **Oscar**'s rules. We have a choice.

CHAPTER TEN

Why We Focus on Irrelevant Things

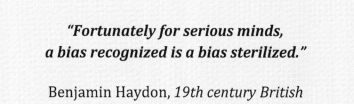

*"Fortunately for serious minds,
a bias recognized is a bias sterilized."*

Benjamin Haydon, *19th century British
writer and painter*

I once received an interesting call from a friend. He told me that he wanted to sell the majority of his stocks right away, and put the proceeds into his money market account. He wanted to move on this quickly, because gasoline prices had gone up lately. He said he noticed that the last few times gas prices went up, stock prices fell shortly thereafter. He wanted to get ahead of the curve this time. He was convinced that gasoline prices at the pumps had a direct and immediate effect on stock prices. He had detected a pattern!

While I might agree that elevated gas prices over a longer period of time may have an impact on stock prices, there is not a direct and immediate correlation. At times it may appear that way, but in reality stocks typically move in one direction or another for a number of reasons, not based on just one variable. There is a big difference between "correlation" and "causation." Two things may become temporarily "correlated" to each other (meaning that they move in the same direction), but that doesn't mean that one is causing the other to change. This is an important distinction.

My friend's conclusion that gas and stock prices are directly correlated is a good example of an "anchoring" bias. Anchoring bias is the tendency to rely on one bit of information or data when making a decision, even though it may be incomplete or irrelevant to the decision that must be made.

As we discussed earlier, humans have a limit on the number of things we can focus on at any one time. We also have an inclination to think that the first idea or thought that pops into our minds is more accurate than later ones. The combination of these two shortcomings is part of the basis for our "anchoring" bias.

These anchors can be pretty powerful and difficult to dislodge once they are in place, even when additional information is presented that may prove it wrong. An example of this is how people view the value of their homes.

I once had a situation where someone bought a home in 2006 for $350,000. A few years after the real estate market collapsed he was transferred out of state and needed to quickly sell his house. The only offers he received were in the mid $200,000 range. Although he had a very small mortgage, he refused to sell because, "the house is worth much more than that." He was anchored to the price he paid for the house, even though the market price was much lower when he was trying to sell. The true value of anything is the price someone is willing to pay for it at that time. He eventually sold the house for $255,000, but only after a year had passed, during which he had paid an additional $18,000 in mortgage payments and property taxes.

The same is true when it comes to investments. Often, people tell me that they will sell a particular investment they own "when it comes back to what I originally had paid for it." Unfortunately the original price that you paid for an investment for has nothing to do with its' value today. GE stock was selling at over $60/share back in early 2000. It hasn't been near that price since then. Someone who is anchored to that price may have to wait a long time before it comes back.

One famous study, done by researchers Tversky and Kahneman, showed just how irrational our anchors can be. They first asked students to write down the last two digits of their social security numbers. Then they asked them to write down the number of countries they thought were on the African continent. Repeatedly, students that had higher social security numbers guessed that there were a higher number of African countries, than those with lower social security numbers.

Obviously there is no correlation what-so-ever between these two numbers, but somehow just the mere task of writing down an unrelated number (anchoring) was evidently enough to subconsciously influence their answers.

In another study participants were shown the following equation:

$$1 \times 2 \times 3 \times 4 \times 5 \times 6 \times 7 \times 8 \times 9 = ?$$

They were then given 10 seconds to guess what the answer was. The average answer in the study was around 500.

The study was repeated with another similar group, but this time the equation was reversed to read:

$$9 \times 8 \times 7 \times 6 \times 5 \times 4 \times 3 \times 2 \times 1 = ?$$

Interestingly, this time the average answer was 4,200! Same numbers only reversed. The real answer is irrelevant (it's 362,880!). The point is that people tend to "anchor" to what they first see or what is easy to understand, regardless of its relevancy. Armed with limited information, people tend to quickly make up their minds.

Anchoring to irrelevant things can prove to be very dangerous when it comes to investing. Most things we observe in life aren't as simple as they may appear. This can be especially true when dealing with your investments and the economy. When a significant event occurs, whether a stock market decline, a sudden interest rate spike, or a recession, there are many variables at play. The event is only a reaction to all of these variables.

When a significant event occurs we want answers, and we want them quickly! The human mind is impatient. It favors simple answers. If you only look at the most recent variables that led up to the event, you are at risk of making an erroneous conclusion that they are the sole cause.

Suppose you're loading logs onto your pickup truck. You load the last log and the axel breaks. So the question is, was it that last log that broke the axel? Someone's knee jerk reaction might be "yes." The correct answer is "no". The weight of all the logs combined contributed to the axel breaking. Loading the last log first, would not have changed the outcome.

The same mistake can be made when examining a financial situation. For example, you may have noticed that the last few times the Fed raised interest rates, the stock market dropped. You could erroneously conclude that when the Fed raises interest rates, stocks will drop, and selling immediately would protect you from these losses. This could be a mistake.

In reality, the Fed's raising interest rates probably was not the sole reason that the stock market went down on those days. There were many events happening. The most visible event was the Fed's action. But it was only the "last log". Your **Oscar** brain detected a pattern. The Fed raises interest rates—stocks go down. It's simple, it's easy to understand, and you have personally observed it. You have now created a *shortcut* filter that is anchored to an irrelevant assumption or correlation— when the Fed raises interest rates it is bad for stocks. **Oscar** created a *faulty shortcut*. Beware, if you rely on it, the next time the Fed raises interest rates, your instinct will be to sell stocks.

INVESTOR LESSONS:

Typically, it's faulty thinking to blame one or two variables as the cause of most financial problems. Usually, the cause is multi-factorial, and difficult to judge in the present. The answer may only be available in hindsight. Avoid the tendency to focus too narrowly when making long-term financial decisions. Doing so could give you a skewed view of the problem. Are the variables you are focused on merely coincidental to the underlying cause? Always try to anchor your decisions to longer-term issues, such as "what is the long-term rate of return I need to achieve to meet my retirement income needs", or "why should this event change my long-term focus?"

Misdirected Focus: "Move along, there is nothing to see here."

> *"What the eyes see and the ears hear, the mind believes."*
>
> Harry Houdini, *magician and escape artist*

As our duel-brain system wages its internal tug-of-war, our focus can be misdirected. We can all relate to instances when we catch our minds *wandering* from the activity on which we are currently working. We must consciously redirect our mind back to the task at hand. A temporary lapse of focus can lead to disastrous results.

Two of the culprits of our *wandering* minds are our limited short-term memory capacity and our attention deficit. As we discussed earlier, our short-term memory has a very limited capacity. Once at capacity, any additional information will have more trouble *sticking*. Consequently what we are exposed to first may take priority.

We know our minds are easily distracted by new information; like a child at Christmas who jumps from toy to shiny new toy, none getting their full attention. The combination of these two tendencies can lead to distorted views of the situation at hand.

This natural tendency can also complicate matters for an investor. When a long-term perspective is distracted by an event, it can revert to short-term panic. Recall Sir John Templeton's observation that "everyone is a long-term investor—until the market has a substantial drop". Especially in times of heightened emotions, examine where you find you focus- don't lose sight of your long-term plan in a moment of panic. When the stock market and the economy appear to be operating *reasonably*, the rational brain has a chance to focus on the longer-term issues.

This is the time to develop plans to address saving for the kid's college tuition, or saving for retirement. Commit to investing for the long-term, understanding that adjustments may be necessary moving forward.

Being able to reference back to the longer-term view can help keep current emotions in check. You can make **Oscar** and **Felix** work together to solve the problem at hand.

Extreme situations, like job loss, death of a spouse and other major life events can trigger a heightened emotional state and additional stress. Or, the trigger could be due to external events like as significant drop in the stock market (and your

401(k) or IRA), major bad news on the economy, or some global political or financial crisis.

As the stress level rises (aided by increasing media coverage) the investor's logical brain may start to get crowded out, opening the door to the impulsive brain's desire to focus on immediate problems. It may tend to focus (or obsess) on one *crisis*, and then another, failing to fully analyze the implications of a rush to judgment. Much like the child at Christmas with all the new toys, in a panic your brain will quickly move from one crisis to the next. I refer to this phenomenon as "crisis surfing."

For investors, the problem can be easily compounded when their focus turns to irrelevant issues, ones they perceive to be significant in their own minds, but which are not. They may recall similar situations in the past (familiarity bias), and erroneously misinterpret the current one. This is similar to attributing the last log being thrown on the truck as the cause of the broken axel.

If this heightened level of stress continues long enough, long-term financial plans may begin to diminish in importance, causing a loss of perspective while critical decisions are being made. If permitted, decisions may be made purely on emotions that are based partly on inaccurate or irrelevant information, with little regard to the long-term consequences.

I'm sure that after the dust settled in March of 2009, smart people looked back in dismay and wondered why they sold their GE stock for under $7/share (it was over $42/share just a few months prior to that). When relying solely on emotions, even smart people can make disastrous financial decisions.

The Art of Misdirection

Being easily distracted is one of our biggest Achilles heels. In the hands of someone who understands this human weakness, it can be a powerful tool to manipulate others for their own advantage.

Magicians are masters at exploiting this weakness. While researching this book I was fascinated to learn how adept magicians are in the art of misdirection. For most magic acts to succeed, the magician must be able to direct the audience's attention towards something that is irrelevant to divert attention from what is really happening. If they can keep you preoccupied, even for a few seconds, they will be successful in fooling your mind. They are basically taking advantage of the "blind spots" we all have. So while you are focusing on the magician waiving his wand over the attractive bikini clad assistant, an elephant appears on the stage!

In the world of finance and investing, we are constantly besieged by misinformation that can distract us from the real issues at hand. As we discussed in the section dealing with the mind's perception, this attempt to influence our focus comes in various forms.

Sometimes the attempts are obvious, such as ads for gold coins, a new super-duper investment, or a testimonial from some washed up actor hawking reverse mortgages. Their goal is to persuade you to buy or use their products by trying to evoke certain emotions, such as fear, greed, or safety.

For example, if you watch these investment ads carefully, you will notice a re-occurring theme. Many attempt to appeal to your greed or fear. These are powerful emotions that feed normal worries about the economy and its impact on our financial security.

One of my favorite commercials shows two men, each in front of several computer screens. One is bragging that he has 20 investment charts open simultaneously, monitoring over 1,000 investments in real time, and how he can trade stocks, options and commodities simultaneously, suggesting that if you buy this program you can get better returns on your money. While that may sound impressive, the average investor would be clueless on as to how to use the information. The misdirection is getting you to focus on how impressive the tools are and not on the fact that they may be useless in your hands, and in some cases it may prove to be downright dangerous!

While there is nothing inherently wrong with advertisers trying to influence your decisions, we as investors must be aware of these attempts to misdirect our attention. This is true for almost all financial products sold, whether they are annuities, limited partnerships, mutual funds, or Exchange Traded Funds (ETF's). Later, we'll discuss how to protect yourself from some of these advertising gimmicks.

Not all the attempts to misdirect your focus are as obvious as advertisements. These other attempts may come in many forms, each having their own agenda. A thorough discussion of this topic is beyond the scope of this book, but to reinforce this problem, let me touch on two common attempts at misdirecting an investor's attention.

WALL STREET: The investment world has a vested interest in how the general public perceives investing. Consequently there may be attempts to persuade people that investing is a fair and logical game; and if you just follow their simple rules, you should be able to stay out of trouble and make some money. Well, how's that fairy tale been working out for the average investor over the past decade or so?

Wall Street's biggest fear should be that if enough investors become sufficiently frustrated, they could decide that the investment game is no longer safe, or they feel that it is somehow rigged. They might decide to take their money off the table, and go home. And even if it were not forever, it could certainly be for long enough that it could severely damage Wall Street's survivability.

Could this be why the Wall Street PR machines go into overdrive when things like a 50% drop in the stock market occur? *Experts* are paraded out, in an attempt to reinforce investor confidence by reminding them that "the market always comes back in the long run." This confidence building was also evident after the May 2010 "flash crash", when the U.S. stock market dropped nearly 600 points (3%) in just 4 minutes, and then recovered over the next half hour. That day, the stocks of some major companies were rendered near worthless in a matter of minutes for no apparent reason, only to see them rebound significantly. The experience left many investors wondering if it was even worth continuing to remain in a game where the rules appear to be in a constant state of change.

U.S. GOVERNMENT: A few years ago I was watching a movie on cable TV. Somehow the sound track was mixed up with that of another movie, so the dialogue had nothing to do with the scene on the screen. I ended up watching it for about 15 minutes because at times it was funny when the dialogue would sync up with the actor talking on the screen, but it had nothing to do with the scene. I recall one scene where the two actors were in a serious romantic conversation, but the dialogue was something right out of a Rambo movie!

At times that's how many people must feel when they hear some of the government economic reports. The Announcer says: "Government reports show that inflation is well under control, with prices going up an average of only 2%." I'm sure there are people who wish they could shop where the government does, since their expenses are increasing a lot faster than that! Or when the government statistics report shows a "significant improvement in unemployment". Try selling that "significant improvement" story to the millions of people that are still unemployed or under-employed.

These are just two examples of "selective data reporting." If people focus on certain data, they may be convinced that the situation may not be as bad as it seems. This is how the theory of animal spirits could be implemented. By using selective data that supports a particular view or outlook, you could theoretically influence people's attitude and opinions towards the economy in general. And technically you are not lying, just simply misdirecting, much like the magician.

INVESTOR LESSONS:

There is an important battle raging between potentially conflicting forces seeking to influence your thinking and behavior. Being aware of it is not enough. One of the best defenses against having someone misdirect your focus is to do your own independent critical thinking. Don't take someone's word on something just because they are in a position of authority or appear knowledgeable. The first question you should always ask yourself when you hear someone being interviewed on CNBC is—what vested interest does this person have in my believing what they are saying.

BONUS! Using Anchoring in the Art of Negotiating

Anchoring is an important concept to remember when negotiating. Many negotiation experts suggest starting from an extreme initial position. The idea is to get the other side to anchor to that number, so in the end they will feel they got a good deal. The art of negotiating is making the other side feel they got the better end of the deal. Getting them to anchor on your number may convince them of that.

Just remember, when entering into a situation where you are the buyer, the salesman will be doing the same to you. This is especially true when buying large ticket items such as cars, electronics and homes.

A good salesperson will try to get you to anchor on another higher priced item, so as to make the one you really want seem like a bargain. Sometimes they may stress all the additional features, even though it may not add a lot of value (or mean that much to you). They are hoping that it will appear to make the overall purchase, of what you really wanted, look like more of a bargain. An example of this would be stressing the 1,000 watt sound system in the new car. Really? Do I need 1,000 watts of thundering bass in my 40 square foot car? Perhaps I could trade it for a back seat barbeque instead!

If you are aware of these techniques, you can actually turn the tables on them. First, always let the salesman state his price and reasons. Now you know his position and can better formulate a response. Counter with a low ball price, anchoring the bottom. Don't be afraid to go too low. The worst that can happen is that they say no. If they want the sale, they will make you a counter offer. Above all, be prepared to walk out. That will send them scrambling for their best deal with all the extras you don't need.

Then, say that you don't need or want all those extras. You find them way too confusing to use. Remember, you're not trying to impress them; you just want to get the best deal. Try this—pull out an old, outdated cell phone, one you used three years ago, hold up the phone and tell the sales person that this is about as technologically advanced as you get. I know this works because I have personally used this many times to make a point. The sad part is that it really was my current phone! I had one guy ask me "where'd you get that, in a museum?" The good news is by now you should be able to hear the air going out of the salesman's balloon, and you're well on your way to getting a good deal!

CHAPTER ELEVEN

Looking to Confirm What We Already Believe

> *"The human brain is a complex organ with the wonderful power of enabling man to find reasons for continuing to believe whatever it is that he wants to believe."*
>
> Voltaire, writer, *historian and philosopher*

As we discussed earlier, the human mind is constantly seeking short cuts to reach quick conclusions, which may be based on incorrect or incomplete information. Once we reach a conclusion, it is very difficult to change it. It is equally as difficult keep an open mind when encountering something or someone new, without imposing our preconceived opinion on the situation. We can become a victim of our own "confirmation bias."

Researchers suggest that once we have developed an impression about something or someone, we tend to selectively filter new information we receive on that subject so that it confirms what we think we know or believe. We are predisposed to focus our attention on information that supports our opinion, and ignore or downplay information that contradicts our opinion. This is why first impressions are so important.

We also seek out new information in much the same way. A good example of this is how some people get their political news. If someone is more conservative by nature, they are more likely to watch Fox News, while if more liberal, they may watch MSNBC or CNN. By doing this, much of the information they receive will simply reinforce their already formed opinions, further solidifying their existing beliefs. This may make it even more difficult to change their opinions, even when confronted with conflicting evidence.

As a result, a person's confirmation bias often results in poor decisions, because reliance on one-sided information skews their frame of reference. This leaves them with an inaccurate picture of the current situation. To compound errors, these faulty conclusions get *uploaded* into your memory for future reference, thereby influencing your future decisions.

On this subject, Charles Darwin was quoted as saying: "I followed a golden rule, namely that whenever a new observation or thought came across me, which was opposed to my general beliefs, I would make a memorandum of it without fail and at once …. for I had found by experience that such facts and thoughts were far more apt to escape from the memory than favorable ones."

From an investors' point of view, this skewed view of the financial world can prove costly. Confirmation bias suggests that an investor is more likely to seek out information that supports his existing position about an investment, and ignore information that contradicts it.

The original opinion may have been formed with incomplete or faulty information, as with the example of the checkout girl with her baby. Consequently, unconsciously seeking out only new information that confirms an investor's faulty conclusion can only strengthen and reinforce that view.

For instance, let's say an investor reads an article stating that technology stocks are poised to go up dramatically. After reading the article, he recalls that when he went to shop for his new computer last month the store was quite full, and people were waiting in line to pay (forgetting that it was a liquidation sale). At this point he may have already formed a conclusion— he wants to buy tech stocks. But, he decides to validate his conclusion. So he fires up his new computer and checks out a few tech company names he recognizes, and sure enough, they are all up considerably over the past 12 months. Then, he does a Google search for "outlook for technology stocks."

After waiting an excruciating 0.2 seconds for the results, he is presented with a list of 20,500 related articles. As he scans the list of articles, what he may not realize is that subconsciously his mind may be *noticing* the ones that appear to be more positive towards tech stocks, and passing over the articles that appear to have a more negative slant.

After finishing his "research" he feels pretty comfortable with his original decision to buy tech stocks. So he logs on to his XYZ on-line trading account and confidently places his *buy* orders.

After all, his original hunch was correct, all his research confirmed it.

If he had been more careful in his research, he would have noticed that most of the positive articles were over a year old. That's a long time in the investing landscape. The more current articles were focused on why computer sales were down, and how tech companies were furloughing some of their manufacturing shifts, and had to severely discount their prices. This could significantly cut into their profits and therefore lead to a substantial drop in their stock prices.

What our investor initially saw as a huge demand for computers was actually a fire sale, which is why the store was so busy when he went to buy his computer. Once his initial perception was set, his subconscious mind tended to reinforce that view.

INVESTOR LESSONS:

- One of the most important things an investor can do is to maintain an open mind when making decisions. Of course, this is much easier said than done, since our brain has a tendency to fight us all along the way. Establish a process to help you make more well-rounded and informed decisions. First, recognize when you are under stress. Be aware of your thought processes. Review at least three contradictory opinions. Make a pro's and con's list. Examine your choices and the impact they can have on your portfolio. If you do this, many times you will find yourself moderating your initial viewpoint. I live by a simple philosophy, "things are rarely as bad, or as good as they appear, the truth is usually somewhere in the middle."

- When doing your own research, especially on the internet, make sure you check the date of the articles! We are all guilty of thinking that we have found that preverbal nugget of gold, only to realize (hopefully not too late!) that it was outdated or obsolete information. Also, check the sources of the articles. Any fool can post an opinion online. Bloggers are no exception. I'm still waiting for Google to come up with a "stupid" filter! I am constantly being forwarded articles that at first glance seem impressive and legitimate. When you do a bit of digging, you realize that it's some guy living in his grandmother's basement, and because he works part time at the local pawn shop, it makes him an expert on gold prices! Check those sources!

- Stick with independent research and opinions. Research done by companies or people that have something to sell may be biased towards a certain viewpoint. It doesn't mean the research is flawed, just be careful with their conclusions. Trust but verify!

CHAPTER TWELVE

When Normal Isn't Normal Enough

> *"There are known knowns. These are things we know that we know.*
>
> *Then there are known unknowns. That is to say, there are things that we know that we don't know.*
>
> *But there are also unknown unknowns. There are things we don't even know we don't know."*
>
> Donald Rumsfeld, *former U.S. Defense Secretary*

Most people have difficulty properly preparing for disasters that may occur at some unknown future date. When people are faced with a potential disaster, human nature can make it difficult to accurately gauge its true probability, its magnitude and possible effects. This phenomenon is known as your "normalcy bias."

This is particularly true for people who have never experienced a certain type of disaster before. People, who have already experienced a similar disaster, will likely have a vivid memory of it, causing them to be more cautious and prepared the next time the threat occurs. People who live in California know what it is like to experience an earthquake and how to prepare. Someone from Ohio likely has no idea!

People who have never experienced a certain type of disaster may have trouble knowing how to react to it. This can result in disaster. An example would be preparing for an impending category 5 hurricane. People who have experienced one before will likely heed the warnings, and take appropriate precautions. People who have not lived through a hurricane may take the threat more casually. Our tendency is to be more optimistic, and down play the risks. They don't know and don't want to know. As the old adage goes, "ignorance is bliss."

Every hurricane season we watch news footage of people throwing hurricane parties in their beachfront homes, and scenes of surfers in the water as the storm approaches. Their actions would suggest they may be underestimating the potential danger. However, if the hurricane were to hit near their home, I'm willing to bet the next time there was a warning, they would be boarding up their windows and heading out of Dodge; not loading up on chips and kegs of beer!

This can also hold true on a much larger scale. The government, either local or national, can fail to properly interpret the magnitude of a potential risk. Hurricane Katrina is a perfect example. Local, state and federal authorities underestimated the potential catastrophes of the hurricane and the levies breaking at the same time.

Although hurricanes occur frequently, the severity and damage of each one tends to be localized, so a particular area may not suffer one for decades, or even generations. During that interval, people who lived through the prior event may no longer be alive to warn current residents. This loss of community memory of a prior event can present opportunities for miscalculations.

Our normalcy bias may also be affected by how people cope with a disaster after it has occurred. The problem may stem from the fact that they are looking at the aftermath with a localized view. It is much easier to accurately interpret damage that you can see for yourself—seeing is believing. It is much more difficult to assess the devastation on a larger scale. To achieve this you must rely on outside sources, such as news coverage. Your final interpretation of the catastrophe will be based more heavily on how it directly affected you, your loved ones, and your immediate surroundings.

For example, a survivor of Katrina will have a much different recollection of the devastation, then someone who only watched it on television. Even when two people experience the hurricane, their experiences may be different. A survivor whose neighborhood was spared from severe flooding will have a different perspective than someone whose neighborhood was wiped out. Although they both lived through Katrina, their different perspectives were based on their specific outcomes. Their personal experiences will affect how they respond to the next threat.

In part, our normalcy bias is determined by how we chose to interpret what is "normal" or expected. Our "normal" expectations are based heavily on our own unique experiences, and our own definition of what is normal. A conflict can occur when a potential situation or crisis arises that falls outside of our normal expectations. Because it falls outside of our normal range, we may be unable to accurately assess the true probability or severity of its occurrence. This *blind spot* that our normalcy bias creates, along with our optimistic tendencies, can cause us to underestimate the true risks involved in a potential crisis situation.

Most catastrophic events occur infrequently. But they can leave a path of devastation in their wake. As we discussed earlier, these black swan events are certainly not limited to natural disasters. We are just as vulnerable to man-made catastrophes such as economic depressions, stock market crashes, prolonged power blackouts, and world wars. As with natural disasters, man-made disasters create a normal range of expectations.

For example, having observed them before, you may expect recessions and moderate stock market declines as normal. Consequently when they do occur (or the warning of one), it's likely you will be able to anticipate what to expect, and perhaps how to protect yourself. In case there is a recession, you may choose to bolster your savings account in the event you may be laid off. If you anticipate a stock market decline, you may decide to decrease your stock holdings.

But what if the warnings fall outside of your normal expectations? What if the predictions call for another possibly prolonged great depression, or a 50% drop in the stock market that lasts for more than a decade? What happens if inflation goes to 14% again, or if the U.S. dollar collapses? How does one plan for extreme outcomes?

The typical response is to simply ignore these black swan scenarios. The tendency to disregard them may stem from the following reasons: First, your perception may be that it won't happen, since you have never encountered it before; and, second, there is no simple way to protect yourself anyway.

Too many people go through life working off of a "best case scenario" financial plan, meaning that everything has to go according to plan for it to succeed. Let's be honest, how many times in your life has your best case scenario worked out? Even once? Yet that is exactly what many people are counting on.

What if the best case scenario doesn't materialize, perhaps because of a black swan?

Much of the problem has to do with misinterpretation of the real risks. Let's call this the "Mr. Magoo syndrome." For those of you too young to remember the cartoon character Mr. Magoo, he was a nice elderly man, nearly blind. He misinterpreted virtually every situation he came across. He would have conversations with mannequins, pet rats on their heads thinking they were cats, and complain about the pizza as he ate the cardboard box it came in. But somehow he always survived the impending disaster he helped create.

Much like Mr. Magoo, many of our financial problems can and do stem from our misinterpretation of financial or investment situation. Sometimes this may be due to a lack of information or experience, other times it may simply be a case of wishful thinking. In the end it can create a problem. But, unlike Mr. Magoo, things don't always work out in the end, and good people don't always win.

As I stated earlier, we may be witnessing one of history's greatest paradigm shifts in global power. U.S. and Western Europe, who have dominated the financial, economic and geo-political systems of the world and benefited for over 100 years, now have to share with the emerging powers of China, India, Indonesia, Brazil and others.

Many people seem oblivious to this shift, and its possible implications. Even when presented with the facts, the tendency is to down play this historical shift and its potential consequences. Some of this can be explained in part by our *normalcy bias*. Since most of the people alive today have only known a world that has been largely dominated by the United States, it is difficult to imagine any other scenario. While the United States will remain a dominant force, make no mistake about it, the shift is already under way. Ignoring or misinterpreting the potential consequences of these changes could have devastating results.

INVESTOR LESSONS:

- Try not to automatically dismiss forecasts or viewpoints that initially may seem far-fetched or out of the normal range. While many situations you encounter will prove irrelevant, it is possible that you may encounter a potential black swan event. When evaluating the validity of information, examine the credibility of the source. Too many times the source may prove dubious.

- If the source is credible, and on second review the information seems more plausible, ascertain the likely impact on your financial plans.

- If the impact could be significant, determine a course of action that might mitigate some of the risks involved. The scope of this book doesn't allow me to cover all potential scenarios and courses of action. Suffice to say if you do identify a potentially serious financial threat, you may want to seek the guidance of a professional.

CHAPTER THIRTEEN

Driving While Staring in the Rear-View Mirror

> *"Right now I'm having amnesia and déjà vu at the same time. I think I've forgotten this before."*
>
> Steven Wright, *comedian*

A basic flaw in our thinking process is the assumption that circumstances from the immediate past will continue indefinitely (good or bad). We have a tendency to look back at what has happened most recently and assume that it will continue for the indefinite future. Armed with that information, we may then make long-term plans based on those patterns continuing. This is referred to as our "recency bias."

This is partly due to our tendency to look for patterns. So when we look back at the immediate past, we assume that a pattern has formed and that it will continue. Even if we do look further back for guidance, instinctively we tend to give more credence to the immediate past over the longer-term past.

The details of more distant past events require more effort to recall. As we know, the brain loves to take short cuts and tends to rely on information that is easier to recall. It may simply be easier for the brain to assume the recent past will continue, than to go through the effort of thinking through alternate scenarios. Our recency bias can be particularly dangerous for investors.

Back in the mid 1990's, the U.S. stock market was growing at an average of over 25% per year. No, that is not a typo! During that particular time period, if you were to ask an investor what a fair rate of return would be for stocks for the next 10 years, it was not uncommon to hear them to say 15% or more. They thought this was a conservative estimate. After all it had been growing at 25%!

Investors were simply looking at the preceding 5 years of the market and projecting forward. Had they looked back a bit further, they would have realized that over the long run, say 50 years, the market averaged around 10%. From 2000 to 2012, the U.S. stock market actually provided a negative rate of return!

Interest rates are dramatic example of how we can be misled by our recency bias. Back in the early 80's, the interest rate on the 30 year U.S. Government bond was over 15%! Ah, the good old days! Let's suppose you retired in 1981 and put your entire $200,000 retirement savings into that 30 year bond. Since then you have been getting $2,500 per month to supplement a pension and social security check. Not a bad retirement!

Now 30 years later, there is good news and bad news. The good news is you are still alive. The bad news is that your bond is maturing and the current interest rate on a new 30 year bond is 2.7% (as of June 2012), that will now pay you approximately $450 per month. That's a drop of more than $2,000 per month! And that's not even taking inflation into account.

Frequently people will ask how to allocate their 401(k) investments. Many times, they will have already circled the options they think they should choose. Guess which ones are typically circled? More times than not, they have circled the ones that have done the best in the past 12 months. Go figure!

The same thing frequently happens when doing reviews. Often, an investor's inclination is to sell investments that have lagged most recently, moving those funds into positions that have a better performance record. It's so easy to forget the simple rule—buy LOW, sell HIGH!

My point here is that all investments move in cycles. It may prove foolish or even dangerous, to assume that how an investment has performed most recently, is indicative of how it will perform in the future. As a matter of fact, one could logically argue that if an investment is coming off of an unusually good or bad period, it could be a sign that it may be ready to change its direction.

INVESTOR LESSONS:

- Just because an investment has recently treated you well, does not mean that it is your friend. Investments are like trained tigers. It is in your best interests to not become too complacent, because they can turn on you in a moment's notice.

- All investments move in cycles. What goes up eventually will come down, and vice-versa. The key is to have an idea about where you are in that cycle.

- Put all of your investments that have done exceptionally well over the past 1-3 years on your watch list. This doesn't mean you need to sell them, but you do need to carefully monitor them for changes that could indicate a new direction.

- Start a second list with types of investments that have done the worst over that same period of time and cycle. This list may contain the next winners. Working from these two lists allows you to develop a longer-term plan with the assistance of your logical brain. This method should help reduce the odds of making a panic move during an anxious period. You have a plan B, some logical options to choose from, in the event of a change in direction. Planning is key.

CHAPTER FOURTEEN

Making Decisions Based on Similar Past Experiences

> *"It seems like déjà vu all over again."*
>
> Yogi Berra, *Major League Baseball player and manager*

A s we discussed earlier, **Oscar**, the impulsive part of the brain, must process an incredible amount of data. It accomplishes this task by creating a wide range of shortcuts that enables it to make snap judgments. These short cuts are formed from things we have learned, observed, and most importantly, things we have experienced personally.

Researchers believe these short cuts are filed away, waiting for the appropriate time to be recalled, in order to make a quick decision. How does the brain know which shortcut to recall in any given situation? Part of the answer seems to be that it looks for things in its memory that are similar or familiar to the situation in question. This is called our "similarity bias," and also its close cousin, "familiarity bias."

At any given time, your **Oscar** brain is searching your memories to see if your current situation is similar to something you may have experienced in the past. If a similar situation is recalled, what was the outcome? Was it pleasurable, neutral or painful? If pleasurable enough, your brain will have a strong impulse to try to repeat it. If it was painful or threatening, the impulse is to avoid it. Remember, this is the impulsive part of the brain, so it is simply reacting to the situation. It reacts proportionally to the amount of pleasure or pain recalled from past experiences.

It also appears that the more extreme or vivid the past memory, the more vivid the recollection will be, making it easier for the impulsive part of the brain to make an immediate decision, without seeking input from the logical side. The more pleasurable the recalled experience, the more you'll want to repeat it, even if it is not necessarily logical or in your best interest. This is our primitive brain, driven by impulse and immediate gratification. This helps explain why some people have such strong vices, sometimes dangerous ones. These strong primitive urges may simply be overruling the logical brain's objections.

The same can be true with extremely unpleasant past experiences. Recalling past pain and/or fear that was involved at the time the memory was formed can drive you to avoid it, regardless of how illogical your current reactions may be.

These primitive instincts were critical to survival for our early ancestors. But assessing threats and possible pleasurable opportunities was a lot simpler back then. Run from the lion. Chase the rabbit. Eat the red berries. Avoid pine cones.

Since then, life has become infinitely more complicated. Threats and opportunities come in many more shapes and sizes. They aren't as easily recognized and categorized. Our lives have become much more dependent on things over which we do not have any direct control.

Just look at how our lives were disrupted by the 2003 blackout. Even if you didn't live in one of these blackout areas, your life may have been severely affected. Millions of homes went without power, businesses were forced to shut down, transportation and communication systems were disrupted. Can you imagine how society would have been affected if the blackout had lasted a few weeks or even months instead of a few days? I don't even want to imagine the chaos that would have ensued if the entire wireless communications system went down for a few weeks or months. Teenagers would have to learn to talk to each other again!

How about the 1979 gas shortage? Do you remember sitting in gas lines for hours, hoping you wouldn't run out of gas before you got your chance to fill up? It only lasted a few months, but imagine if it had lasted a year or more. The threats and opportunities we face today are much more complex, because our lives are much more complex and interdependent. While the complexity of the world has increased exponentially, the part of the primitive brain that deals with perceived immediate threats and opportunities has not. In addition, it is only in more recent times that our brain has had to deal with outside attempts to influence it. Put it all together and it's like trying to run the most recent version of Microsoft software on an old 286 CPU computer.

Consequently, the opportunities for misinterpreting and/or underestimating risk have also increased exponentially, as well as the potential consequences they carry. While the vast majority of these new risks may not be life threatening, they can severely impact our lives in other ways.

Therefore, problems can occur when our minds misinterpret or confuse a past experience with the current situation. Because the situation you may be facing now seems similar to one that you encountered in the past, it doesn't necessarily mean they are the same. Chances are they won't be the same. And even if the situation is similar, that doesn't mean the same outcome will result.

This misinterpretation of a situation by your emotional brain can prove to be costly to your investments. Repeatedly people make quick investment decisions based on little information, other than their recall of a similar situation in the past. In many circumstances, this vague recollection may be enough evidence for your impulsive **Oscar** brain to make a snap decision.

For example, in the late 90's an investor may have experienced making a huge paper profit by buying stock in an initial public offering (IPO) of a new dot-com. This fast and easy success may have left a positive impression. This *easy money* may have enticed them to buy into even more IPOs, based solely on the success of their past experience, and not necessarily on the merits of the individual companies they were buying. As the old Wall Street adage goes, "It's very easy to confuse genius with a bull market." Translation: You made money because the market as a whole went up, not necessarily because you knew what you were doing!

Another aspect of similarity bias occurs when investors find themselves in an uncertain situation. Looking for guidance, they may find themselves searching for a similar past situation or pattern. However, even if a similar pattern can be found, it is important to consider the circumstances that led to the creation of a particular pattern. Usually past circumstances do not mirror current ones. Just because two patterns are similar, if the events that created the pattern are different, the final outcomes may also be very different.

Familiarity Bias: "Hey, don't I know you from somewhere?"

We also have a strong bias toward familiar things. When given a choice, we tend to migrate toward things that seem more familiar. This can be true even if we don't necessarily have a positive recollection of the memory, but simply because we feel that it is somehow familiar.

The Catholic Church conducted a survey of 1000 people. Those that had read the DaVinci code were more than twice as likely to believe that Christ had fathered a child, and 4 times as likely to believe that Opus Dei was a murderous sect. This is in spite of the fact that it flies in face of core Catholic beliefs. Evidence suggests that when information is presented in a *familiar* format, people may blindly process it as being accurate[1].

Advertisers and politicians are keenly aware of this psychological blind spot. Much of their advertising is designed simply to make an initial impression in your mind. Then they reinforce it through repetition. At some later date, chances are you may not remember the specifics of the message, but that's not critical. What's important is that you recall the name. It is familiar. The imprint has been made successfully. Later, when a decision has to be made, your mind may be influenced by the familiarity of the name, even though it may not recall the actual context. How many times have you chosen one item over another at the grocery or electronics store simply because you were familiar with the name? As American songwriter George Cohan once said, *"I don't care what you say about me, as long as you spell my name right."*

This familiarity/similarity bias can also have a strong influence on an investor's behavior. Most investors have a strong tendency to invest in things or companies with which they are more familiar, and stay away from those that are not. This bias can be strong enough that it may influence the decision to choose an apparently inferior investment, simply because the name is familiar.

This bias can also lead to a skewed view of potential investment options. For example, all things seemingly being equal, which are people more likely to invest in? GE or Daewoo? Proctor & Gamble or Henkel? Motorola or LG Ltd.? Many people may opt for the companies whose names are more familiar to them, without examining the details.

It may prove unfortunate when an investor limits investment choices only to only those with which they are familiar. Keep in mind that the best time to have bought companies like Apple, Microsoft, Intel, Google and Starbucks was *before* they were household names. Instead, you may have opted for some *better known, more well established* companies, such as LTV, Circuit City, Lehman Brothers, Chrysler, GM, WorldCom or Enron.

Many attractive investments may not be household names in the U.S., but they may be well known overseas. You may have been able to get away with such a myopic view 40 years ago, when U.S. stocks accounted for nearly 70% of the total stock values in the world. But today, about 65% of the total stock values in the world are beyond our shores. By excluding these companies, you may be severely limiting your investment options.

Companies such as, Siemens (German), Petrobras (Brazil), Total (French), ENI (Italy), Sinopec (China), Novartis (Swiss), TTI (Hong Kong), BHP Billiton (Australia) and Tesco (UK) may not be household names to U.S. investors, but they are major global players. (Note: These are only examples. I'm not recommending these companies.)

As investors, we must resist the temptation to end our research satisfied because we have found something that seems familiar, or *feels* similar to something we have experienced before. When you find yourself in such a situation, try asking these follow-up questions "how is this situation different from the last time", "how could the outcome be different this time", or "how are other investors reacting?"

While it may be tempting to go the quick and easy route, investment history has shown that many times things are not as they appear, and further research is usually prudent.

The Curse of Investor Overconfidence

> *"It's not what a man don't know that makes him a fool, but what he does know, that just ain't so."*
>
> Josh Billings, *American humorist*

By nature, humans tend to be overly confident creatures. According to behavioral finance Professor Richard Thaler, it's in our nature to think we are at least a little bit better, smarter, faster and more talented than we really are. This can create serious problems.

Our tendency to be overly confident stems from the way we determine our own abilities. Often, we do this by evaluating our past successes against our failures. How we attribute those outcomes is what creates the problem (attribution bias). Research suggests that we tend to attribute our successes to our own efforts and talents, but dismiss our failures to others, or to circumstances that we deem beyond our control. For example, a gambler at the race track may attribute a streak of victories to his equestrian acumen, and a series of losses to rain, a poor pole position or an inexperienced jockey.

According to Thaler, studies have shown that over 90% of drivers think they are "better than the average driver." Well, statistically, that's impossible! You simply cannot have 90% of people being better than the average. Our better-than-average bias (BTA) isn't limited to our driving. Research suggests that most people tend to overestimate many of their true abilities. The brutal truth is that most of us have a higher opinion of ourselves than what we actually merit. I know this to be true because my wife often reminds me of it!

Most people tend to be somewhat overconfident in their own views, opinions and predictions. Interestingly, our confidence tends to grow even stronger once we have made a commitment based on that confidence. In a research project using horseracing bettors, researchers R.E. Knox and J.A. Inkster found that people became significantly *more* confident of their choice *after* they had placed their bets. In their 1968 research project, they interviewed bettors before and after they placed their bets on a horse. They found that people became even more confident in their choice right after they had actually placed their bet. This increase in their confidence levels rose, even though no new information was presented.

There is an important lesson for all investors in this research. It may help explain why people have a hard time selling poor-performing investments. The fact that they made the investment may have actually increased confidence in their initial decision. This increased confidence may also increase emotional commitment to their choice, and cloud assessment of future facts that may contradict their original choice. This overconfidence may make it harder at some later date to sell a poor performing investment. Doing so may mean admitting that they could have been wrong. By simply hanging on to the investment, there is always a chance (regardless of how remote!) that the investment could stage a dramatic comeback. Therefore, you can postpone having to admit that you could have possibly made a mistake.

This flies in the face of the conventional investment wisdom that reminds us to *sell our losers short and let our winners run.* Cutting your losses means having to admit that you may have made a poor decision. There is nothing wrong with making a mistake, as long as you learn from it.

These are examples of how financial problems can arise when we make important decisions based on faulty assumptions. In addition, investors need to be alert to misplaced feelings of certainty as to the success of an investment, or the outcome of a situation, when the present circumstances do not merit this level of confidence.

According to Professor Terrance Odean (University of California at Berkeley) overconfidence is one of the biggest obstacles investors must learn to overcome. Odean has spent his career studying the behavior of individual investors. In one study, *"Trading can be Hazardous to Your Wealth,"* he studied the trading patterns of more than 64,000 households at a national brokerage firm. Odean's research has led him to conclude that, **"overconfidence gives people the courage of their misguided convictions."**

Odean has also collaborated with his colleague, Professor Brad M. Barber, on several related projects studying investor behavior. I have highlighted some of their more interesting observations.

"Investor overconfidence" is not necessarily a personality trait. Instead, in many cases it appears to be a result of mere circumstances. Many times, overconfidence tends to be more prevalent when the stock market is rising. It may start with some investors having early successes in the market (remember: Don't confuse genius with a bull market!). As more investors begin to experience these early successes, additional new investors may jump in, pushing the market even higher. They want a piece of the action too!

As the number of investment successes increase, investors may begin to feel more confident that they have discovered a *system* that works. As their confidence grows, the frequency of their trading tends to increase, as well as the amount of their bets. For many investors, this increased trading actually hurts their performance. According to Odean's study of 64,000 family accounts, *active* traders substantially underperformed those accounts that did not trade as frequently.

He attributes some of the underperformance to impatience. As investors increase their trading frequency, they have a tendency to look for a quick return. In some cases, this may lead to selling an investment prematurely, in hopes of finding a more attractive alternative.

Odean's studies also uncovered some additional, interesting trends:

- On average, the investments that active traders *sold* performed better over the next 12 months than the new investments they bought.

- Active traders tended to have much more concentrated portfolios. Their overconfidence in their picks may have encouraged them to make larger and larger bets on their original choices. This lack of diversification and concentration of assets can lead to a much riskier portfolio.

- Men were much more prone to be overconfident than women. As a result, women tended to have a better return on their portfolios than their male counterparts. The results were even worse for single men, when compared to single women. We'll further discuss the gender differences in investing later.

- In another study, Odean found that online traders did substantially worse than telephone traders. In some cases the same investor fared worse when they switched from telephone to online trading. The theory is that it is much easier to act on a whim when trading online than other methods that take more effort. The extra time, required for that additional effort, may have given them pause to reconsider their original impulse.

You can see the complete results of Odean's studies, and much more of his interesting research on individual investor behavior, by visiting http://faculty.haas.berkeley.edu/odean/

A byproduct of overconfidence is the "illusion of control," to which we all are susceptible from time to time. The illusion of control was coined by psychologist Ellen Langer, and is more common in familiar situations, and where a person may know in advance the desired outcome.

For example, according to her research, if you ask people to bet on whether a coin toss will end in heads or tails, most will bet a larger amount if they are allowed to flip the coin. If the coin has already been tossed and the outcome concealed, people will offer lower amounts when asked for bets. People act as if their involvement in the coin toss will somehow affect the outcome. In this case, the idea of having control over the outcome is clearly an illusion. Another interesting example of this effect is found in casinos. When rolling dice in a craps game, people tend to throw the dice harder when they need high numbers, and toss softer for low numbers.

This illusion of control can be even stronger in stressful and competitive situations, including investment trading. According to the research[2], sometimes, investors may become overconfident based on their subconscious illusion that they have some sort of control over the outcome, simply because they thought it was a good buy in the first place.

INVESTOR LESSONS:

An interesting takeaway from research on investor overconfidence is that it is not necessarily a personality trait. Anyone can become a victim, regardless of their personality or experience. As the tech bubble taught millions of investors, anyone can be fooled into thinking that making money in stocks is easy and relatively safe. While experience is the most effective teacher, at times it can also be the most painful. The good news is that investor overconfidence can be cured. The bad news is that it may take a 30-50% drop in the market!

Chapter Footnotes

[1] - "Behavioral Investing" James Montier, 2007
[2] - "Trading on illusions: Unrealistic perceptions of control and trading performance" Fenton-O'Creevy, Nicholson, Soane, Willman, 2003

CHAPTER FIFTEEN

How We Mentally Keep Track of Our Money

> *"Money without brains is always dangerous."*
>
> Napoleon Hill, *American author*

I first met Ted and Alice about 20 years ago. Our initial discussion was pretty typical. We discussed their sources of income, expenses, existing savings, and their goals. What struck me was the large amount of savings they had been able to accumulate relative to the modest income he was earning. In addition, he worked for a very small company that had no retirement plan at all.

At this point, I asked whether they had received any inheritance or some other type of financial windfall. To this he replied simply, "No, I just have a special way of making sure I am saving enough for my retirement." With that he pulled a small index box out of his briefcase. At the sight of it, Alice immediately did an overly exaggerated eye roll and exclaimed "Oh no, not the money box!"

As he opened up the box, I could see a large number of envelopes. He pulled them out. I could see each one had a handwritten note on it, such as "gas bill," "electric bill," "groceries," "car repairs," "vacation," etc.

He went on to explain that every time he got paid, he would deposit his entire check into a savings account. He would then withdraw 75% of his pay in cash, leaving the remaining 25% in the savings account. He would then divide up the withdrawn amount into 15 or so envelopes, including one for "emergencies."

Whenever he had bills to pay, he would write the checks, then go to the corresponding envelope and remove the amount he needed to cover the check, rounded up to the next dollar. He explained that if the bill was less than the amount needed, the remainder would stay in the envelope for future bills. If he accumulated too much cash in any envelope, he would move some of it to the "emergency" envelope. When I asked him what he did when there was not enough in an envelope, he answered that it didn't happen often. But when it did, he would simply take it out of another envelope. At this, Alice sarcastically piped in, "and it usually comes out of my grocery or vacation envelopes."

Then, when he was ready to mail his checks, he would take the cash that he had removed from the envelopes and deposit it into his checking account. I haven't asked him in the past few years, but I believe he still does it this way today. While most people may look at Ted's *system* and chuckle, you can't argue with the results. His house was paid off 20 years ago. He never had a car payment in his life because he had a separate *new car* envelop! They had more than enough money to retire comfortably. His system worked for them.

I share this true story with you to illustrate the behavioral finance concept known as "mental accounting" that was originated by University of Chicago's Richard Thaler. The concept states that basically all of us are like Ted to a certain degree. We all have our own *mental envelopes* where we keep track of our money. While we may not physically move money in and out of envelopes the way Ted does, we do tend to earmark and track our money as it moves from envelope to envelope in our minds.

"Mental accounting" attempts to explain the approach that most people use to mentally keep track of their financial assets. Many create separate mental "financial buckets" for assets and investments. They may categorize these *buckets* based on several variables. Some of these variables may include:

- The source of the money (was the money "earned" income vs. "found' money).

- The purpose of the money (retirement savings, vacation money, etc).

- How to invest it (long-term growth or short-term safety).

Many times this mental categorization and segregation of money can work to our advantage. For instance, creating these mental buckets may be the only way some people can keep their spending under control. It may keep them from spending retirement and college savings on frivolous things, because those accounts are too important to invade. It may also keep some people from selling in panic during down markets, by reminding themselves that this is *long-term money.* They won't need it for a long time.

On the other hand, mental accounting can also be one of the most common and costly mistakes we make with our money. For many people, it can get in the way of thinking logically when dealing with their finances.

Following the Money Trail

One of the biggest mistakes people make is viewing or valuing money and investments differently depending on its source. We tend to assign a different *value* to money, when it is earned vs. when it is found, won or inherited. This is often referred to as *house money* or *found money.* Assigning a lower value to certain dollars makes it easier to spend or risk them on something that they wouldn't normally do. This is really an exercise in self-deception.

For example, people tend to spend found money, such as tax refunds, work bonuses and gifts, much more freely compared to a similar amount of money that came from their normal paycheck. This represents another instance of how mental accounting can cause an illogical use of money.

Logically, money should be considered interchangeable, regardless of how we obtained it. Treating money differently depending on its source defies logic. Where the money came from should not be a factor in how much of it is spent, or what we are willing to spend it on. Regardless of the source, spending it will represent a drop in your overall wealth.

For example, suppose you went to the racetrack with some friends with $1,000 in your pocket. During the course of the day you were incredibly lucky and you parlayed the $1,000 into $250,000! You were so lucky, in fact, that you decided to bet the whole amount on the last race. Your horse lost, and you left the racetrack with nothing in your pocket but the losing betting slip.

How much did this day at the track with your friends cost you? Many people may answer $1,000, the original amount you started with. In reality though it cost you $250,000! At some point in the day you could have cashed out and been $250,000 richer. You could have paid off your mortgage and car loans, you could have set up a college fund for your kids, or put it away for retirement. It was real money! But you chose to keep playing with it and you lost it all. You really lost $250,000. But to soften the psychological blow, you convince yourself that in the end, you really only lost the original $1,000 you left the house with.

Many people also segregate their money in separate accounts designated for specific goals, such as saving for retirement, buying a new house, paying for college expenses, or having a separate stash for emergencies. If an emergency were to arise, you may be willing to *borrow* from a lower priority goal, such as your *new car fund*, while not even considering touching your *new house down payment* or retirement account.

This may hold true even if liquidating some of your investments in the *hands off* account may make more financial sense. This can occur when the asset you are going to liquidate has a penalty or tax consequence attached to it. So while money is theoretically fungible, the mere fact that you have mentally earmarked that particular investment for a specific purpose may override the logic in using it for another purpose.

It is not uncommon to see people making this mistake. I once knew a couple who were willing to pay more than $15,000 in taxes and penalties by taking money out of their IRA to pay off their bills, even though they had access to more than enough money in other accounts that would have carried no penalties. The other accounts had been earmarked for their kids' college expenses. The kids were only in 3rd and 5th grades, so there was plenty of time to make up for the amount they planned to withdraw, but the emotion attached to their children's education accounts overruled their logical brains. Chalk up another victory for the **Oscar** brain!

In addition, many times we may assign different investment objectives to these different accounts. We might be aggressive with one, moderate with another and view a third as our *safe money*. Although I agree that, at times, it may make sense to assign differing investment goals to different pots of money, in the end we are all acting a bit like my client Ted with his envelopes. At the end of the day, it's all your money, regardless of which account it is in, or what you plan to spend it on. The only difference may be that we have chosen to hide our envelopes in our minds and not a *money box*!

A truly self-deceiving action is to mentally spend the same dollar multiple times. We have all done this!

For example, let's suppose your boss informs you that because of the great job you have been doing, you will be receiving a

$1,000 bonus on your next paycheck. Great! Found money! So you go home, and excitedly tell your wife.

It's coming at the perfect time, because you have been driving your car on four well-worn tires. Money's been tight, so you've been putting off buying new tires. The next day you go to the tire store. While you're there, the salesman convinces you that for only $500 more, you can upgrade your old *boring* hubcaps to new sporty ones. The total bill is $1,200, but what the heck, you have a $1,000 check coming in a few weeks. You think, " it will really only cost me a couple hundred dollars." Right? Besides, your new hubcaps will make the car look great! So you put the new tires and hubcaps on your credit card. You tell yourself you'll pay it off when the bonus check arrives.

In the meantime, your wife has been planning to do something special for your anniversary next month. So she decides to surprise you by booking a short junket to Las Vegas for the two of you. The $1,300 is more than she was planning to spend on your anniversary, but with the $1,000 check coming, it is really only going to cost a few hundred bucks. And besides, it's your anniversary! So she puts it on the credit card and figures she'll just pay it off when the check comes in.

A few days later the two of you are sitting in your living room watching TV. It's the 24-inch set her parents got you as your wedding gift three years ago. Just then a commercial comes on and you see *Crazy Eddie* advertising a brand new 52-inch 3D, HD TV for only $1,100. If you order by credit card in the next 30 minutes, it will be shipped directly to your house within 24 hours. And, you will get a cappuccino maker at no extra charge!

You look at each other, and almost simultaneously say, "Gee, with that check coming in, the TV would almost be free"! And besides, we like cappuccino! You can guess what happened next.

A few weeks later your bonus appears in your paycheck— $740. Oops, forgot about those taxes. That evening you sit down to pay your bills. You open up your credit card statement and it shows a balance of $3,600! How the heck did that happen? All you have now is $740. That evening you sit down with your wife to tell her the bad news. You decide that if you tighten your belt a bit, you should be able to pay the balance off in nine months or so.

In the end, including the interest on your credit card, your *found money* of $1,000 ended up costing you $3,175! Let's just hope there are no other bonuses in the near future. You can't afford them!

While we may chuckle at this story, it happens millions of times every year. This, my friends, is only one of the ways that people fall into the insidious debt trap.

Debt is Modern-Day Slavery

To illustrate how powerful mental accounting can be, ask yourself whether you ever borrowed money or charged something on your credit card to pay for something, even though you had the money in your wallet or purse, or in an account somewhere else?

Chances are, if you are like most people, you would have said yes. The fact is that it would make no sense doing that unless the interest you are earning in your savings account is higher than the interest you are paying on the loan or credit card (good luck with that!). While not logical, we take on debt so we don't have to dip into our *envelopes*. It's illogical to have money in a savings account earning little or no interest, while carrying credit-card debt accruing at 10-25% annually.

I am convinced that if credit cards didn't exist, and people had to pay for all their purchases with cash or checks, our country would not be in the economic mess we find ourselves. When the final chapter is written about what ultimately led to the weakening of what was once believed to be the most dominant economy in the world, the finger of blame will point to credit cards, and home equity loans or lines of credit. These two things have allowed ordinary people to live way above their means, for a considerable time.

It allowed people to live a lifestyle that Madison Avenue advertisers convinced them they were entitled to, but in reality couldn't afford. In past generations you saved your money, or at least have most of it, before you bought something. With the advent of plastic money, you can buy it immediately, even if you can't afford it! When you maxed out one card, you could simply get another one!

Credit cards can also make you more generous than you can afford to be, and permit you to become a big spender. People tend to spend much more on gifts when they charge it on a credit card than when they pay cash.

Home equity loans took this potential for excessive spending to a whole new level. No longer were most people burdened with those pesky four-figure credit limits. By tapping into their home's equity, they could spend tens or even hundreds of thousands of dollars they couldn't afford! And boy did Americans spend! Even as the American economy and corporations benefited, individual Americans slowly sunk deeper and deeper into debt, until finally in 2008, the house of cards came tumbling down. For many, debt became nothing more than their own personal modern-day slavery.

INVESTOR LESSONS:

- Before you make a discretionary purchase, ask yourself: is this something I really *need* or do I simply *want* it. If it's a *want*, can you live without it?

- Before you buy a *want* item, divide its price by your hourly pay. When you do the math and discover you will have to work 28 hours to get that new electronic gadget, you may find that it's really not worth it! I've had many clients comment to me on how well this works for them. It's especially useful for younger people whose hourly pay tends to be lower.

- Try to avoid impulse buying, especially on the internet or in catalogues. If you find something you *want*, put it in your shopping cart and give yourself a 24-hour *time out* period. Many times what seemed like a terrific idea then, may seem silly and frivolous in the cold, cruel morning light.

- Before you spend a large amount of found money, remind yourself that if saved and invested it, assuming you could earn a little over 7%, your money will have DOUBLED in about 10 years and QUADRUPED in 20 years! That's money that could be generating additional lifetime monthly income for retirement, or maybe even allow you to retire a few years early!

- Before buying something on a credit card, ask yourself if you wouldn't be better off paying cash for it out of savings. This may help you accomplish two things. First, it may prevent you from running up your credit card balance at an obscene interest rate, while you have cash in a savings account earning 0%. Secondly, you are less likely to buy a want item if you have to pay cash for it.

CHAPTER SIXTEEN

Accurately Measuring Risk

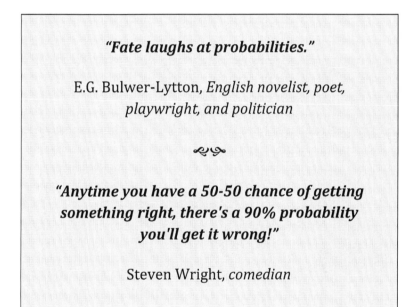

"Fate laughs at probabilities."

E.G. Bulwer-Lytton, *English novelist, poet, playwright, and politician*

❧ ❧

"Anytime you have a 50-50 chance of getting something right, there's a 90% probability you'll get it wrong!"

Steven Wright, *comedian*

Many investors find it difficult to accurately measure the true risk of an investment. This can lead to all sorts of problems, including inadvertently taking on more risk than planned, which can cause a disastrous result.

One culprit of misinterpreting risk seems to be the inherent inability of many people to properly estimate the true probability of an event happening. Some of it may simply be due to our own carelessness and ignorance, but some of it may be due to our brain's hard wiring. Earlier we discussed how for the sake of speed and efficiency, the brain may be programmed to take short cuts. This is its way of dealing with the enormous amount of data that it has to process simultaneously. Taking a short cut when calculating the probability of the occurrence of a critical event can be devastating for investors.

A common miscalculation is applying the "law of large numbers" to a small sequence of events. Simply put, it means coming to a conclusion based on the results of a relatively small set of events. For example, we all know that if you flip a coin you have a 50/50 chance of it being heads. But suppose you flipped a coin ten times and it came up heads nine times. If you had to bet $10 on the next flip, which would you bet is more likely to come up, heads or tails?

Some people may say tails, reasoning that since there is a 50/50 chance, and heads has shown up 90% of the time over the last 10 tosses, thus it was *due* to be tails. Others may conclude that a trend has emerged and therefore believe is likely to continue. In reality, it's still a 50/50 chance, regardless of the number of past tosses. Thinking that a trend is more likely to reverse itself is known as the "it's overdue" fallacy. In either case, the mistake is in believing that the odds of a subsequent toss will be affected by the outcome of the previous tosses. In the same vein, an investor may feel that the market could reverse direction in the near future, simply because of a longer-term trend they may have detected.

Misinterpreting the true probability of an event is also known as the "gambler's fallacy." It's mistaking the true odds of something happening simply because an expected pattern has not materialized thus far. It is a common mistake to which many gamblers fall victim. The most famous example of this occurred in Monte Carlo in 1913, when the ball in a roulette wheel fell on *black* 26 times in a row, an almost-unheard-of event. It is reported that the gamblers at the table lost millions betting on *red,* assuming that the pattern would surely reverse on the next roll, since red was *overdue.*

The same danger may hold true for investors who assume the market is likely to change course, simply because it is *overdue.* A lot of money can be lost in the short-term, waiting for a long-term expectation to materialize. As economist John Maynard Keynes once said: **"The markets can remain irrational much longer than you can remain solvent."**

While it may be useful to compare short-term to long-term trends, one has to be careful not to erroneously detect a *trend* that doesn't really exist. Doing so could lead an investor to become a victim of overconfidence.

Simultaneously, this feeling of overconfidence can be even further heightened by your **Oscar** brain's tendency to jump to quick conclusions, many times based on limited knowledge. Before you know it, you have absolutely convinced yourself that you are on to something big. Overconfidence usually precedes carelessness.

Another danger of overconfidence is that it can lead one to assume a greater amount of risk than they are aware of or can actually tolerate. This hubris can lead to dangerous results. This was never more evident than during the tech bubble of the late 1990's. In the late 90's, the skyrocketing stock market gave investors all the confidence they needed to make bigger and bolder bets. Their early investment successes may have further fed their basic instincts of greed, and seeking patterns. For many, the *pattern* they thought they detected was too tempting to ignore. When the stock market reversed and the bubble burst, it left millions of investors angry, confused and substantially poorer.

One significant shortcoming of "trend analysis" is that it can be used to verify just about any preconceived notion an investor can dream up. It's all in the interpretation. For example, an investor may feel they have detected a longer-term pattern for a stock. Looking at its current price, they may feel that it is at a short-term low. Based on the stocks longer-term trend, they erroneously conclude that the stock should now be poised to go up, failing to consider the impact of other factors at work. .

Years ago, I met an engineer named Karl who worked at the local gas company and owned a considerable amount of his company's stock. He told me that he had recently retired and was trying to decide what to do with his company stock.

He proceeded to pull out what seemed like dozens of pages of green graph paper (all you engineers and accountants know exactly what I'm talking about!) On these sheets were dozens of handwritten graphs and charts. He went on to explain how he had been charting his company's stock daily for the past 10 years or so. At this point, he pulled out a chart that consisted of four scotch-taped pages from one end to another. He excitedly went on to explain how he had detected a long-term pattern for his company's stock price. At this point he was speaking in a very low voice, almost whispering, very confidentially.

He explained how for the past several years he had periodically been buying and selling his company's stock with about half of what he had in his 401(k) plan. Every time the stock price would start getting near the top of the range of the *pattern*, he would sell all of it. When the price approached the bottom, he would buy it back. He had done this several times over the past few years and the strategy had worked out well for him. In fact, the portion of this 401(k) that had been in his company's stock had done much better than the other half, which was invested in diversified funds. Overall, he had built his 401(k) account to over $1,000,000.

He went on to explain. He was getting frustrated because over the past few months his account was down below $900,000. He noted that the half that was in the company stock had held up much better than the other half. Because he was in the middle of retiring, he had not sold the stock off at the last *peak* a few months ago. Instead he rode it all the way down this time. But guess what, it was now trading near the bottom of his chart! So this was his opportunity to make up for lost ground.

He was going to immediately roll his 401(k) into an IRA and then quickly sell all the funds. With the proceeds he was going to buy additional shares of his company's stock. He was speaking excitedly at this point, and he could barely contain himself. He did not want to miss the next wave!

Most financial professionals would advise people that such a move could prove to be very foolish. Putting virtually all your

230 | MONEY BRAIN

money into a single company's stock, regardless of how stable it may appear, is very risky. Concentrating his entire retirement assets in one individual stock was not worth the potential gain. Unfortunately in his state of mind, the advice would have probably fallen on deaf ears.

He did end up staggering the sales of the funds in his 401(k) over a few months, rather than all at once. He ended up selling about $150,000 of his funds, and with the proceeds he bought the company stock at about $27/share. This was in early July 2002.

For the next few weeks the stock market continued to go up, but the company stock went up even higher. It was up over 20%, to $33/share. During this time he pointed out how much better he would have done had he sold all of the funds at the same time. He was also anxious to buy the rest of the stock before it went up too much higher.

Over the next month or so the stock market dropped about 13%. The price of his company' stock dropped even more, by about 27%, to about $24/share. By late September the stock was trading near the bottom of Karl's *pattern*. At that point Karl immediately sold the remaining two-thirds of the mutual funds in his 401(k), and bought his company's stock with the proceeds. Karl now had 100% of his nest egg in one individual stock.

Over the next few weeks it looked like Karl may have been right. The stock was steadily moving upwards, and by early October it was trading over $26/share again.

Then it happened.

The company made an announcement that it would be selling $1 billion in additional stock in an effort to strengthen its weakening balance sheet. The news was not taken kindly. That day the stock dropped 13%, and by the next day the stock was trading at around $19/share!

By day three, Karl was in outright panic. His **Oscar** brain was now calling the shots, and **Felix** was nowhere to be found. Karl felt that he could not afford to lose any more money, so he decided to sell ALL of his stock immediately. In less than 3 ½ months Karl had lost more than $190,000, or 22% of his entire retirement nest egg.

There are several lessons an investor can take away from Karl's experience. One is to recognize how dangerous it can be to rely too heavily on long and short-term trends. When attempting to extrapolate the future from any current trend, be mindful of two key pitfalls.

First, virtually all trends will eventually change direction. It's just a matter of time. In addition, most people don't even take notice of a trend until it is well under way. So every week, month or year that goes by, only increases the odds that the current trend may be getting closer to an end. And when it does, you may be caught on the wrong side.

Second, trend cycles are not consistent. At times they may fall into what appears to be a fairly predictable pattern, only to abruptly change direction, increasing or decreasing in either magnitude or duration, or possibly both. If an investor picks up on the trend during a fairly stable period, they may incorrectly assume they have detected a longer-term predictable pattern.

For example, after doing some research Ed noticed that for the past three years, Acme Delivery Express' stock price tended to go up in early in November, as the holiday season approached. Based on this "predictable pattern", in late October, he confidently purchased the stock. However, this year the shipping company is embattled in a bitter union negotiation. Consequently, the company is expected to have a large reduction in profits. On this news, the stock price dropped dramatically. The *pattern* Ed thought he had detected was only temporary, and changed with the circumstance at hand. As mentioned earlier in the book, humans appear to be hard-wired to eagerly look for patterns, even where there may be none.

Perhaps both Karl and Ed were unwitting victims of this human trait (you can also throw in some greed and stubbornness). They believed they had discovered a predictable pattern. Confident that the pattern would continue, they were convinced to take on a much larger bet. The *pattern* didn't factor in what could happen if some unexpected event materialized.

In Karl's case, when the pattern deviated, the stock price temporarily plunged, reflecting investors' fears. When the price dropped well below Karl's expected range, he panicked and quickly sold. Chalk up another victory for **Oscar**.

The final chapter to Karl's story is that the stock price did fully recover within nine months, and went on to set new highs over the next few years. Unfortunately for Karl, by that time, he didn't own any shares.

INVESTOR LESSONS:

- Before you attempt to beat the odds, be sure you could survive the odds beating you.

- It's important to understand that regardless of what precedes an event, the odds of a specific outcome occurring on the next turn may be very different.

- Investors need to remember that it is the long-term fundamentals of an investment that count. The markets are driven by the fundamentals and human behavior. Buying or selling an investment because you believe that a prolonged trend is likely to reverse soon is irrational. Investment decisions must be based on the fundamentals and not on random short-term trends.

- Don't put too much faith in trends. Remember, we tend to see trends where there are none. Always hedge your bets when acting on an investment trend.

- Be wary of trends that are getting long in the tooth. All trends will eventually change direction.

CHAPTER SEVENTEEN

The Devil You Know is Better Than the Devil You Don't

> *"Courage is simply the willingness to be afraid and act anyway."*
>
> Dr. Robert Anthony, *motivational speaker and personal development coach*

While we've all heard the saying "the more things change, the more things stay the same," there may be much more to it than first meets the eye. There may actually be a strong psychological reason why things don't seem to change very quickly. This holds true for just about everything, from science to politics, from sports to personal relationships, and of course, investments.

As we have already discussed, human nature leads most people to be risk-averse. With almost any potential change there is an element of risk. To minimize this potential risk, it appears we have a built-in bias to prefer the status quo. Consequently, most people are comfortable with the status quo, even when they know the current situation could be much better. The devil you know is better than the devil you don't.

For many people, any change that ushers in the unknown may present too much risk for them. "Who knows, the change may actually be worse than my current situation." All of a sudden, they've convinced themselves that the current situation may not really be all that bad after all.

Generally speaking, our "status quo bias" leads most people to prefer that things remain the same, or if they must be changed, that the change be as little as possible. This is why change is so difficult to achieve at times. This hesitancy is only made worse when there is a general lack of trust or confidence. In addition, change tends to be difficult because we are apt to overestimate the value of what we already have and underestimate the value of what we have to gain. When you combine all these psychological factors together, is it any wonder why achieving change is so difficult?

Many years ago, I knew someone who was stuck in a miserable marriage. She was young when she married more than 30 years earlier. The few times I met her husband, he came across as pushy, condescending and arrogant. He took particular pleasure in belittling his wife in front of others. He reminded me of your typical schoolyard bully. Not the kind of guy you would want your daughter to marry.

On several occasions she would come in alone for a meeting, and she would tell me she was fed up with him, and going to divorce him. She was angry and determined. She had had enough. She was finally going to leave him. She would discuss how horrible her life was with her husband, and how she couldn't imagine spending the rest of her life like that. The psychological abuse she was subject to was quite evident.

When she finished going over his latest antics, we began to discuss her options, and how her new life might look. We would talk about her job options, other sources of potential income, and possible housing arrangements. It was at this point she would hesitate.

Once the realization began to set in that her life would change dramatically, I could actually see her whole demeanor change right in front me. Her voice went softer, she wouldn't make eye contact and she even physically hunched over. She confessed how scary all this was for her. She had never been alone in her entire life.

By the end of our meetings, she had convinced herself that her situation "maybe, really wasn't that bad after all". Maybe she made a mistake coming in. She was visibly embarrassed and apologized for wasting my time "over such a silly matter."

Looking back at this situation now, I have no doubt that Mary would have been better off leaving the jerk. But, each time she built up enough nerve to finally do something to help herself, the fear of the unknown overwhelmed her and she reverted back to the status quo. The devil she knew was evidently better than the devil she didn't.

Reflecting back, my biggest regret is that I didn't know then what I know now about human behavior. Had I understood how powerful our psychological baggage can be at times, I might have handled the situation differently. Who knows, maybe she would have had enough nerve to take the risk to change her miserable life. As you can probably tell, this still bothers me.

Our status quo bias may be one of the major reasons investors have such a hard time adapting to changing economic and investment conditions. Once an investor gets comfortable with a situation, possibly because of a series of short-term successes, it may lead them to believe that the current trend or streak will continue indefinitely.

One of the key's to investing is to successfully anticipate changes, and act to stay ahead of the curve. Many people ride the *wave* too long, only to suffer the inevitable crash. Cashing out of a successful investment can be difficult for many investors, even if they have already surpassed their original profit targets. Often it doesn't seem to matter how specific or definite the plan was at the outset. It appears that given the chance, your **Oscar** brain can slowly rationalize away the most logical of goals and plans.

Many investors are fighting two psychological battles simultaneously—reliving their past regrets while struggling with the fear of making decisions that could lead to more regrets.

Their regrets over making poor investment decisions in the past can serve as a painful reminder of the potential consequences yet again. As a result, there may be a tendency to put off making an important decision for as long as possible. Subconsciously, we may be hoping that the situation will resolve one way or another, on its own, before we have to make a decision. By letting nature take its own course, we might avoid the responsibility for having made the decision!

I have seen this phenomenon hundreds of times in my career. When working with a new client, we typically discuss their financial goals and determine the available options to meet those goals. One task is to determine what rate of return may be required to reach those goals. We'll cover this in more detail later.

Once a required rate of return is established, a portfolio should to be designed to achieve that goal. This new portfolio is then compared with an investor's current holdings to determine if any changes are required. This is where the wheel will, at times, fall off the wagon. Sometimes, an investor may have several existing holdings that they know should go. But, when the time comes to pull the trigger, impulsive **Oscar** suddenly appears out of nowhere!

All the time spent with **Felix** to determine the logical steps to meet our long-term goals comes to a screeching halt. This is when you may hear all the emotional (irrational) reasons to keep the *dog* holdings that they agreed should be sold. "Let's just wait until XYX comes back to what I paid for it" or "I really like ABC because it did great last year," or "let's hang on to Dead Dog Fund because after the last three terrible years, it's really due for a great year." Any of this sound familiar? Go ahead, you can be honest, we've all done it!

With some luck and enough patience, **Felix** can usually be invited back into the discussion. And for a time, and the sake of compromise, a few dog positions may end up staying. **Oscar can be such a royal pain at times.**

INVESTOR LESSONS:

- Our status quo bias may convince us to prefer that things remain the same. If something needs to be changed, the least amount of change would be preferable. Once a person becomes aware of their status quo bias, they can take steps to reduce its influence on their decision-making. An important step in keeping this bias under control is to be deliberate and specific in your decision-making process. Be brutally realistic and specific when evaluating the current situation with a potential alternative. Try to minimize any emotional influences that may be present, such as greed and fear. They may lead you to be overly optimistic or pessimistic. Embrace the practice of questioning your assumptions.

- Set specific growth targets for your portfolio. These targets should be realistic and determined by what is required to meet your overall financial goals, and not some arbitrary goal such as the S&P 500 index. After reaching the specified goal, reassess the situation to see if it wouldn't make more sense to lock in a substantial portion of those gains by reallocating to a more defensive position. While certainly not foolproof, this forces you to look at a potential change with a more logical eye, and possibly avoid riding the wave all the way back down.

- Don't become emotionally attached to your investments. You are not married to your investments, you are simply dating them. Sometimes dates work out, other times they don't. If you are going to end a relationship, it's better to end it sooner rather than later (before you end up married to it!).

- One of my favorite sayings is by Theodore Roosevelt: "The best thing you can do is the right thing; the next best thing you can do is the wrong thing; but at times the worst thing you can do is nothing at all."

SECTION III

CHAPTER EIGHTEEN

How Investment Bubbles Occur and Why They Eventually Burst

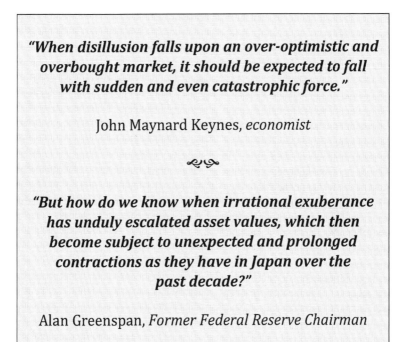

> *"When disillusion falls upon an over-optimistic and overbought market, it should be expected to fall with sudden and even catastrophic force."*
>
> John Maynard Keynes, *economist*
>
> ∂৶৹
>
> *"But how do we know when irrational exuberance has unduly escalated asset values, which then become subject to unexpected and prolonged contractions as they have in Japan over the past decade?"*
>
> Alan Greenspan, *Former Federal Reserve Chairman*

Over the past 100 years there have been at least several hundred examples of irrational investor behavior. Extreme movements in the market, both up and down, are often driven more by emotions than circumstances. For the purposes of this discussion, I would define an example of irrational investor behavior as *"an extreme movement in the market that is not driven by the current underlying fundamental economic environment."*

Former U.S. Treasury Secretary Larry Summers wrote in 1989, "Over half of all the largest moves in the stock market appear totally unrelated to fundamentals. Of course if it isn't fundamentals that are driving the markets, then it must be sentiment." He wrote this paper before the two biggest stock market declines in 2000 and 2008. The largest in recent history.

Using this definition, in this section we will explore some of the possibilities that could lead large numbers of otherwise rational and intelligent investors to simultaneously head right toward the proverbial "lemmings cliff."

The two most recent investment bubbles were the 1990's tech bubble, followed by the real estate boom and bust, which in part led to the 50% stock market plunge of 2008-2009. Both serve as excellent examples of how irrational investor behavior can cause extreme movements in the markets. In addition, these are recent enough so that most of you will be able to easily identify with the events.

If we start with Larry Summers' premise that most extreme market moves are driven by "investor sentiment" and not market fundamentals, the question is "what drives investor sentiment?" The answer to *that* question lies in our minds.

Many times we don't act on the facts as they really are, but rather on the facts as we *perceive* them to be. As we have discussed throughout this book, our perceptions may be based on incomplete, distorted and biased information—information that may have been heavily influenced by our subconscious minds, as well as by external forces.

These distortions are created in our subconscious and may be influenced by several factors. Some of these may include our initial *framing* of a situation, or some of the many psychological influences to which we are susceptible. As we discussed earlier, they may include our confirmation bias, familiarity bias, our anchoring tendencies, hindsight bias, focusing bias, recency bias, and loss aversion. That's just to name a few. To this, add one heaping portion of emotion—whatever you happen to be dealing with at that time, such as fear, greed or grief.

Throw all that baggage into one big pot, stir it all up, and presto—you have your overall perception of a situation at that specific moment. It's a psychological cocktail that at times has the potential to be a toxic recipe for disaster. And those are just the internal battles we have to wage.

Additionally, we are affected by the many outside forces trying to influence our behavior. As we've discussed, these forces may include the media, business, government, and a host of others. All of whom are trying to influence our decisions and opinions, with their own agenda in mind.

Given all this, should we really be surprised that on occasion we stop and wonder, "What in the world was I thinking when I did that?" As one of my favorite comedians, Flip Wilson, used to say, "The devil made me do it!" But in this case, the devil is your own mind! While this may conveniently help explain how an individual investor could make a horrendous investment decision from time to time, how do we account for *millions* of other investors simultaneously doing the same thing?

The answer to that question may, in part, be due to our social behavior. Humans are social animals, and our behavior can be heavily influenced by what others around us are thinking and doing. Naturally, our own actions are shaped by the *cues* we pick up from others in *our group*.

When the influencers are perceived to be those with superior knowledge, critical information, or in a position of power, respect and authority, these influences can be especially strong. In a time of crisis, confusion or indecisiveness, we may seek out their opinions or guidance, consciously or subconsciously.

Some of these *experts* may include people we see on CNBC, writers from credible publications, economists, politicians, or possibly even your brother-in-law, because "he's a pretty smart guy." Regrettably, these *experts* are also humans, subject to the same psychological pressures and shortcomings.

We may fall victim to several subconscious social forces. These include our strong desire to be socially accepted—to be one of the *group*. We have a natural tendency to find safety in a *herd* and sometimes (often?) succumb to *group think*. We may be especially vulnerable to these social pressures when we are under stress or in an emotional state. When our thinking starts to become cloudy, these social behavior pressures may exert an even greater influence over our decisions. We may even find comfort in being wrong, so long as a lot of people are in the same boat. If I have to be wrong, I don't want to be the only guy in the room holding my hand up.

Keeping all this as a backdrop, let's move forward to explore how investment bubbles can occur. Investment bubbles don't begin as irrational movements—they develop into them. These extreme investment movements typically start out quite innocently.

'Normal' Operating Times—A Market in Equilibrium

In *normal* operating times, the number of buyers and sellers of a particular investment tend to be fairly equal. In other words, the number of people coming into the market to buy is roughly equal to those who are coming to sell. In times of general equilibrium, the price of that investment—whether it be a stock, real estate, or a commodity—is likely to remain relatively stable.

For example, if 1,000 people show up to sell their IBM stock, and there are 1,000 people who wish to purchase IBM, then, all things being equal, the price should remain relatively stable. In this example, there are enough people to buy the shares being offered for sale, and there are enough shares available for those who wish to purchase them.

If, however, on a certain day, 1,000 people show up to sell their stock, but only 900 show up to buy, the price of the stock is likely to drop, since there are fewer buyers. If there are sellers who are more anxious to sell, they may be more inclined to accept a lower price to make sure their shares are sold. The most anxious seller at any given time will set the new price for the next share sold. The more anxious sellers there are, who want to unload their shares, the lower the price may drop. At the end of the day, it's simply a matter of supply and demand. If there are more sellers on a given day than there are buyers, the stock price will drop.

Conversely, if 1,000 buyers showed up, but only 900 sellers, the price should go up. On that particular day there would be more buyers vying to own shares than there were sellers willing to part with them. At any given time, there may be some buyers so committed to owning shares, they may bid the price up high enough to ensure that they will get their desired allotment. On those days, the price moves up.

I know this is basic stuff. Too simple, you may even be thinking. But stay with me. As Warren Buffet said, "Investing is simple, it's just not easy."

So the question is, on any given day, what might influence the numbers of willing buyers or sellers to dramatically shift from one side to another?

Decisions, Decisions—Do I Buy, Sell or Hold Today?

"Every morning in Africa, a gazelle wakes up. It knows it must run faster than the fastest lion or it will be killed. Every morning a lion wakes up. It knows it must outrun the slowest gazelle or it will starve to death. It doesn't matter whether you are a lion or a gazelle, when the sun comes up, you'd better be running." So it is in the investment world.

Every morning investors wake up and they have to decide what they are going to do that day. This includes people who may not even consider themselves as *investors*. If you own a mutual fund, participate in your company's 401(k) plan, or even if you just decided to buy a CD at your local bank, you are an investor. Whether you like it or not, the investment decisions you make today may impact the rest of you and your family's financial life.

So every morning investors have to decide whether they are going to "buy", "sell" or "hold." For most typical individual investors, the answer is usually going to be *hold*. We are very busy. Our days are filled with tasks and distractions—going to work, chauffeuring the kids to practice and recitals, dealing with their school issues, paying bills, taking care of the house, and getting ready for vacations and holidays. Maybe, if you're lucky, you can even get in a round of golf on the weekend! Life certainly has a way of filling up our days.

Consequently, the day-to-day activities of the investment world don't even show up on most folks' personal radar screens. Oh, they may hear how the stock market finished for the day on their way home from work or when they watch the nightly news, but that's usually the extent of it. Unless the market suffers a particularly nasty plunge that day, or has been dropping for several weeks or months, most people are satisfied just to hold to the status quo. "Besides, it would take a lot of time to decide what changes to make in my portfolio, and I simply don't have the time right now. I'll get to it later, when I have more time." Sound familiar?

We have already discussed several possible psychological reasons for this status quo bias. If the investment has lost money, there may be a strong tendency to hang on to it in hopes that it may miraculously recover one day (loss aversion bias). "And who knows, the new investment may end up being worse than the existing one!"

If you combine all the psychological influences at work, it's no surprise that the average individual investor has a tendency to keep things as they are, even if at times they may have a nagging gut feeling that is telling them they should do something. Again, does this sound familiar?

Typically when most average investors are in the *hold* mood, larger institutional investors—such as mutual funds, pensions, endowments and hedge funds, are likely to be driving the direction of the market. This crowd tends to be much more active, and will typically make frequent changes. They are the lions and the gazelles, running and chasing each other, in hopes of being the victor that day.

They are likely to come to work each day and pore over reams of data, opinions and information, trying to gain even the slightest advantage over their competition. Based on that information, they have to make a quick judgment call as to whether they are going to buy, sell or hold that day.

At this point it may be beneficial to step back for a moment, and look at how these institutional investors may arrive at their decisions. Again, I'm going to keep it simple.

What Can Influence a Stock's Price?

Let's suppose an investment company is thinking about adding XYZ Technology Company to their portfolio. Before they decide to buy shares of the company, they decide to more closely scrutinize the company, as well as the overall economic conditions. If things appear to be reasonable, they may go forward with the purchase. Let's examine the possible decision-making process a little more closely.

There are two basic methods of valuing current stock prices— fundamental analysis and technical analysis, as well as various combinations of the two. In general terms, a fundamental analyst will first evaluate company specifics, the industry involved, and the overall economic situation. They develop projections as to how the company might fare under the current overall economic conditions. This is called a "bottom-up analysis", examining the company first, and then looking at the larger industry or economic picture.

Another fundamentalist approach, called "top-down analysis" starts in the opposite direction. They look at the larger overall health of the economy first, and then try to determine what types of companies or industries may do well under those specific conditions.

With either approach, the important basic theory to remember is that the long-term performance and profitability of a specific company should ultimately determine its current stock price. If a company's profits are projected to steadily improve over time, theoretically the price of their stock should also increase. Conversely, if profits are projected to decline, the stock price should drop as well. For a fundamental analyst, the projected profits should determine a company's current stock price.

The other basic method of valuing stock prices is called technical analysis. A technician may be more interested in the recent direction and momentum of a company's stock price, than in the actual performance of the company. In addition to watching an individual stock's price performance, they would also be likely to closely follow the movements of the entire stock market. A technician's theory is that the more recent direction and momentum of a stock or the market will give them an indication of where their prices may be heading in the short-term.

Fundamental Analysis

When researching a company's stock price, a fundamental investment manager may look at factors like a company's current and projected sales, current expenses, market share, cash flow, and how much debt is owed by the company. They may also look at some intangible factors, such as, how well the company is run, how their customers and suppliers are performing, what new products are scheduled to be introduced, and how their competitors are doing. The purpose of this "company-level" analysis is to determine what the company's profits are likely to be in the future. Anything that may affect a company's future profitability would be of considerable interest. A few examples of these key issues may be:

- Slumping sales due to poor product satisfaction
- Possible loss of key customers
- A competitor coming out with a better or more desirable product
- A potential labor dispute that may cause production problems
- Expenses that are increasing faster than sales
- Large amounts of debt that the company may have trouble refinancing in the near future.
- Potential disruptions by key suppliers that may slow production.
- Regulatory changes that may impact that industry.
- Large increases in key commodity prices that are used in production of their products.

Any one or a combination of these issues could cause a company's profits to be substantially reduced, thereby reducing the potential future value of the stock. Conversely, a major improvement in these variables could cause the stock price to increase.

In addition to company level research, the analysis may also include an examination of overall economic conditions and how they may impact upon profits. Some economic indicators may include current interest rates, the inflation rate, the growth of the economy, the unemployment rate, inventory levels, consumer confidence levels, the U.S. trade balance, the strength of the U.S. dollar and many others. The following are examples of how some economic variables may impact a company's overall profitability.

- Rising interest rates may make the company's debt load more expensive.
- Declining consumer confidence may result in customers curtailing purchases.
- A slowing economy may further signal a slowdown in overall consumer spending.
- A weakening U.S. dollar may make it more expensive for retailers to buy their goods.
- Rising unemployment may signal a decline in consumer discretionary spending.
- Bad weather conditions during key holidays may discourage people from shopping.

In a poor economic environment, even a well-run company with a terrific product line can suffer substantial profit reductions. As a result, most money managers are likely to closely monitor both overall economic conditions and individual company results.

IMPORTANT NOTE: The goal of fundamental analysis is to accurately forecast a company's profits for the near and foreseeable future. This projected future profit stream will help determine what price someone may be willing to pay today for a share of that stock. The goal is to determine how much profit each share of stock may be entitled to. This is known as a company's "earning per share" (EPS).

In general, the higher the projected future profit stream of a company, the more someone may be willing to pay for that stock. In addition, the current price may be increased even further if that future profit stream is expected to be more stable or reliable. Keep in mind that this forecast of future profits is based on currently available information. Those projections would be quickly altered were the circumstances to change.

This is an incredibly important concept to remember. Anything that could possibly change the outlook of a company's future profit stream can also dramatically affect its current stock price.

Consequently, a company's forecast may change as new information and economic data are analyzed. When the forecast is adjusted either up or down, the company's stock price will be adjusted. Any new information may result in a change in the earnings forecast, and even a small reduction in expected profits could have a significant impact on stock price.

If you start to look at the investment world from this context, it begins to explain why at times there is so much volatility, and erratic behavior in stock prices. As new information becomes available, opinions can change quickly and dramatically. These fluctuations can become even more extreme during challenging and turbulent economic times. These conditions can make investors particularly vulnerable to emotional decision-making based on incomplete or misinterpreted information.

In the next section we'll contrast the philosophy of fundamental analysts with that of the technicians.

Now Meet the Technicians

Technical analysts or investment managers are less interested in the fundamentals of an individual company or that of the economy. Rather, they tend to be shorter-term investors, who are more interested in the direction and "momentum" of the stock market, or of a particular stock. To forecast where a stock price may be headed, they look to the immediate past performance of the stock price, and project forward. In *very* simplistic terms, the theory suggests that the present momentum of a stock, either up or down, is likely to continue until something acts to change its direction. This is similar to the familiar physics theory that "a body in motion, will remain in motion, until acted upon."

Many technicians use charts and the "moving-day averages" of a stock price or index in an attempt to gauge where a stock price may be headed. Basically they chart the daily price of a stock or index over a designated period of time, such as the past 50 or 100 days. Then they superimpose a second line on the chart representing a longer period, such as 200 days. The second line will give them the longer-term trend of the stock price. A technical analyst will be looking for the times when the two lines "cross." These crossover points may give them a *signal* to either buy or sell the stock. The subsequent chart is a hypothetical example of what a technical analysts chart may look like. (*See following chart.*)

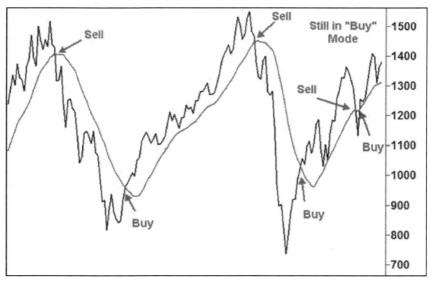

Source: Les Szarka, CFP®, ChFC®

For example, if a stock is currently trading above or below the longer-term trend line, it may be signaling a potential change in the direction of that stock price. Typically a technician may consider buying a stock if it is trading below its moving average, or selling it if it is trading above it. While overly simplified, this explanation will suffice for our current discussion.

Buy, Sell or Hold?

On any given day, when the lions and gazelles of Wall Street come to work, they are looking for anything that may change their current outlook (or perception) of a particular investment, or the investment world in general. At any given time, there will always be some individual key indicators that are positive, and others that are negative. The difficult task is determining which of these indicators in critical at the time.

Let's go back to our example of throwing logs into a pickup truck, where the last one thrown on the pile breaks the axel. Did that last log that you threw on the truck really break the axel? Of course not, it was a combination of ALL the logs that caused it to break.

It's the same with financial and economic indicators. Many times a single economic indicator changes right before a major move in the stock market. At times that particular economic indicator may get too much of the blame (or credit) for the change in the market. At other times, these indicators may negate each other, and end up being a wash, with little effect on the stock prices.

As a consequence, investors may come to expect to have the same result the next time the same variable changes. They may be surprised when something different happens (misdirected focus bias). This is why it is unwise to overweight any single indicator, since the impact on the market may be different the next time.

Occasionally you will see several indicators start to turn in the same direction, either more positive or negative. These are the times that you may see stock prices react accordingly. So as an increasing number of indicators start to look more encouraging, you may expect to see stock prices start to move upwards, or vice versa.

We will now look at how these financial and economic basics, combined with human behavior, can possibly explain why investors behave irrationally at times. For the balance of this section I will use stock prices in my examples, but the same principle can apply to other investments as well.

Stage One of an Investment Bubble

A Market Moving out of Equilibrium—Stock Prices Start to Move Up

As I discussed earlier, when the number of buyers is roughly equal to the number of sellers, the market should be in equilibrium, with prices remaining somewhat stable. But, when key financial or market indicators begin to turn more optimistic, stock prices could start to move upward. Initially this upward movement may be minor. Keep in mind that at any given time, there are dozens of key financial and economic indicators that can initially cause stock prices to rise or fall.

To further complicate matters, any single variable may prove critical in one situation, only to be insignificant in another. For example, the Federal Reserve may decide to raise interest rates and the market may panic and sell off. In another situation, the exact same move by the Fed may not have any effect at all. Typically, a single indicator won't have a dramatic effect on the markets. It will usually take a number of indicators to change to positive or negative to cause a corresponding reaction in the markets.

As these indicators change, some investment managers may begin to see a more positive pattern emerge, and it may prove to be enough of an incentive for them to start buying. Of course, not all investors will see the pattern emerge at the same time. Some may pick up on it earlier, and as the buying momentum begins to build, prices will start to rise (more buyers than sellers in the market). As prices continue to steadily increase, other investors, who were initially less perceptive or not as optimistic, may decide to start buying.

Keep in mind that at this early stage in our example, typically there won't be a large increase in new buyers jumping into the market. But it doesn't take a large number to begin to tilt the scales.

At this point in the market move, initial buyers are likely to be larger institutional buyers (mutual funds, investment banks, pension funds), rather than individual investors. Larger institutions are more likely to be closely monitoring key financial and economic indicators. Most individual investors are still being distracted by their normal lives, so they may be content to stay in a holding pattern.

At this early stage in the market move, you will typically see little news coverage of the stock market increase in most of the general media outlets. You may, however, start to see some coverage appearing in those outlets that are dedicated to business or investment topics, such as the *Wall Street Journal* or CNBC.

At this point, the market increase may be small enough that investors believe it could be a temporary increase, which it could turn down at any time. Much of the price increase could be attributed to *fundamental* improvements, with very little of it being driven by investor emotions or behavior.

Stage Two of an Investment Bubble

The Market Continues to Build Momentum—Up, up and away!

As new buyers fuel the market, the momentum begins to feed on itself. At this point, as some of the "moving day averages" may turn positive, and additional technical analysts may decide to join the party, buying stocks, or adding to their existing holdings.

As other economic indicators point in a more positive direction, coupled with the market increase, *buy* signals may start to appear on more investors' radar screens. This will continue to fuel the market increase. As the number of new buyers grows, they come to outnumber willing sellers, pushing prices even higher. As more and more buyers jump in, some evidence of the effects of *herding* and *group think* begin to register among some institutional investors. These influences will become stronger as more and more investors jump into the market.

At this point in the market increase, most of the business media will likely be spending considerable time dissecting the market's every move. The general media, however, may be oblivious to it, since they may have far more important things to cover—issues such as the identity of the most recent person voted off American Idol, or which rehab facility Paris Hilton was recently admitted in to.

The market gain, up to this point may be attributed largely to institutional investors, since individual investors may be distracted by their lives, and struggling with their *status quo bias*.

Stage Three of an Investment Bubble

The Market Kicks into Overdrive—Full steam ahead!

Fueled by the ever-increasing number of new buyers, the market is likely to accelerate its upward movement. Frustrated by missing the early movement in the market, and fearing that their performance numbers may begin to suffer, the remaining institutional buyers who had been holding off, may now start buying as well.

By now, the *herding effect* and *group think* may also be playing a greater role in the market increase. Some investors who jumped in early may also fall victim to other powerful subconscious bias, such as their "confirmation bias", "recency bias" and "hindsight bias." Based on their recent successes, they may also be fighting some investor "overconfidence" issues as well.

At this point, even the most skeptical institutional investors may feel compelled to join in, at least to some degree. They may be starting to feel the pressure from their shareholders who may be jumping ship because of their lagging performance numbers. In addition, ridicule for missing the market surge may be starting to take its toll.

The business media is likely to be all over the market surge. Words such as "soaring" and "bull market" are being used more frequently. Every nuance of the market increase is likely to be dissected, comparing the current run to every run over the past century. The only question remaining is, "How high will it go"?

Now, even the general media begins to pay attention to the market run-up. A few stories start to appear pointing out the "nice run in the market." Fortunately for them, there are some good, hard news stories out there that also need to be covered. Charlie Sheen is rumored to be dating Lindsey Lohan, and one of the Kardashian sisters was just admitted into a rehab facility. (Just in case you haven't noticed by now, I'm not a big fan of the media!)

At this point in the market cycle, an increasing number of individual investors may also take notice of the market rise. Frustrated by missing out on the earlier gains, they may start to move some of their assets into the stock market. Others, who have been burned before by sudden drops in the market, are content to wait a bit longer, "to make sure that this time it's the real thing." Some may be ready to make a change, but more pressing matters must be attended to first. "I'll get to it when I have some time next week..."

While being driven primarily by financial and economic fundamentals, human behavior (greed) may now exert an increasingly greater influence on the market surge, as evidenced by more individual investors buying into the market, due to the increasing media coverage.

Stage Four of an Investment Bubble—Alternative #1

The Market Reverses Course—Uh-oh!

Most often, the market surge will start to run out of gas at this point of the cycle. Although the number of individual investors may continue to increase at this stage of the bull market, there are likely to be a number of institutional investors who begin to slowly exit.

Yet, more investors may buy into the market, partly due to their regret about missing the early part of the run. In addition, media coverage highlighting the recent success in the market may also reinforce investors' belief that the market will continue to go up (confirmation bias).

Meanwhile, institutional investors that bought in the early stages of the surge may be sitting on a 50-100% gain. For them the greater risk would be to hold on too long. Having a nice gain at risk, these institutional investors may start to slowly sell their holdings, or begin to exit at the first hint of trouble.

One of my colleagues compares it to a person who is sitting in the front row of an old theater, and sees smoke billowing from under the curtain. He is worried that if he jumps up and yells fire, he may not make it out alive, since everyone will try to get out at the same time. He worries that since he is in the front row, he may be among the last ones out. So instead of bringing attention to the risk, he slowly and quietly gets up and moves toward the rear of the theater, hoping not to alert anyone else, so he can get out before others catch on to the potential disaster.

In the same manner, some institutional investors, sensing the potential for fire, may decide to slowly and quietly exit the market, hoping not to draw too much attention to themselves. Their selling volume may not necessarily cause the market to drop, due to the increased buying by individual investors who have now decided to get in. At this point the market surge may begin to lose momentum, since the buying and selling volume begins to go back toward equilibrium.

As the market surge slows, individual investors may continue to buy, seeing the market leveling off as simply a temporary pause, hoping it moves on to new highs. These late stage buyers are especially vulnerable to losses, having missed the entire market increase up to this point.

If enough institutional investors decide to cash in at this point (also called a "crowded trade"), you could end up with considerably more sellers than buyers. In that instance the market could quickly reverse course, bringing an abrupt end to the bull market run.

Stage Four of an Investment Bubble—Alternative #2

The Market Continues to Surge and Develops into a "Bubble"—Oh happy days!

In rare cases (at times more than a decade apart) the market does not retreat from these lofty gains, but continues to surge. This is what we saw in the tech bubble in the late 90's and again with the real estate bubble in the 2000's.

In this scenario, the market may already be up 100% or more, but the momentum continues to feed on itself. Instead of taking profits, institutional investors continue to buy. The continuing institutional demand, along with the ever-increasing number of newly inspired individual investors, can accelerate the increase in the market. When you examine most investment bubbles, the prices dramatically accelerate near the end of the run, at times ending in a feeding frenzy.

As the market continues its increase, and investor confidence continues to rise, there are likely to be fewer and fewer sellers. Buyers are willing to pay unreasonably high prices just to assure they get their allotment.

By this time, some investors throw caution to the wind, buying more and more, with little thought to the actual value of the underlying investment. Fundamental analysts are left scratching their heads, trying to figure out why people are willing to pay inflated and outrageous prices. At times there appears to be giddy, almost euphoric, even invincible feeling in the air. Nothing can stop me now!

We saw this phenomenon with the tech bubble build-up in the late 90's, as people were buying stocks in companies where the only requirement seemed to be that they ended in dot-com. In extreme cases, some of these new tech companies, with no real earnings or profits, were being valued significantly higher than large, well-established international manufacturing and industrial companies.

The NASDAQ stock market, which represented most of the newly formed dot-coms, rose 235% in about 18 months, from

October 1998 to March 2000. It was up over 85% in the last six months of that period alone. Talk about "irrational exuberance"!

Then in the mid 2000's, we saw it happen all over again, but this time with real estate. At its fever pitch, people were putting down large deposits to reserve the opportunity to buy a house or condo in a building complex that had yet to be built. Those who bought at inflated prices were still able to sell out at a handsome profit, before the construction was even completed, because the boom continued. There were numerous shows on cable TV dedicated to showing how easy it was to *flip a house* and make a fortune. The term "flipping" was being used more with real estate, than with hamburgers!

The Greater Fool Theory—Emotional Oscar Takes the Driver's Seat!

Most investment bubbles are driven by emotional buying (greed), and not the underlying fundamentals of an investment. Many buyers who jump in at the later stages of a bubble doing so out of blind faith that the market will continue to rise, regardless of and market company fundamentals.

This is what is referred to as the "greater fool theory." So long as there is someone behind you who is foolish enough to pay more than you did for an overpriced investment, the market will continue to rise, and the game will continue. The second you look behind you, and there is no one left, YOU HAVE BECOME THE GREATER FOOL. It's like a game of musical chairs. When the music stops, if there are no empty chairs, you're out of the game.

So the question begs, why would seemingly intelligent people, including many institutional investors, keep playing this game of investment Russian roulette? That's exactly what it is, because the longer you stay in, the greater the odds become that you will hit the loaded chamber. The simple answer may be that the adults left the room, and **Oscar** was left in charge.

As I stated earlier, the two greatest threats to your investment outcomes are the emotions of fear and greed. Greed can take prices and markets to levels they have no rational reason to reach. When **Oscar** gets excited and **Felix** is nowhere to be found, it's not going to end well!

Stage Five of an Investment Bubble

Someone Yells "Fire" in the Theater—The Bubble Finally Bursts!

> *"Markets tend to go up like an escalator,*
> *but drop like an elevator."*
>
> Author Unknown

At the tail end of an investment bubble the feeding frenzy reaches a crescendo. At this point, nearly everyone who intended to buy into the market has already done so. There may only be a relatively few new buyers. Existing investors may have pretty much exhausted their ability to buy any more. This may occur because either they don't have any new additional money to invest; or, in the case of institutional investors such as pensions, endowments or mutual funds, they may be prohibited by their own policies from increasing their allocation any further. As the money on the sidelines continues to dry up, a dangerous situation can start to emerge.

The market is on thin ice. All that has to happen for it to dramatically reverse course is for a few early, large institutional investors to decide to cash out and lock in their profits. Investors who started buying in at the earliest stages of the bull market have the biggest gains at stake. They are the ones who start selling to lock in their gains. This situation would be similar to what I described earlier, when the markets reverses direction before it gets into bubble territory. The difference may be how quickly and how much the market may decline in a very short period of time.

The initial reason (or excuse) investors begin selling may be fairly benign. It may be triggered by a few disappointing earnings reports, some bad economic news, or possibly an international incident. My point is that it may not take much negative news for them to begin to sell.

With little new money available on the sidelines to absorb the increase in shares for sale, prices begin to fall. If the selling volume continues to increase, and prices continue to drop, more and more investors who got in early may begin to sell as well.

At this point the bubble has not yet burst. Though prices have begun to decline, possibly significantly, it may not be enough to alarm investors. Those who jumped into the market late, and have little or no gains to protect, may be less likely to cash out at this point. They're hoping the market is in a temporary lull, and stocks will soon resume their rise. Additionally, many investors receive their investment statements monthly or quarterly, so they may not have even noticed how much their accounts have dropped yet!

These late-stage investors may also be encouraged by stories in the media promoting the easy riches being made, to stay in the market. This was certainly the case in the late 90's. Remember the stories about individuals who quit their jobs to become "day traders"? "It's so easy to make money in the market—why work!"

Based on perceptions, and biases, there may be enough of a *consensus opinion* that this is only a temporary pullback, and that "this may simply be a buying opportunity for those who got in late." Others may decide to jump ship, hoping to salvage at least some crumbs from the bull market run.

If prices continue to decline sharply over the proceeding days or weeks, the selling will hit critical mass. At some point in the selling frenzy, prices may decline severely enough that it may scare off many of the few remaining buyers.

With the system overwhelmed by sellers, and so few buyers, the market may end up in a free fall. This is when the bubble is likely to burst. It's similar to yelling "fire" in that old crowded theater. There are simply too many people trying to exit at the same time, and people get trampled. At this stage of the cycle, the market may already be down 30 to 40% or more from its highs. Many investors may become victims of the "death grip of fear." The only thing on some investors' minds may be "how quickly can I get out and still have something left?"

At the same time, something else may also be starting to happen. With the sharp decline in prices, and in the midst of all the fear, some seasoned investors may see some attractive buying opportunities. These investors may be the ones that got into the market early, and sold out with large profits, so they would certainly have the ability to start buying if they wanted to.

What may hold them back at this point is the concern that the market may continue to drop because of continued irrational selling. As the old Wall Street adage goes, "Buying in a declining market is like catching a falling knife. The goal is to grab the handle. If you move too soon, you may catch the blade instead, and you'll get cut."

So even though there may be some willing and able buyers, they may choose only to nibble for a while before making any large commitments. Strategically, if prices do continue to fall, they will be in a position to buy shares at even lower prices, "So let's wait and see if the fools continue to panic and sell."

It is not unusual to see the market hit what are called "false bottoms." This is when the selling temporarily subsides and some buyers jump in and start to *nibble*. These temporary reprieves are also referred to as a "sucker's rally." They may lure in some buyers, only to have the selling resume, driving the market even lower.

Eventually the market simply runs out of investors wishing to sell. Those that were in a panic have probably already sold out.

Some may have held out to the bitter end, only to eventually throw in the towel after it appeared that "the market will never recover." Those left in the market may be convinced the market will eventually rebound, or they are so despondent they figure, why bother selling now.

Once again, the market seeks and reaches equilibrium—the number of sellers now roughly equals the number of buyers. This equilibrium stage at the bottom of a cycle may be short-lived. As investors move from panic to calm, buyers who were holding back, waiting, now start to aggressively buy those attractive deals they identified earlier. Some of these opportunistic investors are affectionately called "vultures." As the vultures move in, and with relatively few sellers left, the market may quickly move out of equilibrium. But this time there are more buyers than sellers, so the prices may start a move up—at times dramatically.

Historically, when you look at the stock market after a substantial drop, the biggest gains tend to come early in the recovery—often in the first few weeks or months. This typically happens because these early investors know that their aggressive buying will drive up prices. Their hope is that not too many people will have caught on yet, so they have more time to buy more! But as prices continue to increase, additional buyers may start to jump in, hoping to get in on the early stages of the recovery. As the prices continue to move up, the market cycle starts all over again.

Meanwhile, some poor investor is licking his wounds from the pounding he took just a month ago when he sold off a large portion of the stocks in his 401(k). "How could I have lost over

35% in such a short period of time? Everybody was so sure it was going to continue to go up. How could everyone have been so wrong?"

As he's driving home from work he hears on the radio that over the past few weeks the stock market is up over 20%. "No way" he mumbles to himself. "No way I'm jumping back in yet. I'm going to wait this time until I know for sure this market is for real! Besides, we're leaving for vacation next week. If I have some time, I'll look at it when we get back."

And the market cycle starts all over again...

Rationalizing the Creation and Implosion of an Investment Bubble

The following is a recap of some of the psychological forces to which investors may be susceptible during dramatic investment swings, both up and down. These contribute to investor irrational behavior. Investors will be affected in varying degrees. No one is immune. This list is certainly not all-inclusive, but represents how easy it may be for investors to become vulnerable to these psychological forces during strong market movements.

Bubble Building Phase

"Irrational Exuberance"

Bubble Bursting Phase

"Death Grip of Fear"

Confirmation Bias

Exuberant investors actively seek out additional information to reinforce their already optimistic attitudes, while discounting any information to the contrary.	Panicking investors actively seek out information to reinforce their already pessimistic attitudes, and discount information to the contrary.

Recency Bias

Investors' tendency is to look at the immediate past to get an indication about where the market may be headed. Near the end of a bull market, the immediate past will tend to look amazing, and may add to an already euphoric state of mind.	The same recency bias that pushed the market upward, is now moving it in the opposite direction. In the middle of a sharp market decline, the immediate past may tend to look downright frightening.

Herding Effect

Humans tend to seek safety in numbers. So investors may mimic other investors. As the number of people doing the same thing increases, it only reinforces their decision to buy, and can escalate very quickly. Even if they are proven wrong, at least they weren't alone!

Seeking safety in numbers goes in both directions. Investors tend to do what other investors are doing, so if they see a herd running towards the exit, they may find it hard to fight the urge to do so themselves.

Group Think

This is the tendency for people to fall in line with consensus thinking. As market momentum builds, the consensus feeling grows stronger. For some institutional investors, there may be a greater professional and financial risk being outside the consensus.

When analysts and investors turn pessimistic, and the forecasts become grim, there is a strong tendency to fall in line with the group think. Even large institutional investors may be susceptible to this phenomenon.

Optimism Bias

When we are in a positive frame of mind, we tend to be overly optimistic, and over-estimate favorable outcomes. If investors are already in a positive mood and expecting the market to rise, there is a tendency to be overly optimistic about their potential investment gains, and downplay the risks.

Pessimism Bias

Focusing too heavily on selective negative data and opinions may give an investor a strong sense of doom, leading to the conclusion that the market will continue to drop. This pessimism can lead people to make more emotionally-based investment decisions.

Immediate Gratification

Our tendency is to want immediate results, with minimal pain. The latter stages of a raging bull market can certainly have that illusionary appearance. Let's get rich quick!

Our instinct is to reduce pain or stress quickly as possible. In a dropping market, our minds way of reducing pain quickly may be to sell those assets that are causing the pain—even if not logical.

Anchoring Bias

Anchoring bias is our tendency to anchor to an irrelevant number or event, such as having a goal to "beat the S&P 500 index," even if it has no bearing on your specific financial goals. This may lead some investors to stay in too long, simply to "beat the market."

At times investors may find solace in the fact that "it could have been worse." So if the market is down 40% and you're down only 30%, you beat the market by 10% points (even though you're down 30%!) This is basically putting lipstick on a pig!

Bandwagon Effect

Acting on the feeling that "if everyone else is buying, they must be right."

Having the feeling that "if everyone else is selling, they must know something I don't."

Framing Effect

Looking at the investment world from a very optimistic perspective. If someone's initial perspective is already highly confident, most of what you see thereafter will have a more positive slant to it.

Looking at the investment world from a negative perspective. If your initial framing is already pessimistic, much of what you observe may be tainted by that negative outlook.

Gambler's Fallacy

Not realizing the true probability of an event occurring. Inaccurately interpreting that the current market will continue to surge, and discounting the probability that it may reverse direction.

In a severe down market, this tendency may lead investors to conclude that the downward trend will likely continue. So they bail out to salvage what they can.

Availability Heuristics

Your brain takes short cuts based on limited or partial information. Investors run the risk of jumping to a conclusion that the market will continue to increase based on limited, biased or inaccurate, information.

Many investment decisions are made out of fear. Investors run the risk of jumping to the conclusion that the decline is likely to continue. They fail to consider the reasons for the fall. "Don't bother me with the facts, I've already made up my mind."

Pattern Seeking Bias

Investors' looking for patterns or trends may find them even where there are none. Detecting a "pattern" that leads them to believe the market will continue to surge may lead an investor to become overly confident.

In a highly emotional state, when the market is dropping, investors may start to see patterns that they believe confirm their already existing beliefs that the market will continue to drop.

Overconfidence Bias

Focusing on selective data and opinions can give an investor a false sense of security that the market will continue to rise. This overconfidence may lead them to assume more investment risk than they might otherwise have taken. This can encourage an investor to stay in the market, even though they may feel that the market is already overpriced, hoping that it will continue to rise for the near term, and believing that they will be able to bail out before it drops.

Loss Aversion Bias

The tendency for investors to hang on to their investment losers too long. In many scenarios they would have been better off selling earlier. Many investors may inhibit a tendency to avoid selling their investments at a loss to avoid having to admit that they made a mistake. By not selling it, they think they still have a chance the market will recover. The risk is that an investor rides the bear market all the way to the bottom, and then panics and sells.

INVESTOR LESSONS:

As we've discussed, there are times when the investment world is driven by logic and reason, and then there are the times when emotions rule the day. One of the keys to successful investing is to recognize when enough investors are starting to cross over from the logical to the emotional side.

Investors must exercise more caution when an investment's price increases dramatically over a relatively short period of time. The greater the short-term increase, the greater the corresponding correction may be. As we discussed earlier, there may be a simple and logical reason for this. The longer an investment or bull market runs, the higher the gains that are at stake for those investors who bought early. The more they have at stake, the greater the incentive to sell at the first sign of danger. A sharp increase in sellers at any one time can send prices plummeting.

For example, let's say you have a 20% gain in your portfolio over a relatively short period of time. You see some potential risks ahead, but you also see the possibility of the market continuing to go up. You may decide to sell a smaller portion of your gains. This way, you are hedging your bets. You're still hoping the market will continue to go up. But if it drops, you have locked in at least some modest gains. This approach, if widely adopted, may reduce the market's incentive to sell, thereby limiting overall selling volume.

Now let's suppose you have a 100% gain over that same period of time. Two things will have changed. First, with the market already up 100%, there is a greater chance that market prices may have gotten ahead of themselves, and may be ready to reverse course.

Second, since you already have a 100% gain, you now have less incentive to stay in the market. So at the first sign of any trouble, instead of just selling a small portion of your holdings, you may decide to substantially cash out. A large gain over a relatively short period of time means that there may be more investors willing to substantially cash out, causing a sharp drop in the market. Remember the Wall Street adage, "pigs get fat, but hogs get slaughtered."

There are some powerful psychological currents that investors must fight as they try to stay grounded in a raging market. When you see a large number of investors stampeding in the same direction, it is easy to get caught up in the emotion of the moment. It is far easier to do the wrong thing if everyone else is doing it, than it is to do the right thing, if you are standing alone!

The Anatomy of an Investment "Bubble"

The Greed-Hope-Fear Cycle of Emotional Investing

The 1990's Tech Bubble by the Numbers

The Bull Market Phase

- In January 1995, the NASDAQ Index* stood at around 800 points.

- In a little over three years (Jan 1995 to March 1998) the NASDAQ was up an impressive 130%, to approximately 1,800 points.

"Bubble" Phase

- In early October 1998, the NASDAQ stood at 1500 points.
- By early March 2000 it was 5,000—another 230% increase in just 18 months!
- It increased over 72% over the last 5 months alone! (Irrational exuberance)

The "Bubble" Bursts

- In just 16 days (March 24 to April 14), the NASDAQ dropped an astounding 34%!
- By April 4, 2001 it was slightly above 1,600—a 68% drop in 12 months.
- By Oct 2002 it hit bottom at 1,100—a total drop of 78% in 18 months.

---

* Indices are unmanaged and investors cannot invest directly in an index. The NASDAQ Composite Index is a market-capitalization weighted index of the more than 3,000 common equities listed on the NASDAQ stock exchange. The types of securities in the index include American depositary receipts, common stocks, real estate investment trusts (REITs) and tracking stocks. The index includes all NASDAQ listed stocks that are not derivatives, preferred shares, funds, exchange-traded funds (ETFs) or debentures.

CHAPTER NINETEEN

Understanding Risk and the Pain of Losing Money

> *"I am more concerned with the return OF my money than the return ON my money."*
>
> Mark Twain, *author and humorist*

We all hate losing money, but at times, the decisions we make to avoid it can be illogical, and even senseless. As we discussed earlier, some of this can be attributed to our brain's basic desire to avoid risk, and seek out safe havens. From this perspective, it can make sense that investors would go to great lengths to avoid risks, especially when they are already nervous. The difficult task is to be able to accurately assess ALL the risks involved, not just the obvious ones.

The understandable goal for most investors is to minimize potential losses in their portfolios. While this sounds like a reasonable (and obvious) goal, it should be balanced against other risks as well. A drop in your portfolio is not the only way you can suffer a loss. As we discussed earlier, inflation and the loss of purchasing power can be just as devastating as a significant loss in your investments.

From the perspective of your retirement income and lifestyle, the doubling of your expenses due to inflation is comparable to losing half of your portfolio's value. In either situation, you can only buy half as much as you could initially. If you doubt it, here's an example.

Let's suppose you have $500,000 in an IRA, and you are withdrawing 4% each year to supplement your Social Security and a pension. The distribution from your IRA would work out to approximately $20,000 per year ($500,000 x 4%). If you lost half of your account value, you could now only draw down $10,000 per year ($250,000 x 4%). Thus, a loss of 50% of portfolio value will force you to cut your spending in half (from $20,000 to $10,000).

Now, let's suppose you still had your $500,000, but instead, your expenses had doubled from $20,000 to $40,000 because of inflation. You were eating the same, driving the same car, and taking the same vacations, but everything is now twice as expensive. Although your income was the same $20,000 ($500,000 x 4%), you would now need $40,000 to buy the same amount of goods that $20,000 bought you earlier. In either case, the net result is that you must cut your expenses in half! This is what is referred to as "inflation risk."

Inflation risk is insidious, because it's not as apparent as a sharp decline in your portfolio. But make no mistake about it— it's the silent financial killer. It is every bit as real as a 50%

drop in the stock market. The main difference is that it is not as obvious—you don't get a monthly statement to remind you of the risk and pain. Instead, it quietly goes about its business, slowly stealing away the purchasing power of your savings. As Ronald Reagan once so accurately described it, "Inflation is as violent as a mugger, as frightening as an armed robber and as deadly as a hit man."

Below are some real-life examples of inflation, and their devastating impact on purchasing power.

ITEM	1990	2010	20-YR % INCREASE
Postage stamp	$0.25	$0.44	76%
Loaf of bread	$1.29	$2.49	93%
Gallon of milk	$2.05	$3.39	65%
Gallon of gas	$1.08	$3.50	224%
Doctor's appointment	$40	$95	137%
Avg. new car	$9,437	$21,750	130%
Avg. new house	$128,000	$242,000	89%

Source: Congressional Budget Office
(National averages; prices will vary from region to region)

On average, consumer prices have nearly doubled in the past two decades. And keep in mind this was a VERY moderate inflationary period. In the 1980's, inflation was nearly twice that rate. Ask anyone who has been retired for the past 20 years if their expenses have increased considerably. I think it would be safe to say most people would respond with a resounding "yes". Now ask them if their sources of income, such as social security and pensions, have gone up as much as their expenses. I'm confident they would respond "no way"!

By now I'm sure the problem is obvious. What do I do if my expenses go up and my sources of income don't keep up with the increase—where will the difference come from? This is the dilemma millions of people face every day.

In a well-planned retirement, the increased income would come from the retiree's investments. As their expenses increase they could increase distributions from their portfolio, as needed. This assumes, of course, that there are sufficient assets to be able to generate enough additional income.

However, if the value of a retiree's investments has not increased enough over that same period of time to generate the additional income required, it is likely their standard of living will have to be reduced, and in some cases the reduction may be significant.

This is the predicament many current and future retirees must face. Their retirement expenses may increase at a faster rate than their investment income. At some point they may face a difficult decision—can I cut my expenses enough to keep pace with the income my investments can generate; or do I attempt to increase my investment income. Some retirees may not have the option of reducing their fixed expenses any further. Attempting to increase the income from the investments introduces a whole new set of problems, in that it would entail having to increase portfolio investment risks. This is where many people may encounter a problem. At this stage in their lives, most retirees will not feel comfortable increasing their investment risk. In fact, given the volatility of the past decade or so, many would probably prefer to decrease it. Given their circumstances, they may not have a choice.

It is possible that even more people may be facing this difficult situation in the future for two primary reasons. First, it is likely that inflation may be even higher in the decade to come, primarily due to the incredible amount of new money that has been created by the Federal Reserve over the past few years. Historically, the unfortunate consequence of excessive money creation by government has been higher inflation rates. This may create a situation where a retiree's expenses increase faster and at a higher rate than they have in the past few decades.

In addition, retirees are being punished by historically low interest rates. In 2007, money market rates were over 5%, whereas currently they stand near zero (as of 7/15/13). To illustrate the devastating impact this has had on retirees, take for example a couple who in 2007 were receiving $35,000 in Social Security and $25,000 in interest income from bank accounts ($500,000 x 5%), for a total annual retirement income of $60,000.

By 2012, that same couple's total annual income was reduced to $40,000, because their interest income was slashed to from $25,000 to $5,000 ($500,000 x 1%). The devastating combination of increasing expenses coupled with historically low interest rates has forced many people to assume greater risks in their portfolios, in their quest for higher yields. In many cases, retirees may not even fully understand the true risks they must take.

Earlier, I stated that inflation, in certain instances, may be even more dangerous than a severe portfolio loss. Here's why. If your portfolio suffers a substantial loss (as it may have in 2000 or 2008), you always have the chance that it may recover sometime in the future. For instance, many portfolios may be higher now than where they were in March of 2009, when the market bottomed out. So there is always a possibility that your portfolio may recover those losses.

Inflation, on the other hand, is cumulative and compounded. It rarely ever goes down. So when prices go up, it is added to all the previous yearly increases. If inflation averages 3% per year, that means prices will be up 34% after just 10 years, and 80% after 20 years. At a 4% inflation rate, your costs would be up 48% after 10 years and 119% after 20 years! That is why inflation is so dangerous.

Even with *mild* inflation, because of the cumulative and compounded effects, rates and prices can go up dramatically, with little chance that they will ever decline. As a matter of fact, you really don't even want to hope to see prices drop. When prices decline, it's called deflation, and that usually happens when an economy is in a depression.

It is a tragic situation when we have millions of retirees in this country living their lives in quiet desperation. At times, they must make untenable choices like whether to pay their electric bill or buy their prescription medications, because they can't afford both. People, who worked hard all their lives, raised their children, paid their bills and saved their money, are now trying to make ends meet by cutting their prescription pills in half and skimping on their meals. They have simply outlived their incomes. As stated earlier, for many people the REAL risk in retirement may not be dying too soon, but rather living too long!

Measuring the Total Real Risk in a Portfolio

When measuring the total REAL risk in your portfolio, the actual question should be: Which is the greater risk—waking up one day and finding your portfolio is down 20%, or finding you can no longer pay your bills.

Many investors tend to fixate too much on protecting the *value* of their portfolios, and not enough on its real purchasing power. This is especially true today. More than a decade of financial devastation has left many investors' psyches in shambles. It has been a fertile environment for their **Oscar** brains to successfully mount a hostile takeover of logical **Felix**. And not without reason. Many people are in a state of investor paralysis from repeated market losses and the extreme volatility we have witnessed for more than a decade.

Consequently, many investors may find themselves vulnerable to hardship in the future. People who in the past could reasonably handle a 10 or 15% drop in their 401(k)'s or IRA's are now stampeding into Money Market accounts at the first hint of a drop in the market.

This comes at a time when inflation is already starting to rear its ugly head, and may be worse in the future. In inflationary times, investors must take measures to assure their investments provide enough growth to offset inflation. Sadly, driven by our "risk aversion" bias, we may delude ourselves into believing we have chosen a *safe* investment, unaware we are simply exchanging one risk for another.

So at a time when inflation appears to be on the rise, we also have historic low interest rates, and a volatile investment world. Is it any wonder that many investors are frustrated, angry and scared? Later in this book we'll deal with how to cope with these challenging times.

A Dollar Gained Does Not Equal a Dollar Lost (At least not in your mind)

Extensive research and experiments, conducted by Professors Kahneman and Tversky in 1979, indicated that it is much more painful for people to lose money than it is pleasurable for them to gain it. To be more precise, they found that losing a dollar is about 2 ½ times as painful as is the pleasure of gaining one dollar.

In their experiments, which have since had numerous variations, Kahneman and Tversky asked two similar groups to make a choice between two options.

The first group was told that they had $1,000, and asked to choose between:

1. A sure gain of $500, or
2. A 50% chance of gaining an additional $1,000, and a 50% chance of getting nothing more.

The second group was told that they had $2,000, and asked to make a choice between:

1. A sure loss of $500.

2. A 50% chance to lose $1,000, and a 50% chance to lose nothing.

The outcomes of either choice are identical for both groups. If either group chose option #1, they would have $1,500. If either group chose #2, they would have either $2,000 or $1,000.

Despite the identical potential outcomes, the preferences of the two groups were surprising. The first group, facing potential gains, selected option #1, the certain gain, more than 84% of the time. Interestingly, the second group, the one facing a certain loss, chose option #2, indicating that they would rather risk losing $1,000, than take the certain loss of $500.

The research, which was coined the "Prospect Theory," suggests that people tend to be more interested in trying to avoid prospective losses, even if it means foregoing greater potential gains. Said another way, it seems that people in general are more willing to take on additional risk to avoid *losing* money, than they are to secure a potential *gain*! According to the research, the pain of a potential loss of a dollar is more than twice as great as the pleasure of gaining a dollar.

In other studies, people were asked to bet $20 of their own money on a single flip of a coin. In most of these experiments, the participants required at least a $45 payoff to take the bet, even though there was a 50/50 chance of winning! Again, to offset the potential pain of losing $20, the participant needed at least a potential $45 payoff.

Based on the results of these and similar studies, it should not be a surprise that people have so much difficulty evaluating the actual risk/reward with their investments. Subconsciously we tend to be more motivated by avoiding losses than we are achieving gains. Keep in mind these experiments were done in controlled, non-stressful settings. Add a little stress to the situation, such as a stock market in a free fall, and it's no surprise why people do irrational things with their investments.

I've seen this play out many times over the years. Frequently you see people holding on to investments that have outlasted their usefulness. When questioned, the response may be something like, "When it gets back to my original investment value I am planning to sell it." In some instances it may take a long time to "come back," and in some cases it never will.

Investors who bought GE stock at the peak of the market in 2000 for $60 per share are still waiting for it to "come back" after it hit a low of $6 per share in 2009. As of this writing, it is selling for around $23 per share (as of 7/15/13). Ford was at $30 in 2000; currently it's at around $17 (as of 7/15/13). Intel was $71, currently its $23. Microsoft was $55, it's now $35. Those unfortunate investors that bought Kodak at $50/share, later watched it file for bankruptcy. Stockholders of these well respected companies have been waiting over 12 years for them to "come back"!

Here's the problem with the "wait until it comes back" strategy. The investment that is currently held may take longer to get back to its original value, than if you had sold it, and reinvested it in something more promising. At times, an investor may be in denial—"If I don't sell it, I didn't really lose any money," (at least not yet!)

When faced with this dilemma, I always invoke the "Templeton rule."

Sir John Templeton, one of the original icons of investing, had a simple strategy when it came to deciding what to do with a disappointing investment in his portfolio. He would simply ask himself: "If I had new money to invest, would I buy more of that investment"? If the answer is NO, then you are admitting that there are other investments that look more attractive than the one you currently own. In which case, you must ask yourself: "Why would I want to continue to own it"? If you wouldn't buy more of the investment in question, you may want to consider selling it, and investing the proceeds in something that you would have used new money to buy.

This psychological block may also explain why people are so hesitant to sell their *loser* investments. By selling, they are acknowledging a loss, which is painful. By holding on to it, they don't have to acknowledge the loss, yet. There is still hope of a miraculous recovery, regardless of how improbable.

The other interesting aspect of Kahneman and Tvresky's study was that people WERE willing to take more risk to potentially minimize the risk of a loss. Recall how nearly 70% of the second group chose option #2, which meant they had an equal chance to either lose $1,000 or nothing, instead of taking a certain loss of $500. So they were willing to accept MORE risk in the hopes of losing less money.

What is surprising is that the research suggests we have a tendency to be more risk-averse when faced with the potential for a gain. Yet, when faced with the chance of reducing or avoiding losses, people tended to be willing to accept even more risk. To complicate matters, investors may not even be fully aware of all the risks involved in the investments.

There are several investment implications to this research. First, when investors are faced with potential losses, they may be inclined to take on additional risk in an attempt to minimize their losses. This may come at the very time when they need to reduce their risk exposure. In an attempt to quickly recoup their losses, they may be tempted to "double down" (buy additional shares at the lower price) on an investment that has dropped significantly. While this strategy may be appropriate at times, it should be done based on fundamental reasons, and not because of an urge to quickly recoup losses.

This phenomenon was quite evident when LTV Steel went bankrupt. In the waning months of its existence, many LTV stockholders continued to hold on to their stock hoping for a miracle, a "stay of execution." I'm confident that most of these investors, who owned LTV stock, would NOT have bought additional shares if they had an additional $10,000 to invest. Yet they were willing to ride their investment down to zero. There were a few brave (foolish?) souls that did buy additional LTV stock at the very end. As a matter of fact, LTV continued to trade for a short while even AFTER it declared bankruptcy. The CEO of LTV had to publically appeal to people to stop buying the stock since it was worthless. Now *that's* investor denial!

Reviewing Your Investments from the 10,000-ft View

As we discussed earlier, people tend to be much more upset when they incur investment losses, than they are pleased about their gains. For example, an investor may have 12 holdings in their portfolio, ten of which may be up, one that is even, and one that is down. Guess which one they want to discuss? You guessed it, the one that is down.

This would be like your child excitedly bringing home their report card because they had a 3.5% GPA. They have 10 "A's," 1 "C" and 1 "D." Instead of celebrating with your child on their 3.5% GPA, the only thing you can think about is, "How the heck did you get a 'D' in art"?

As we discussed earlier, one proven way to reduce risk is to make sure that your portfolio is well diversified. Diversification does not mean simply investing in a large number of different things. In general, you don't want all of your investments fluctuating in the same direction at the same time. By design, you may want to have some of the investments in a portfolio moving in the opposite direction. Investments that don't move lockstep with each other have a "negative correlation" to each other.

The logic behind this strategy is that certain investments tend to do better than others under certain economic conditions. For example, you may choose to use short-term bonds in a portfolio to offset some of the risk in the event of an anticipated stock market plunge. In this scenario, the bonds would be intended to act as a shock absorber, and hopefully limit the decline in overall portfolio. In a severe stock market decline, you would probably be happy that you owned the bonds. As a matter of fact, you may wish that you had owned even more.

If the opposite happened, and stocks soared, the bonds may act as a drag on the portfolio, and reduce the potential gain. In this scenario you may regret having any bonds at all. The goal of diversifying a portfolio is not to eliminate the risk (that's impossible), but rather to reduce the wild swings in your portfolio. In other words, hedge your bets.

So here's the question: What is more important to you, trying to maximize your gains, or potentially limiting your losses?

The reality is that an investor's answer is rarely consistent. The answer will vary depending on the current situation. Typically, when the market is doing well, an investor may be more willing to focus on trying to maximize returns. They may somehow feel cheated if they underperform the market. However, when the market drops, their mood may quickly change, and they may suddenly be much more concerned about limiting any potential losses. Remember, as Templeton said, "Everyone is a long-term investor, or at least until the market drops!"

Hopefully this investor fickleness should make perfect sense to you by now. At any given time we are viewing the future through different lenses, generating new perspectives. Sometimes we are optimistic, other times more fearful. Your future outlook is heavily influenced by the current situation (recency bias). As the investment environment ebbs and flows, so do investment outlooks and goals. It is important to be aware of these potential changes in your outlook, and to make sure your decisions are based on your long-term goals, and not short-term emotions.

In most cases, it would be wise to find some middle ground in a portfolio. Your investment objective should be to achieve the growth needed to meet your long-term financial goals. At the same time, care should be taken to minimize the damage a severe market downturn could cause. It can take years to recover from large portfolio declines.

The most effective way to reduce volatility in a portfolio is to properly balance it. In a properly balanced portfolio, at any given time, some investments may underperform and others may outperform. Those that underperform are not necessarily poor investments, since not all investments perform the same in different economic conditions. There is simply no way to avoid occasional disappointment with some of your investments.

Consequently, there will be times it will help to remind yourself that each investment in your portfolio plays a specific role. If a particular investment is a disappointment, it does not necessarily mean it was a bad choice. That particular investment may not have been expected to perform well under those specific economic or investment conditions. For example, a money market would not be expected to perform as well as stocks in a booming market.

It's not unlike evaluating the players on a sports team. A wide receiver tends to be slight and fast, and is built differently than a massive defensive lineman. Each one has a specific role to play on the team; one is on offense, the other on defense. It wouldn't make sense to judge them by the same criteria.

For example, you would not judge your wide receiver by how many tackles he had that year; just as it wouldn't make sense to judge the lineman by how many touchdowns he scored. That wasn't the role you asked each one to perform. It's the same with your investments. It's not reasonable to love your stocks and be disappointed in your bonds when the market is soaring; or to love those same bonds and hate the stocks when the market drops.

This is certainly not to say that adjustments will not be required to a portfolio on an ongoing basis. Adjustments to the allocation will have to be made periodically. Ideally the adjustment will be based on the current facts and circumstances, and not on emotional whims.

INVESTOR LESSONS:

- Make sure you are not focusing exclusively on the volatility of your portfolio. Inflation risk should be a critical component of making any financial or investment decision. At times this may require that you go outside your investment comfort zone. However, ignoring the long-term effects of inflation on your lifestyle could prove even more costly.

- Be aware of the tendency to be more sensitive to losses than to gains in your portfolio. This phenomenon may, at times, encourage you to sell your winners too soon and hold on to losers too long. Be willing to admit to a poor investment decision and cut your losses short.

- Use the Templeton Rule. When evaluating an investment in your portfolio, ask yourself: "Would I buy more of this investment now"? If not, why do you still own it?

- Make sure your portfolio is always properly balanced and diversified. This means that you will want to have some of your investments *negatively correlated* to each other.

- A properly balanced portfolio may result in disappointed with some of your individual holdings. Don't make changes simply because an investment didn't perform well compared to some others in the portfolio. It may not have been expected to perform well under those conditions.

CHAPTER TWENTY

Clearly Defining Your Financial Goals and Investment Objectives

---

"You got to be careful if you don't know where you're going, because you might not get there."

Yogi Berra, *Major League Baseball player and manager*

≈⁹≈

"A perfect plan poorly executed, is as effective as a poor plan that is perfectly executed."

Vince Lombardi, *NFL Football player and coach*

One observation I've made repeatedly over the years is how many investors confuse having specific financial goals, with simply having vague dreams. The basic difference between the two is that goals have legs by which they can move forward. One step at a time, they get you closer to your financial objectives, whether that's retirement, saving for a new home, or making sure your children have the opportunity to go to college. At times it can be frustrating since it is hard to see small incremental progress being made. But if you stick with it, believe me the results can be amazing. Most of the people I have met, that had been disappointed with their financial situation, never had any specific goals that they were trying to achieve, and no plan to do so. Instead, they had vague dreams, such as "I would love to be able to retire early and have a comfortable life", or "I would like my kids to go to a good college." The problem with vague and ill-defined goals is that they are too general. Without specific goals it is difficult to establish benchmarks to measure progress, to make sure that you are on track to achieve those goals. A financial plan without specific goals is simply a dream with no legs. To have the best possible chance of reaching your financial goals you need to quantify them.

An example of a clearly stated financial objective and goal would be:

"I am planning to retire in 6-8 years with approximately $75,000/year in after-tax annual retirement income, indexed for inflation. To meet my goal, I need to save $24,000 per year in my 401(k), and my overall investment portfolio return needs to average 7% per year after-taxes."

Another might be:

"I plan to send my child to a 4 year college that today costs approximately $22,000 per year, hedged for inflation. To meet my goal, I need to accumulate approximately $122,000 by saving $595/month in a 529 education plan for the next 11 years, and

my investment portfolio return needs to average 7.5% per year."

Clearly stating your goals and objectives makes it easier to track and monitor your progress. Closely monitoring your progress along the way allows for smaller incremental changes, if necessary, to keep you on track to meet your specific goals. Waiting too long to check on your progress may leave you well short of the goal, with not enough time to make up the difference.

In addition to setting specific benchmarks, visualize your goals in vivid images. Remember, the mind tends to recall vivid images more easily. So when you think about retirement, imagine the specific things you would like to be doing, such as traveling to exotic places, having more time for your hobbies and passions, and being able to spend more time with your children and grandchildren. Imagine having friends and family over to your new dream house, or seeing your children walk down the aisle to receive their college diplomas.

Vividly embedding those images in your subconscious can be that little extra push you may need to help you reach those goals. This may be especially important when self-imposed *behavior modification* may be required to reach those challenging "stretch" goals. Recalling those pleasant, vivid images may help you get through the tough tasks that may be required to meet those goals, such as working longer hours, cutting back on your current spending to save more money in your 401(k), or maybe even delaying retiring by a few years.

Having a well thought out specific plan doesn't guaranty that you will meet all your financial goals, but it does go a long way toward increasing the odds. It is psychologically easier to stay on course when you have specific goals and measurable results.

After 30 years of helping people with their retirement goals, I can make the following observation. Financial plans are not maps, as they are sometimes described, but rather more like a compass. You can set a general course, but there are simply too many unpredictable and shifting variables to be able to set out a specific course in advance. These variables may include your income requirements, inflation rates, investment returns, your employment status and your health. As these variables change, you may need to make adjustments to your plan.

There are many good financial planning software programs available. They can also be misleading. Because of the level of detail in these programs, people could be easily misled to believe that they are roadmaps to specific outcomes. Many may even have a trip or journey theme to them, implying that you will be able to "set your own specific course."

This all feeds into the misconception that we somehow have more control over our specific financial outcomes than is really the case. Remember, our human nature is that we like to make projections and have plans—we just don't tend to be very good at them. One reason is that we tend to be overly optimistic with our projections, and then seek out information that may reaffirm them, while ignoring the facts that may challenge them.

The truth is we don't have as much control over our financial lives as people may be led to believe. Take this from someone who has been doing it professionally for a long time. There are simply too many uncontrollable factors, both personal and economic, that affect our financial lives.

THIS DOES NOT MEAN YOU SHOULDN'T MAKE A FINANCIAL PLAN! I'm not going to let you off the hook that easily. What it does mean is that you must focus on the things over which you have control, and avoid depending on things over which you have no control.

Basically it's the Serenity prayer said by investors:

"Grant me the serenity to accept the things I cannot change;
the courage to change the things I can;
and the wisdom to know the difference."

In reality, regardless of how thorough you think your financial plan is, at best you are simply setting a general direction for your trip, and will need to make many adjustments as you move through your life, to compensate for personal and external changes.

Some of the obstacles you encounter in your personal life may put substantial pressures on your finances. These unexpected road bumps may come in several forms, some of them may include:

JOB RELATED – You may not be able to work as long as you anticipated due to job layoffs or health issues. Maybe you depend on two income earners, but due to circumstances beyond your control, only one of you is able to work, due to death or a divorce. It also could be that the level of income you were anticipating did not materialize, so the amount of savings you were projecting could not be achieved.

ADDITIONAL FINANCIAL OBLIGATIONS – You may find yourself in a situation where someone else becomes financially dependent on you, such as an elderly parent, an adult child or grandchildren. These additional obligations could substantially reduce your savings and investments, and may further reduce your ability to save for the future.

HEALTH ISSUES – Many times a health issue may arise that can cause major complications even in the best thought out financial plans. These complications can create severe financial strains in the form of depleted savings and diminished earnings potential. It may also change the life expectancy or quality of life that either you or a partner may anticipate. In some cases this may cause you to substantially alter your long-term financial plan.

Larger issues may also require adjustments to your financial plan. Some of these may include:

ECONOMIC ISSUES – Changes in long-term interest rates and inflation rates may necessitate making adjustments to your financial plan. Long-term financial plans are very sensitive to even small changes in these assumptions. These variables must be carefully monitored to make sure that they are realistic with the current outlook. It is better to err on the side of caution, rather than being caught by surprise by being overly optimistic.

INVESTMENT UPHEAVALS – Severe stock market drops can wreak havoc on any financial plan. As we have seen several times during the past decade or so, in a blink of an eye, a large market drop can wipe out gains that may have taken years to achieve. If a portfolio suffers a substantial loss, it may require that adjustments be made to the plan to compensate for those setbacks. We'll discuss how to help reduce these risks later on in the book.

THINK GLOBALLY – It is important to remember that we do not live in an economic vacuum. Events that occur overseas can have tremendous consequences to our economy and markets as well. It is important to monitor world events, as well as domestic issues.

Every financial plan needs to be adjusted periodically to assure the goals and assumptions are reasonable given the current environment. As you progress through your plan, making smaller, incremental changes is easier than waiting too long, and then having to make larger, more painful adjustments.

There are typically four basic variables that can determine the success or failure of your financial goals. You need to carefully examine each of them to make sure that your assumptions are not only accurate today, but also reasonable for the future.

Here's an example of the four variables of a well-thought-out financial goal.

1. **The Stated Goal**
   "I would like to have $6,000/month of total retirement income, after taxes, and indexed for inflation."

2. The Time Frame
"I would like to retire in 8 years when I'm age 62."

3. The Required Savings
"To meet my goal I need to save $1,900/month in my 401(k) plan, and pay an extra $100/month on my mortgage, so it is paid off by the time I retire."

4. The Required Investment Return
"To meet my retirement goal my investment returns will need to average 7.5% per year, after taxes and fees, between now and when I retire in 8 years, and then 6.5% after I retire."

Let's dig a little deeper into each one of these four variables, and see what planning is required for a successful outcome.

1. Your Stated Goal

"I would like to have $6,000/month of total retirement income, after taxes, and indexed for inflation."

When you are setting any type of financial goal it is important to be as specific as possible. You need to take a vague statement such as, "I would like a comfortable retirement," and quantify it. You need to define exactly what it means for you to be comfortable, and then assign a realistic amount to it.

The best way to do this is to play the "Sears's catalogue at Christmas" game. If you are old enough, you will remember getting those big catalogues from Sears, Penney's or Spiegel, right before Christmas time. As soon as they arrived, I would take them up to my room and go through my ritual of marking off my "wish list." My hope was that my parents would notice the big circles around my dream gifts when deciding on what to get me.

Well, planning your financial goal is your opportunity to play the Christmas catalogue game again. It may be helpful to sit down and determine what it is that you are hoping to accomplish in your life. There was a great movie called "The Bucket List" starring Jack Nicholson and Morgan Freeman. In it the two stars are facing death, but before they die they establish their own "bucket list", or in other words, "things I want to do before I kick the bucket."

I encourage people to develop their own bucket list of things that they would like to accomplish in their lifetimes. Things that they may look back on later in their lives and regret not having done or accomplished. Unlike Nicholson and Freeman's characters, you may want to do it well before you are actually dying! The sooner you start, the better the odds of completing your list.

At this point, you want to let your imagination go. That doesn't necessarily mean you will be able to meet all your goals, but you need to have a starting point. So you might as well aim high. As I used to tell my daughter when she played soccer, "you're guaranteed to miss 100% of the shots you DON'T take."

For example, if you are setting retirement income goals, many financial advisors suggest starting with the amount that you are currently living on, and then making some appropriate adjustments to it. This is referred to as the "cash flow method."

I usually recommend starting with your current NET household cash flow. This is the amount that goes into your checkbook every pay period, AFTER all your deductions have been subtracted, such as taxes, 401(k) contributions, and healthcare deductions. The amount left over is what you have available to pay all your bills, and keep you and your family at your current standard of living. This assumes you are NOT debt financing your standard of living—meaning that your overall debt balance does not increase every year. If your debt increases year by year, you are living a lifestyle you can't really afford!

Starting with your current net income, you will need to make some adjustments to determine how much income you will realistically need in retirement. These adjustments would be the expenses that are likely to change, either higher or lower, between now and when you plan to retire. This assumes, of course, that you wish to continue to maintain your current standard of living in retirement. Here are some common adjustments that you may need to make to your current budget.

Possible deductions from your current expenses

- Your house is paid off before or shortly after you retire. For example, if your current mortgage is $1,000/month, and it will be paid off before you retire (or shortly thereafter), you can subtract the $1,000 from your future budget. If your payments include your property taxes, make sure you are not subtracting them, since those will continue even after your mortgage is paid off.

- College expenses are finished. For example, if you are currently paying or contributing $1,200/month to your child's (or your own) college expenses, these would likely end by the time you retire, or shortly thereafter. Also, don't forget to add the incidentals you may be paying as well, such as books, pocket money, living expenses, car payments and insurance. The tricky part will be trying to determine which of these expenses you are paying out of cash flow, and which are paid out of savings. For example, if the total costs you are paying add up to $17,000 per year, and you took out $5,000 from savings or from other investments; you would only subtract $1,000/month from your current budget. Calculation: $17,000 total paid – $5,000 (came from savings) = $12,000 (from cash flow).

- Financial support to family members. Many people have found themselves in a position of having to financially assist their grown children or parents. In the past, these budget adjustments were typically made for younger children who were still living at home. In today's harsh financial conditions, I see many people having to help out their adult children who may be out of a job, or parents who may not have enough income to pay their necessities, because of record low interest rates. Again, these are expenses that may be subtracted if the support may end sometime in the near future.

- Home equity line or some other loan is paid off. For example, you could subtract the $500/month you are currently paying on a home equity or other type of loan if it is scheduled to be paid off by retirement. As a side note, you may not want to subtract a car loan, even assuming that it will be paid off. You may want to keep some sort of payment in your retirement budget since you will likely need a new car in the future. If you are currently paying a $500/month car payment on a three-year loan, and you typically keep your cars for six years, you may want to include a continuous $250/month car payment in your retirement budget. (Calculation: 3 years of $500/mo payments and 3 years of $0 = average of $250/mo over the 6 years you keep the car.)

Possible additions to your current expenses

- Additional healthcare insurance and expenses. This is typically going to be one of the largest additions to your retirement budget. You will need to estimate how much your health insurance and related health care expenses may be in retirement. These expenses vary widely from one situation to another depending on several factors. It could vary if you work in the private or public sector, if you work for a large corporation or a small employer, or if you are self-employed. It may also change dramatically if you plan to retire prior to Medicare eligibility (currently age 65). For someone over age 65, we typically recommend budgeting approximately $300-$400/month per person. This amount may vary depending on your specific situation. If you plan to retire prior to age 65, you may need to budget an even higher amount until you become eligible for Medicare.

- Additional discretionary spending (fun money!). Most people tend to spend much more money while on vacation than they do while they are working. Your retirement is like a 52-week vacation. Most people's idea of a perfect retirement is not sitting at home all day watching the Food channel or working in the yard. For this reason you will want to increase your discretionary retirement spending budget, to allow for those things you will want to do more of, in retirement. Again, you will want to give it some thought, not just increase it by some arbitrary number. Think about the things you envision doing in retirement and how much it may cost, and then you can create a realistic number.

- Housing arrangements. Some people plan to own a vacation home, or have the ability to "snow bird" in the cold months to a warmer climate once they retire. If this is the case, calculate how much this may realistically cost, and see if it fits into your retirement budget. It's better to know early on what it would take to make it happen. In other instances, people anticipate downsizing from their current house, to something smaller. If so, you need to see how that may impact your overall cash flow. As a side note, just because you may be downsizing, doesn't necessarily mean that it will be less expensive. After you have completed your cash flow projection, you should have a number that will be relatively close to what you are likely to need to meet your desired standard of living in retirement. Keep in mind that this is the NET income, AFTER expenses, and BEFORE income taxes. Just because you've retired doesn't mean Uncle Sam doesn't want to continue getting his fair share! Make sure you allot enough in your retirement budget to cover your taxes. The next step would be to calculate how much you need to add to cover your taxes. You may want to talk to your accountant or financial advisor to see how much you should be budgeting for taxes.

Measuring the effects of inflation is one of the more difficult aspects of calculating your long-term retirement cash flow. Death and taxes aren't the only sure things in life—so is the fact that your expenses will continue to increase over time. Rising prices have destroyed the retirement dreams of many people.

Inflation over the past 30 years has averaged approximately 3% per year. During this period we have seen both extremes. We had very high inflation rates in the late 70's and early 80's inflation (over 13%), and very low rates over the past few decades (at times less than 2%). If that average rate of approximately 3% were to continue throughout your retirement, your expenses would approximately DOUBLE over the next 24 years. Think about that for a second. If you currently need $6,000 per month to live on, you might need over $12,000 per month to enjoy the same life style in 24 years! The key question is, where will that additional money come from?

Determining what to estimate for inflation is critical. Even a small miscalculation can have a dramatic effect over a long period of time. For example, that $6,000/mo current budget would grow to $12,000 at 3% over 24 years. However, if inflation averaged 4%, you would need over $15,000/mo! Using a realistic inflation rate is critical.

One of the biggest planning mistakes you can make is failing to factor in the need for an INCREASING income stream in retirement. One common mistake people make is to simply look at the estimated income they will have in that first year of retirement, and if it's close to what they think they may need to live on, they assume they are good to go!

The reality is that they may be fine for the first few years, but as time goes on, and their expenses continue to rise, they will start feeling the pinch. At first it may not be too bad, because they will be able to cut it from their discretionary budget. But eventually it may start cutting into their fixed expenses, such as utilities, medications and taxes. At this point, their retirement lifestyles may drastically decline with little hope of ever improving. Once you start down that slippery slope, it's difficult to turn it around. For many retirees, the greater financial risk isn't dying too soon, but living too long, and not having enough income.

To avoid this frightening scenario, we typically recommend using at least a 3.5% annual inflation rate (if not higher) for your retirement income calculations. This number should be reviewed periodically to make sure it remains an accurate estimate. Under the current economic conditions, and with the massive amount of money that the Federal Reserve has pumped into our economy over the past few years, it is possible that we may experience even higher inflation rates in the future. If you wish to be even more cautious, use a higher inflation rate figure. But, be aware that even a small increase in the assumed inflation rate may substantially reduce your projected retirement income.

For example, for a couple retiring at age 65 with $750,000 in assets, and total retirement income from social security and pensions of $5,000 per month, their total projected retirement income could be approximately $7,000/month (assuming 3% for inflation and a 7% investment return).

By increasing the assumed inflation rate to 4%, and keeping all the other variables the same, their projected retirement income would drop from $7,000/month to just $6,200. That's a reduction of $800/month in spendable income! (This assumes that in both scenarios the original $750,000 remains intact after 30 years.)

We'll further discuss the effects of inflation in the next chapter.

2. The Time Frame

"I would like to retire in 8 years when I'm age 62."

Another important variable in retirement planning is estimating the age at which you would like to retire. Often this can cause internal conflict. While most people may want to retire while they can still enjoy life, they may not want to risk going too early, and put themselves into potential financial jeopardy.

Sometimes the fear of running out of money can cause people to delay retirement. If that fear is great enough, it may cause them to work longer than they really need to attain sufficient retirement income. This may be exacerbated if they have personally witnessed someone close to them, such as a parent, who has suffered financially in their retirement years. For them, the psychological fear of not having enough money is greater than the displeasure of having to continue to work. (Remember, first-hand observations leave stronger, more vivid memories.)

I have seen many people who continued to work well beyond the time they really needed to. Their fear of not having enough money, or possibly losing their independence, was too strong a deterrent. To these people I would say: "Why are you waiting to start enjoying the fruits of your hard earned labor"? As Will Rodgers once said, "I've never seen a Brink's truck in a funeral procession." Simply put, you can't take it with you after you're gone. And believe me, the people who eventually inherit your money will have no problem spending it for you!

On the other hand, there are those who choose to retire too soon. As I stated earlier, it may take a few years to realize the gravity of their mistake, but eventually inflation may catch up with them. It's only when they start having to continually cut back on their spending that they realize their mistake. By then it may be too late.

At times this miscalculation may be unwittingly aided by their employers. Some employers have a policy of allowing their employees to retire at an earlier age, if they are willing to take a reduction in their retirement benefits. For some, this option may prove to be too tempting to pass up (immediate gratification). My recommendation to anyone contemplating early retirement is this—"just because you CAN do something, doesn't mean you SHOULD do it." Here's a simple question to ask yourself when facing this dilemma: "Is your job really so unbearable that you are willing to risk sentencing yourself to a lifetime of pinching pennies, just to get out early"?

In some cases the honest answer may be "yes", especially if continuing to work may prove detrimental to their health. In those situations leaving their job may be a necessity. For many of those people, continuing to work part-time in something less stressful and more enjoyable can be a financially acceptable compromise. But retiring early from your job, just because you don't like it, may prove financially devastating.

If you need an incentive to avoid this potential mistake, here's a vivid psychological visual for you. "What's less appealing to you, working a few more years at a job you don't like, or potentially having to move in with your kids one day." For many that's a no-brainer!

Setting a reasonable retirement age is critical in developing your financial plan. While most people would rather be retired than working, you don't want it to be at the expense of an enjoyable and fulfilling retirement.

3. How Much Will You Need to Save?

"To meet my goal I need to save $1,900/month in my 401(k) plan, and pay an extra $100/month on my mortgage, so it is paid off by the time I retire."

One of the key variables in any retirement projection is calculating how much you will need to save to meet your goals. This is typically done by assuming that you will be able to save a fixed amount between now and when you plan to retire. Life has a habit of getting in the way of our plans.

Most people are able to save the most towards their retirement, during their peak earning years. Their children have left the nest (hopefully!). As a good friend of mine frequently laments, "It doesn't seem to matter how old they are, they never seem to get off my payroll!"

The ability to save for retirement can be affected by other issues as well. Consequently, the amount someone actually saves over the years won't typically be a steady, level amount. Instead, most people tend to save the majority of their retirement nest egg in the last 5 to 10 years of their working lives. This typical uneven and later-in-life saving pattern makes it a bit more difficult for a young person to estimate how much they may need to save.

One way to compensate is to take the amount you are currently saving, and increase it by a certain percentage, say 3 or 4% per year. This may more closely reflect what is likely to occur. In addition, if your children are already older and nearer to moving out, you may consider using a higher percent increase, since your expenses would theoretically decrease sooner. The bottom line is that you want to be as realistic as possible with your assumptions about what you can actually save towards retirement. In general, the best advice I can give you is to save until it hurts a little, and then give some more! I've never had anyone tell me they saved too much for retirement.

324 | Money Brain

4. Target a Realistic Rate of Return for Your Investments.

Example:

> *"To meet my retirement goal, for the next 8 years my investments need to average 7.5% return per year, after taxes and fees, and then 6.5% after I retire."*

As stated earlier, every investor should have clear and measurable objectives to reach their financial goals. These objectives should directly reflect your specific overall financial goals. Stating a general goal, such as "I want my portfolio to beat the S&P 500 index," won't ensure that you will meet your goals. Even if you would have met your objective of beating the S&P 500 from 2000 to 2012, you would have missed meeting your financial goals. That's because the S&P 500 suffered negative returns for that period of time.

Investors must clearly define the rate of return their investments must earn to meet their specific financial goals. That number is what should be used to measure their portfolio results and not some arbitrary goal or index. It is also critical to target a rate of return that is realistic based on the current economic conditions.

It is possible that the long-term targeted rate of return may need to be adjusted from time to time, in response to changing economic and general market conditions. Changing the long-term rate of return may also necessitate making changes to the overall financial plan. For example, let's assume you feel that it would be wise to use a lower long-term rate of return on your investments. To continue to be able to meet your long-term financial goals, you may also need to adjust one or more of the following variables.

- You may need to reduce your retirement income goals.
- Increase your savings rate, and/or:
- Work longer than originally planned.

Using a higher rate of return would have the opposite effect. That is why you always want to assume a realistic rate of return on your investments. You don't want to be too optimistic with your projections, only to be disappointed that you were unable to meet your goals, simply because the markets or interest rates didn't cooperate.

There is no *standard* rate of return that can be used reliably in a retirement calculation. Unlike the inflation rate assumption, which tends to affect most retirees equally, the assumed investment return may vary considerably from person to person. The rate someone assumes should depend on their own facts and circumstances, as well as their own tolerance for risk.

As a general rule of thumb you would want to use a number less than 8% per year. Many financial advisors would suggest that using a number ranging from 6% to 7% may be more appropriate. For more risk averse people, a lower rate may be more appropriate.

Due to the current low interest rate environment, and lowered expectations for higher-risk investments such as stocks, many investment professionals anticipate that portfolios may experience a lower than historic average rate of return for the next several years. In this investment environment, it may be prudent to assume a lower rate of return. In general it is best to expect the best, plan for the worst, and prepare to be surprised.

INVESTOR LESSONS:

"Architects don't win awards for their plans,
but rather for the buildings that are actually built."

Developing a sound and realistic financial plan is only the first step. Over the years I have observed a common mistake some people make. They take the time, money and effort to develop a financial plan, only to ignore it. Typically the failure isn't in the plan, but rather it's a failure to implement the plan.

The success of your retirement years will, in large part, be determined by the accuracy of your financial plan assumptions, and how well the plan is executed. A failure in either area can easily derail your retirement goals.

It is critical that the plan's assumptions are both realistic and obtainable. A miscalculation in any of the four variables can have significant consequences. Simply assuming (or hoping) something will happen won't get it done. Underestimating inflation, overestimating investment returns, or your ability to save money, may leave you well short of your retirement goals. You don't want to look down one day, and think you are near the end zone, only to find out you're only on the 50-yard line with a long way to go!

While research may suggest that humans love to make plans that don't always turn out to be accurate, we aren't necessarily doomed to failure. Making practical and realistic assumptions, and then faithfully executing and carefully monitoring your progress along the way, will go a long way in helping you successfully meet your own retirement goals. A plan without action may prove *futile*, but action without planning may prove *fatal*.

CHAPTER TWENTY-ONE

How Men's and Women's Attitudes Differ Towards Investing

> *"Men Are From Mars, Women Are From Venus."*
>
> John Gray, *author*

It is interesting to observe the differences between men and women regarding their attitudes and behavior toward investing and finances. While these differences can be subtle, and are certainly not universal, they are nevertheless worth noting. Some of these attitude differences could be the result of past disparities in job and pay opportunities between men and women; and the different roles assigned by society and adopted by the different sexes.

Some of the difference in attitudes towards investing can be attributed to confidence, or more specifically, overconfidence. Research done by professors Terry Odean and Brad Barber of the University of California Berkeley in 2001, which examined the trading patterns of 35,000 households over a five year period, suggested that "...there are significant differences between the investment trading habits of men and women", and "Overconfidence permeates the ranks of investors, especially men." In addition, "Psychological research demonstrates that, in areas such as finance, men are more overconfident than women."

Their research suggested that "men claimed to have greater investment ability than women do, perhaps related to an upbringing of being more confident in traditionally viewed 'masculine tasks', such as math, science and finance." To illustrate this, the research showed that men traded 45% more actively than women, and single men traded 67% more actively than single women. More importantly, the payoff for all this activity was that the men's portfolios underperformed those of more patient women by a large 1.4 percentage points per year. So it appears that frequent trading and "over managing" can be detrimental to an investor's bottom line results.

While overconfidence tends to be a problem for both genders, men seem to suffer from it more often. In addition, research suggests that gender differences in overconfidence may also be influenced by the task at hand. (Lundeberg, Fox, & Punc'ochar', 1994). Men are inclined to feel more competent performing certain tasks, than do women. These differences in overconfidence tend to be with tasks that are perceived to be in the "masculine domain". (Beyer & Bowden, 1997; Lundeberg, Fox, & Punc'ochar', 1994). An example of this is in the financial services industry, where male advisors far outnumber female advisors.

These studies do not imply that men are better at dealing with financial matters; they simply suggest that men tend to be more confident in their own abilities. Whether this overconfidence is merited is another matter altogether. In fact, Odean and Barber argue that women may actually be better suited for investing because they tend to be less overconfident; and as a result, they tend to be more cautious and less impulsive.

Attitudes toward certain tasks perceived to be in the "masculine domain" have certainly changed. More and more women are becoming the main income earners in a family, and in many cases, the sole breadwinner. Often, they also hold the reins of the family's finances and investments. Life-changing events such as a divorce, illness or death of a spouse may necessitate the change. Research shows that because of life changing events, over 80% of all women will be solely responsible for their finances at some point in their lives. (*National Center for Women and Retirement Research*). This suggests that women need to be better prepared to assume the financial reins if necessary.

In another study, researchers examined men's and women's attitudes toward investing. The study, "Gender Differences in Investment Behavior," was funded by a grant from the Education Foundation Grants Program in 2006. The study was based on the responses of U.S. households with annual household incomes of $75,000 or higher. The data was collected through telephone interviews conducted by the staff of the Center for Survey Statistics and Methodology (CSSM) at Iowa State University.

Here are some interesting findings from that survey.

- While more women held the responsibility for daily money management tasks, such as paying bills; men were more likely to be in charge of investment-related activities.

- Women tended to be more patient with their investments. They were less likely than their male counterparts to sell an investment that did not perform as expected in the short run. As we have discussed earlier in the book, at times being patient with an investment can pay off in the long run. Knee jerk reactions to short-term movements in the markets can prove to be detrimental. In this regard, being patient may have its advantages. In addition, women were more likely than men to consult with an advisor before making an impulsive change.

- More than half of the women who responded to the survey reported that their involvement in financial and investment decisions had gradually increased over the years primarily as a result of a critical life incident such as marriage, divorce, or death or illness of a spouse. In addition, many more women than men reported that they were involved in assisting aging parents with their finances.

- The research also suggested that there was a slight gender difference between attitudes toward investing. Men were more likely to say that they found investing "exciting" or "satisfying." Women were more likely to say that they found making investment decisions more "stressful", "difficult", and/or "time-consuming." This could also help explain why women were more willing to seek assistance from a friend or advisor.

- Men were more likely to describe themselves as being "confident" or "knowledgeable" about investing; and far more men reported that they regularly reviewed and compared their investment performances with market benchmarks, such as the Dow or the S & P 500.

- Women tended to be more conservative with their investments, and were less willing to take big risks. This may, in part, be explained by low self-confidence, which could lead to more caution in decision-making.

- The single, most preferred means of learning about investments for both men and women was to consult with a financial advisor. The majority of the survey respondents said that they found financial advisors as a good source of information, and that they were good listeners. But again, there were gender differences. Women were significantly more likely to consult with a financial advisor before making an investment decision.

- The survey found that women were more likely to receive their investment information from personal sources such as friends, colleagues or advisors. Men, on the other hand, were more likely to do some of their own research using computer-based investment tools and the Internet.

As stated earlier, there is a strong chance that a woman may have to manage family finances sometime in her life. So it is very important that a woman feels comfortable in that role.

While most women already participate to some degree in their household's finances, it tends to be the daily financial tasks, and not necessarily with investments. In many cases, their spouse or partner may be the one making the investment decisions. While everyone's goal should be to become more comfortable in making financial decisions, this is especially true for women, particularly if they don't currently play an active role.

According to research, only 20% of women felt "very prepared" to make wise financial decisions, more than 50% indicated that they "need some help," and one-third felt that they "need a lot of help." *Financial Experience & Behaviors Among Women,* Prudential Research Study, (2010-2011).

In addition there are several factors that could require a woman to be more careful with their finances than a man. For example:

Income – The median wages for women are approximately $650 a week, compared to $800 for men, or approximately 20% less than men earn on average (The Bureau of Labor Statistics, 2010). This means that after paying fixed expenses such as mortgage, utilities, insurance and food, the average single woman has less discretionary income, potentially leaving less to fund important savings needs such as retirement, children's college, and emergency cash reserves.

Life Expectancy – The average life expectancy for women is 81 years, compared to 73 years for men. (The Social Security Administration, 2011). This may put an additional strain on a woman's retirement investments, since on average longer life span would require greater savings in order to provide income for that longer horizon.

Being a Widow – The average age at which a woman becomes a widow is 55. (U.S. Census Bureau, 2010). The death of a spouse often significantly reduces the widow's income, due to a reduction in retirement income, such as social security, pensions or other benefits. If the widow is under age 65, and not eligible for Medicare benefits, it could also mean an increase in the cost of health care insurance due to a loss the husband's employer sponsored insurance.

Caring for Family – On average, a woman loses approximately 15% of her working career caring for children and/or elderly parents, compared to 1.6% for men. (National Center for Women's Retirement Research). This has two major implications. First, it typically reduces the amount of the pension benefits she could have earned had she been working outside the home. Second, it would likely reduce the amount she could have saved on her own for retirement during her working career. Both will reduce her potential retirement benefits.

Single Parent – A woman is much more likely to be a single parent raising children. (U.S. Census Bureau, *American Community Survey*, 2008). This often, though not always, interferes with her ability to earn and save at the same level as her male counterpart.

Life Events – Nearly two-thirds of U.S. women ages 40 to 79 have already dealt with a major financial *life- altering* crisis, such as a job loss, divorce, the death of a spouse, or a serious illness. (*Understanding Women's Financial Needs and Behavior*, AARP Survey, 2007).

When you factor in all the variables, it becomes apparent why many women face a challenging financial future. A potentially longer life expectancy, coupled with a lower average income, a shorter time in the workforce, and the potential of living on a single income can seriously hinder a woman's ability to achieve financial security. A woman who finds herself in this situation will likely need to be even more careful and diligent with her finances, and will want to take steps to assure that she has a secure financial future.

INVESTOR LESSONS:

- One of the most important things a woman can do to improve her financial situation is to take the steps necessary to become comfortable with making important financial and investment decisions. This is especially important if she has not previously been actively involved in making those decisions. Becoming more informed about financial matters is critical. The more you learn about a topic, the less daunting it becomes. The following are some of the financial areas everyone should be well versed in:

  - Family budgeting and wise debt management.

  - Establishing an effective savings program.

  - Developing and implementing an investment strategy that will meet your financial goals.

  - Planning for retirement at a reasonable age and with a comfortable lifestyle.

♦ Determining the proper insurance needs: Life, disability, health and long-term care insurance. Auto and homeowner's insurance should be included.

- Make sure your loved ones are properly provided for in the event of an unexpected death, illness or accident. Having the proper estate planning documents in place is critical. These may include the following documents: a will and trust, a general and a healthcare power of attorney, and a living will.

- Research suggests that many women feel most comfortable learning new things either one-on-one or in small groups, while men prefer doing the research on their own. There are many great resources available: adult education programs through a local university or community college, AARP, local seminars or workshops, or speak to a qualified financial planner. The important thing is to become knowledgeable and comfortable with the subject. You don't need to become an expert, but you do need to learn enough to know what questions to ask, and to avoid being taken advantage of. In the appendix you can find information on how to choose a qualified financial advisor.

- Research suggests that women may have a tendency to be more cautious with their investments in an effort to reduce large losses and volatility. In itself, this doesn't necessarily present a problem. Where this may become an issue is when being too risk averse hinders the ability to meet financial goals. All the life challenges women may fact, including potentially lower income, shorter working years, lower retirement benefits, and a longer life expectancy, may actually require *more* aggressive investment than male counterparts. Meeting their financial goals may necessitate assuming higher risk in order to get a higher rate of return on their investments. A higher rate of return requires taking higher risks.

- However, generally it is not wise to attempt to solve a financial shortfall by becoming more aggressive with your investments. It is usually more prudent to adjust the variables over which you have more influence, such as working a few years longer, increasing your savings by reducing current expenses, or targeting a lower retirement income. You have much more control over these variables than you do over your investment returns.

CHAPTER TWENTY-TWO

Overcoming the 13 Most Common Investor Mistakes

(Finally, the good stuff!)

1. We Love to Predict the Future (We just don't do it very well)

> *"Those who have knowledge don't need to predict. Those who predict don't have knowledge."*
>
> Lao Tzu, *sixth century B.C. poet*

Research suggests that while we love to try to predict things, we simply aren't very good at it. It would appear that most people like to forecast future events, regardless of how poor their previous success has been. The question is, if most people are not very good at predicting the future, why do we insist on continuing to do it?

In their 1979 research, professors Kahneman and Tversky, whose work culminated in a Nobel Prize, found that most people's judgments tend to be overly optimistic. They suggested that this could be caused by our bias toward being overly confident and fail to consider *all* potential outcomes of a situation. Instead, we are predisposed to focus on the outcomes we expect, and discount the ones we don't.

In addition, since we are more likely to take note of information with which we already agree (confirmation bias), we may incorrectly perceive that there are more people who agree with our point of view than is actually the case (a product of our frequency illusion bias).

For example, if you feel the stock market may soon decline, you may be more willing to believe information that confirms the likelihood of a market drop, than information that contradicts it. The fact that you *notice* articles that agree with your point of view may only further strengthen your initial viewpoint. Thus, it becomes a self-reinforcing loop.

Kahneman and Tversky referred to this error in judgment as taking an "inside view." That is, a person focuses on the expected outcome instead of objectively considering all possible outcomes based on similar experiences in the past. They concluded that misreading the true probability of an event occurring is perhaps the major source of forecasting errors.

Research also suggests that this desire to predict may also help explain why gamblers tend to be more excited when they place a bet, than they are after winning it. It appears that trying to predict a winner, whether it is horses or stocks, can provide a greater thrill for many people than being right. This thrill of predicting events seems to apply to investors and businesspeople alike.

Research shows that many of the forecasts done by analysts, economists and businesspeople at the beginning of the year, may end up being well off the mark by year end. But, as the year progresses and revisions are made, subsequent forecasts tend to be more accurate. There are two factors that may contribute to this: First, as new information is factored in, the outlook tends to become clearer; and second, the time horizon being predicted becomes shorter.

For example, on January 1st, based on the current sales and economic conditions, an analyst may forecast the annual earnings of XYZ Company to be $3.57/share. However, by the 2nd quarter, the economy appears to be struggling, causing a slowdown in XYZ sales, so the estimate is revised downward to $3.15/share. As the year progresses, sales continue to falter, so by the 3rd quarter the estimate is reduced even further, this time to $2.55/share. As it turns out, the company actually made $2.50/share for the year. But, based on the most recent 3rd quarter forecast, it was pretty accurate, since it was only off by about 2% ($2.50 vs. $2.55). But if you were to compare it to the initial forecast on January 1st of $3.57, it was off by a whopping 30%! My guess is that an analyst is only going to highlight the accuracy of their most recent forecast.

In defense of investment forecasting, much of the error can be due to changing circumstances, irrational behavior by investors and consumers, and other unforeseeable events. Events such as economic slowdowns, natural disasters, plant strikes and geopolitical unrest (e.g. a threat of conflict may cause a spike in commodity prices) can significantly impact anyone's ability to forecast the future. In addition, an analyst may need to identify a specific company's critical data to make an accurate forecast. But if the analyst receives compensation from that company, the stage is set for a potential conflict of interest. The data may also be presented in a way that makes the company's situation appear better than it actually is. This is my way of saying that sometimes they lie. The Enron and WorldCom disasters come to mind.

Forecasters and analysts can fear departing from the consensus view and becoming *outcasts;* or they could become victims of a herd mentality. That may explain why forecasts tend to cluster around a fairly tight range. It's rare to find an analyst who is well outside the consensus. There is some comfort in being wrong within a group. When you stand alone with your opinion, there is no place to hide. This may make you vulnerable to ridicule. Forecasting is a very risky business. This is why most estimates come with a laundry list of caveats that can be as long as the side effects of some prescription drugs.

Being too trusting may be another reason for poor forecasting results. Unless we already have a strong opinion on a matter, we may be too willing to accept information from an expert or some other allegedly reliable source. Keep in mind that these so-called experts may only be stating their opinions, and being human, they may be wrong, or at times even self-serving.

Also bear in mind that some people have a hard time dealing with failure. Consequently an analyst's most recent forecast or opinion may be an attempt to justify, defend or reinforce something they may have stated in the past.

As we discussed earlier in the book, humans have a tendency to actively seek out patterns, even where there may be none. Think about when you were a child and you were staring up at the sky. At times you would look at a cloud and see faces, animals or other objects. They really weren't there, but we may have detected a pattern that allowed our minds to fill in the blanks so we could "see" them.

Similarly, we may think we have detected an investment pattern that may not be real. We may be subconsciously looking for a pattern that will fit our already established opinion. Finding a pattern that fits our desired conclusion may further reinforce belief and confidence in our forecast.

After reviewing this phenomenon, my approach to research is to assume that all forecasts are going to be inaccurate to some degree. Nothing is gospel and no one is always right. The key is to remain as open-minded as possible and question everything with a healthy dose of skepticism. As John Galbraith once said, "There are two classes of forecasters: Those who don't know— and those who don't know they don't know."

INVESTOR LESSONS:

- Don't believe every forecast you hear. Remind yourself that the people making the predictions are prone to all the same shortcomings as the rest of us. Just because they are on TV or quoted in *Money Magazine* doesn't necessarily make them correct. They are only predictions!

- When you are evaluating a forecast, go out of your way to find an opposing viewpoint. This is especially important if the opinion agrees with a viewpoint you may already have. If this is the case, you may want to seek out several differing viewpoints to make sure you don't become a victim of your confirmation bias.

- If you are working in a group setting, such as an investment group, you'll want to encourage people to voice opposing viewpoints. Refrain from aggressively or personally attacking minority views. This may stifle open discussions and opposing viewpoints. You don't want to become a victim of *group think* pressures.

- Go out of your way to find the *lone wolf* forecasts, even if they are painful to hear. It takes a lot of guts and conviction to be willing to stand alone with a viewpoint, and the ridicule it may invoke. Sometimes these lone wolves can be can be dead-on accurate.

- Never make large investments or make dramatic shifts based on a single opinion. I've seen investors make significant changes to their portfolios after hearing someone make a remark on one of the business shows. In some cases, they couldn't even recall who the person was—"but he sounded like he knew what he was talking about!"

2. We Don't Know as Much as We Think We Do (Our Illusion of Knowledge)

> *"Confidence is ignorance. If you're feeling cocky, it's because there's something you don't know."*
>
> Eoin Colfer, *author*

Many investors have an insatiable thirst for gathering more and more information. The feeling may be that you cannot have too much information. But that is not always the case. "Information overload" can often lead to the dreaded disease of "paralysis by analysis." This terrible affliction affects millions of investors. Its symptoms include a strong desire to seek out large amounts of information, often as an excuse to delay making a decision. While said with tongue-in-cheek, it is a serious problem for many investors. This condition tends to get even worse during periods of high anxiety, when critical decisions may be not only more difficult to make, but more pressing.

It may be normal for investors who find themselves in a stressful situation to want to delay making a difficult decision. While saying that they are merely "looking for additional information" may be a legitimate reason, investors should be careful not to fall into the paralysis by analysis trap. Researching can simply be a convenient excuse.

To compound the problem, much of the investment research we gather may be incomplete, biased, or from a source that later turns out to be dubious. Consequently, important investment decisions may be made based on inaccurate information, rumors and unqualified opinions. That rarely ends well.

The explosion of the internet has further compounded the problem. Thanks to technology we have a seemingly unlimited amount of information right at our finger tips. Valuable research is now easily accessible to individual investors that, in the past, may have only been available to sophisticated investors and large institutional managers. The downside to easy access to this vast amount of information is that much of it is inaccurate, misleading or outright fraudulent. Almost anyone with a computer can develop a newsletter or blog and start spewing out their investment and economic opinions and advice. At times the information is incorrect, based on a lack of understanding or misguided conclusions. In some instances, there may be more calculated, self-serving or nefarious intentions at work.

In the elite echelons of the investment world, where tens or hundreds of millions of dollars may be at stake on a single trade, deception and the art of misinformation are not uncommon. At certain times, large concentrations of money, such as hedge funds, sovereign wealth funds, as well as other "dark" pools of money (monies of unknown sources) may be vying to gain an advantage over a competitor or in a specific transaction. In the end, an investor may end up being the unwitting victim of some well-placed rumors or misinformation.

Rarely a week goes by without someone sending me an article or link on some "confidential" information or some "hot tip" they received. Many of these forwarded hot tips come from "free" investment newsletters that someone received. They typically start off with some outrageous claim to whet an unwitting investor's appetite, such as "5 stocks that are poised to triple in the next 6 month." Then comes the pitch, "for the ridiculously low price of just $3 dollars a day, you too can learn the secret to incredible financial wealth." Sometimes the information may be partially accurate, to help give it some plausibility and credibility.

In many instances, a quick Google search on the article may quickly reveal that the author or source is either unknown, unqualified, or of a dubious nature. At times, however, the information may appear credible and legitimate because it is sourcing a well-known economist or other expert. When further investigated, it turn out that the original source was taken out of context or misquoted, to better serve the story.

There can be several reasons why investors may easily fall for this kind of information. First, we tend to have an overwhelming need to feel that we are in control (our illusion of control bias). Gathering information can give us a false sense of control, since by doing homework, we somehow have a better grasp of the situation at hand.

Armed with a false sense of confidence, an investor may incorrectly conclude that they may be able to influence the outcome of their investment results. For example, an investor may diligently research some internet stocks. Based on his extensive research, the investor may now feel empowered to pick some winners. This false sense of security may lead an investor to become overconfident, and willing to accept a greater degree of risk than may be prudent.

In addition, because of **Oscar's** impatience, our minds are always in a hurry. As we discovered earlier, we are prone to making snap judgments, often based on very little information. Consequently, we may jump to conclusions based on perceptions and interpretations of information that may not be accurate.

When making crucial financial or investment decisions, it is typically unwise to depend on a few key variables or events occurring. For example, buying a stock based solely on a company's successful introduction of new product; or because you think their profits will rise because oil prices will soon fall, is not a sufficient basis for a crucial investment decision. The risk is that should the single expected action fail to occur as anticipated, the whole scenario may unravel, and the investment outcome may backfire.

Having several good reasons to make a specific investment decreases your risk, in the event that one or two don't happen to work out as planned. It is important not to become too distracted or caught up in a potentially exciting piece of news.

Investor Lessons:

- One of the smartest things you can do is delete the words "I know" from your vocabulary, and replace them with "I believe." Doing this may get you much closer to the truth. Most of what we think to be *true* is in reality only something we *believe* to be true. The mind's perception and interpretation of the facts can lead to the belief that something is *true*. But, those *facts* are only beliefs based on the limited information available at that time. As new information is acquired, we are apt to change our views. Think about how many times in your life you thought something to be absolutely true, only to change your mind because it was later proven to be incorrect. In the early 80's there were credible predictions that interest rates would likely remain in double digits for the foreseeable future. In the late 90's, many believed that the "new economy" would keep driving dot-com stocks into the stratosphere. Neither of these proved accurate, and the same can be said for something that you currently hold to be true. It is only hindsight that fills in the gaps!

- Develop several reputable resources for financial information. Develop your own trusted network of resources. Start with a few well-chosen sources. Expand that network by studying the source to determine where they get their information. For example, if you like a few particular columns in the *Wall Street Journal*, or a specific CNBC reporter, see who they credit for their information. Chances are the sources used by larger credible news outlets have been vetted. It may also be helpful to perform a similar check on the sources of various industry blogs, websites or newsletters. In a short time you will be able to develop your own *go to* team to check up on the latest rumors, or in a time of high anxiety.

- When you find a new potential information resource, review some of their old commentaries and predictions to see how accurate they were. While this certainly is not foolproof, it can give you an idea of their track record and accuracy.

- When developing your resources, always ask one critical question: Where may their bias lie? Or as they say in Texas, "Do they have a dog in the hunt?" For example, if you are researching someone who is associated with a gold trading firm, they may have a bias towards gold. If they trade stocks, they may be partial to stocks, and so on. While they may have a great deal of knowledge in a certain niche that you find useful, it would make sense to be aware of any biases they may have. Looking at the sources of a firm's revenues may also give you an idea of where their bias may lie.

- When doing research on the internet, it is easy to be distracted by provocative and flashy headlines, even from unknown sources. Before you know it, you've ended up wasting a lot of valuable time chasing down dead end leads. Ignore the flash and stick with your trusted information resources.

3. Don't Confuse the Opinions of "Traders" with Those of "Investors"

> *"Investing is not a game where the guy with the 160 IQ beats the guy with the 130 IQ. Once you have ordinary intelligence, what you need is the temperament to control the urges that get other people into trouble in investing."*
>
> Warren Buffett, *business magnate and legendary investor*

Occasionally someone will ask me a question regarding a comment they recently heard, or a story they have read. It usually goes something like this: "I just heard a guy on CNBC that sounds pretty convinced that the stock market (or bonds, gold, etc.) is going to soar (or crash). Should I do something?"

If you find yourself in this situation, ask yourself if the person making the comment is an "investor" or a "trader." There is a world of difference between the two. It isn't that one is good or bad, but rather they involve very different objectives, skill sets and time horizons.

Generally, investors tend to be people such as a Warren Buffett, who take a longer-term view of investing. They typically make investments based on what they think may happen months or years down the road. They normally don't try to predict the short-term direction of the market, but rather feel more comfortable focusing on the longer-term trends. Their goal is to make money by making longer-term investments.

Traders, on the other hand, generally make shorter-term investments. Their investments may last for only weeks, days, or in some instances just hours or even seconds. A trader's view and investment decisions are based on what may happen in the short-term. Their goal is to generate and/or take advantage of volatility in the markets caused by significant news events and by the irrational behavior of investors. But, attempting to predict how investors may react to a specific event or news story is very difficult and entails substantial risk.

How traders and investors view and react to the same financial data and news may be very different. Investors tend to look at current information and news, and attempt to determine what effects it may have on longer-term trends. They may choose to discount the importance of news or information that may have only a temporary effect on the markets or the economy. For example, if the unemployment rate increased from the previous month, a longer-term investor may wait for a few more months' worth of data before concluding that the economy may be getting weaker. Even though the market may have an immediate knee-jerk reaction to the news, a longer-term investor may choose to wait before making any changes in their strategy.

Traders, on the other hand, may look at that same unemployment information and see it as an opportunity to take advantage of a short-term negative overreaction by the market. A trader may decide to "sell the market short" in anticipation of a short-term decline, even though they may think the market will eventually continue to move upward.

Generally, investors tend to think more long-term and be more patient, choosing to focus on longer-term trends. Traders tend to be more opportunistic, with a greater focus on attempting to take advantage of a market that may be mispriced in the short-term. Traders also tend to trade much more frequently than their long-term investor counterparts, who may be more likely to employ a longer-term buy-and-hold philosophy.

Even if you are not a trader, monitoring their views and opinions may prove helpful in understanding the underlying psychology of why a market is behaving in a particular way in the short-term, even though the longer-term view may look different.

For example, let's assume your plan is to slightly increase your stock holdings to take advantage of some positive longer-term trends. However, the market has gone up substantially over the past three weeks, and some traders feel it is due for a short-term pullback. Based on that sentiment, you may choose to wait before increasing your stock holdings to see if indeed a pullback occurs.

However, adjusting the current holdings in your portfolio in an attempt to match short-term trader sentiments may be difficult for several reasons. First, traders tend to move IMMEDIATELY on their hunches. By the time you hear it on CNBC's Squawk Box or read about it in the *Wall Street Journal*, they may have already made their move, and are likely contemplating their next trade. By the time you react to their comments, the opportunity (or risk) may have already come and gone.

Second, you don't really know their true motivation for voicing that specific opinion. Is it what they really feel, or is there another reason? There may be instances where their actions do not match their public comments. I once heard a great piece of advice—"Don't listen to what they say, watch what they are actually doing." This is especially true when it comes to the investment world.

Third, even with discount trades, frequent trading can significantly diminish your portfolio's return. Making frequent portfolio moves based on breaking news can substantially decrease your returns. This is especially true in the current environment, where interest rates are near historic lows, and stock market returns may continue to lag the long-term averages. In this type of environment, keeping investment expenses low is crucial.

INVESTOR LESSONS:

- When researching and evaluating expert investment opinions and advice, it is critical to evaluate and understand the expert's perspective. Distinguishing between traders and long-term investors is crucial, since that may determine whether or not the information matches your style and objectives. If you are a long-term investor trying to meet your long-term financial goals, the opinions of a short-term trader may be less relevant to your portfolio decisions.

- While traders' commentaries and information may not be as useful in making your long-term investment decisions, they may help explain some short-term market disturbances.

4. Thinking You Know Something Others Don't (Psst, I know a secret!)

> *"An educated person is one who has learned that information almost always turns out to be at best incomplete and very often false, misleading, fictitious, mendacious—or just dead wrong."*
>
> Russell Baker, *writer*

At times an investor may feel that they have found a special "golden nugget" of information that could reap them big rewards. The temptation is to believe that the information is somehow privileged, and very few people are yet aware of it. In reality, by the time an individual investor becomes aware of this information, it has likely to have already been widely disseminated.

Often the information may have come from a co-worker, friend, family member or someone who knows someone who works for a specific company that someone may be perceived as "in the know" and likely to have good information. It could be a rumor of a stock split, a raise in the dividend, or a merger or acquisition. It could also be negative news. Whatever the story, the temptation may be to buy or sell the stock of the company based on this "inside information." Sometimes the news may not even be noteworthy, but having the inside information may be exciting enough to tempt someone to act in it.

Most of the time, if you were to do a simple internet search of this inside information; you would realize how widely the news had already spread. There may be some truth to the news, but as it spread through the proverbial grapevine, it may have been blown out of proportion. Other times the news may be correct (even if not "secret"), but the ramifications of it may be completely misread. This is another frequent problem—the facts are correct, but the conclusions are questionable.

There is a story about a psychologist who was doing research on the potential reasons for insanity. He spent several years interviewing thousands of people who were institutionalized. What he found was that every single one of those patients had eaten a banana in their lifetime. So he concluded that bananas must cause insanity. He may have gotten the facts correctly, but his conclusion was questionable. This is a classic case of confusing correlation with causation.

Frequently you will see rumors masquerading as facts. And with 24/7 news and the internet, misinformation can go viral, and quickly become *truth*. This can present a serious problem for companies of all sizes. At times you may observe a company's stock price fluctuate dramatically during the trading day because of a rumor. By the time the company is aware of the rumor and addresses it, the damage (or ill-gotten profit) may have already been done.

INVESTOR LESSONS:

Most of the time when an investor stumbles across a golden nugget of inside information, the best course of action may be to simply ignore it. Chances are that it is inaccurate, or has already been reflected in the price of the stock. Other times, as we discussed in an earlier section, it may have been *planted* misinformation. Too often, it will turn out to be fool's gold. Unfortunately, most hot tips only get investors burned. In the rare event that you do have some truly *inside information*, you should be aware that it is illegal to trade on that knowledge. Ask Martha Stewart!

5. I "Herd" it Through the Grapevine

> *"If everyone is thinking alike, then somebody isn't thinking."*
>
> General George S. Patton, Jr., *U.S. Army Commander*

One of the strongest human instincts, rooted in evolution, is our tendency to "herd." It's far safer being in the middle of the herd than on the outskirts. The herd offers protection. But it has its downsides too. This basic instinct allowed our primitive ancestors to survive attacks from the outside. In more modern times, this herding instinct may have evolved to help humans become more social animals. Research suggests that this social instinct is so strong that we may actually feel the pain of being a "social outcast" in the same part of the brain where we feel real physical pain.

(Source: "The Social Outcast: Ostracism, Social Exclusion, Rejection, and Bullying",
Edited by Kipling D. Williams, Joseph P. Forgas, William Von Hippel, 2005)

This social herding behavior can also interfere with our investment decisions. Often, we can find comfort in being wrong, as long as others were wrong as well. "Yes I lost money, but so did everyone else." At least we aren't the only fool!

There are psychological and emotional risks of publically disagreeing with the herd. The fear of being ridiculed for expressing an unpopular view or opinion may be enough for some people to modify or mask their true beliefs. This modification may not even be a conscious decision, but rather the result of some subconscious influence. The desire to belong may be greater than the desire to be right or to express true opinions.

As discussed earlier, this may help explain why most financial analysts, economists or business people will avoid diverging from the consensus opinion. The social and financial benefits of being accepted by the herd can be significant. These benefits may come in the form of high incomes, generous benefits and perks, and social status. Disagreeing with the herd could make you an outcast, and jeopardize your acceptance in the group. It's very difficult to be the lone wolf. It's far easier to go along to get along, or simply remain silent.

The same fears and desires can apply to many investors. Some may blindly buy or sell into a market simply because it seems to be the accepted thing to do. "If everyone else is doing it, they must know something." Unfortunately, by the time many individual investors notice a trend, it may already be nearing the end of that particular short-term cycle. This is why many investors end up buying near the top of a market, and selling near the bottom. At times, it's like watching a herd of lemmings go over the cliff.

There may, however, be a logical reason for this "lemming" phenomenon. When there are an unusually large number of investors moving in the same direction, either buying or selling, prices may temporarily move out of equilibrium. Therefore, at least in the short-term, it can become a self-fulfilling prophecy. These are the times when investors may tend to become overly confident, and the emotions of greed and fear take precedence over careful analysis.

INVESTOR LESSONS:

- Don't be afraid to be a contrarian. Don't rely on the consensus opinion alone to determine your investment decisions. Investing is not a public sport. If you make a mistake no one else needs to know about it!

- Go with your gut instinct. After careful research, base your decisions on what feels right. Often it's like the advice we got in school when taking a test—go with your initial gut feeling. The more you analyze the situation, the more hesitant you may become. Just make sure that gut instinct is based in facts and not emotions. Of course this doesn't mean you'll always be right. But if you are wrong, at least you won't beat yourself up for not listening to your gut instinct.

- Be careful about adding positions in your portfolio when the current trend seems to be getting a little long in the tooth. All cycles eventually change direction. It may make sense to be a bit more cautious when a market is already up or down by more than 20% over a short period of time. That doesn't mean that the trend will soon reverse, but there may be an increasing number of investors who decide to take their profits and sell off. The same would be true in a declining market. A significant number of investors moving at the same time, in the same direction, could change the direction of the market very quickly.

- Be aware of your herding instinct. If you catch yourself contemplating a sudden investment decision that you haven't fully thought through, you may be reacting to a subconscious herding instinct, based on what others are doing. **Oscar** has a tendency to drink the Kool Aid!

6. Don't Invest Looking in the Rear View Mirror

> *"History does not repeat itself, but it does rhyme."*
>
> Mark Twain, *author and humorist*

While driving your car you spend most of the time looking out the windshield (hopefully!). Occasionally though, you'll glance into your rearview mirror to see if there is anything coming up on you, of which you should be aware. For the most part, if there is any lurking danger, it will typically be right in front of you. That's probably why they made the windshield so much bigger than the rearview mirror!

Often investors focus too much on looking into the rearview mirror, hoping to glean clues about what may lie ahead. What lies behind us typically can't hurt us anymore and is not always a good way to predict the future. It's what's ahead that can cause problems.

So why do we tend to fixate on the past? In part, the brain focuses on what is most easily understood. It is easier to accept simple answers, than struggle with developing more complex ones. The past is easier to explain, and the information is readily available. It is far easier to look backward, than it is to attempt to predict the future. You won't find too many graphs and charts that accurately forecast the future.

Looking in the rearview mirror cay help satisfy our brain's desire to identify patterns. When a pattern is identified, our recency bias creates a trap that can cause one to assume that the pattern will continue. The pattern may be more of a perspective than a reality. If an investor feels that they have identified an important pattern, it could mislead them to become overly confident with their decisions, and lose track of other potential risks.

Just to be clear, I am not saying that studying cycles and patterns is not a useful tool for investing, quite the contrary. Top-tier money managers track short-term trends very closely. But investors should recognize them for what they are—short-term trends, which can shift in direction at any time. Ideally one would be able to identify a trend early on, buy early, and sell before it's too late. Yet, even the best money managers find this a very difficult task. Sadly, many investors don't tend to pick up on a real trend until it too late and the end is around the corner.

- Always be aware of your recency bias. Your mind may play tricks on you by convincing you that you have discovered a pattern that will continue into the future. If you feel you may have fallen into this trap, remind yourself of at least two or three occasions when past trends have suddenly reversed. Using visual reinforcements such as charts and graphs should help to drive the point home.

- Use past experiences as a compass and not as a detailed map. What happened in the past is only one of several possible outcomes that may happen currently or in the future.

- If you feel that you have found a genuine trend, always remember that it will end at some point. Determine how far into the trend the market may already be, and be prepared for it and you to change direction at any moment.

7. Don't Watch CNBC Daily! (Get a life instead)

> *"The one function TV news performs very well is that when there is no news; we give it to you with the same emphasis as if there were."*
>
> David Brinkley, *former news anchor*

In the heat of the economic turmoil in 2008, someone told me: "I've been watching the stock market on CNBC everyday now, and the market is STILL dropping." To which I replied, "Well if you're watching it and it's still dropping, you might as well quit watching and save yourself the grief." He didn't appreciate my humor.

Watching the business channels all day will not necessarily make you a smarter investor. As a matter of fact, I would argue it may just add to your confusion. I keep CNBC on at work all day to keep up with important breaking information that may impact the investment world. And while that does happen occasionally, most of the air time is filled by mundane news stories, and guests postulating their views. But much of the time, it's the same old blah blah, blah blah blah.

Monitoring breaking financial information is important, and frequently a business program will present segments highlighting two opposing viewpoints. Although hearing differing opinions is necessary, it often can lead to confusion if both arguments are equally compelling and both are presented by presumed experts. In some cases, the viewer may walk away from the experience even more unsure of what to do.

Business programs and guest interviews can be a great source of information. But information is only useful if it is interpreted correctly. For many investors this is where the wheel may fall off the wagon. An overload of investment information and data can be overwhelming and at times contradictory. Recall how the mind operates—it reverts to preconditioned shortcuts, especially when it is on overload or in an emotional state. It is not wise to overload your system at these critical times. Typically, smaller doses of accurate information from reliable sources will be much more useful than a massive information "dump."

Keep in mind the goal of your typical business show is to sell advertising. To maximize advertising dollars these shows must increase the number of viewers. To increase viewership, the content must be entertaining and provocative. To be entertaining and provocative they will say things to grab a viewers' attention. Therein lies the problem. By its very nature, the world of finance can be quite dull. It's full of numbers, charts and opinions, regurgitated by people in dark suits and glasses. Not typically the type of people you associate with the words *entertaining* and *provocative*. So how DO you sell dull?

One method to grab a viewer's attention is to spout alarming or outlandish "lead-ins," such as "our next guest is predicting the stock market will crash next Tuesday," or "he will share with us 10 stocks that will double in the next two weeks." But it's only after you've been sucked into watching the segment that you realize how misleading the promo was.

Another technique used to create excitement is to stir things up between guests who have differing opinions. At times, it can be humorous watching a host try to turn the segment into something that resembles a Jerry Springer episode. Fortunately for Jerry, he had guests that were willing to mix it up on air. Watching two economists verbally duke it out is about as exciting as watching a chess match in slow motion!

I always encourage people to become educated about investing and economics. Education is the most powerful defense against making poor financial decisions, or being taken advantage of by unscrupulous salespeople. However, there is a thin line between being well- informed and being obsessive. I've seen many people retire from their jobs, only to take on a new fulltime job—obsessing about their investments!

Obsessing about the markets will not change anything. Do your homework and then go enjoy your life before it's too late!

INVESTOR LESSONS:

- Determine the level of investing knowledge you would like to achieve. If your goal is to ultimately make your own investment decisions, this will require you to devote sufficient time each week to reach that desired level of knowledge.

- To make informed decisions, every investor should strive to achieve a certain level of financial knowledge. Be sure to communicate to your advisor your desire to become more educated. Most advisors will be pleased to learn this and can become a great source of information for you.

8. Don't Invest in Things You Can't Easily Explain to a Friend

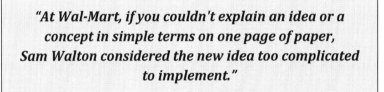

> *"At Wal-Mart, if you couldn't explain an idea or a concept in simple terms on one page of paper, Sam Walton considered the new idea too complicated to implement."*
>
> Michael Bergdahl, *author and former Wal-Mart Director of "People"*

A good rule of thumb is to only invest in things that can be easily understood. It may be wise to steer clear of complicated investments with many moving parts. If we have learned anything from the 2008 financial meltdown, it's that a lot can go wrong with complicated and esoteric investments.

The investments that were at the heart of the financial meltdown, such as collateralized mortgage obligations (CMO) and collateralized debt obligations (CDO) were some of the most complicated instruments ever conceived by Wall Street. They were designed by PhD mathematicians and other "quants" (quantitative analysts) with the goal of maximizing profits while attempting to minimize risk. They got the first part right, but severely underestimated the risk part. Even former Fed Chairman Allan Greenspan admitted that he and his team of financial experts didn't fully understand them.

Of course this does not mean that simpler investments don't have risk. As we discussed earlier, all investments entail some form of risk. But, complex investments are more risky and have a greater potential to go wrong. The more complicated the investment, the more it needs to be continually monitored.

Yes, a simpler investment philosophy may mean that occasionally you pass up on some fabulous short-term opportunities. But, you may also be sparing yourself the pain of a devastating loss. As for me, I've learned to appreciate the delicious simplicity of "plain vanilla" investments!

INVESTOR LESSONS:

- Don't invest in anything you don't fully understand. After reviewing an investment you should have a good idea of the potential gains and risks. You should also be able understand the conditions under which the investment will perform well, and when you can expect it to lag behind.

- When shown an investment, make sure that the person presenting it fully understands what they are recommending. In some instances they may not fully appreciate all the associated risks with the investment. They should be able to clearly and concisely explain the risks and benefits, and why they are recommending the investment. You should do your homework as well. Be extremely wary of anyone who simply dismisses or minimizes the risks, or who seems hesitant to discuss them. Remember, ALL investments carry some risk.

- You should be able to identify the role an investment will play in your portfolio. Is it designed for growth, for income, principal preservation, or tax benefits? This will help determine whether this is a suitable investment for you. Don't add an investment to your portfolio simply because it looks interesting or "ranks" well. Check to see if you already own several similar investments. You don't want to be over-weighted in a specific area. Diversification is a key strategy. Avoid the mistake of putting all your eggs in one basket. Don't hesitate to ask a lot of questions. An investment advisor should never take offense at someone asking questions. If that happens, find a new advisor! After all, you stand to lose a lot more than they do.

9. Analysis Paralysis

The state of over analyzing or over-thinking when faced with too many choices that lead to paralysis in decision-making.

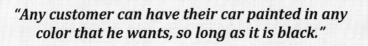

> *"Any customer can have their car painted in any color that he wants, so long as it is black."*
>
> Henry Ford, *American industrialist*

Over the years, numerous studies have attempted to measure the impact of the number of choices on a person's ability to make a decision. In one study, a taste-testing table was set up in a grocery store with a selection of flavored jams. After sampling the jams, the test subjects had an opportunity to purchase their favorite flavor. One group was offered five flavors, while the other group had more than 20 flavors from which to choose. Interestingly, the groups with fewer choices made more purchases, more often, than the groups with more choices.

This study has been repeated many times in several variations with similar outcomes. While we may prefer to have many choices, this often leads to "decision paralysis", where the choice is overly complicated and so a choice is never made. This may also result from the need to find a "perfect" choice or fear of making the "wrong" choice. More recently, these study results have encouraged 401(k) plan sponsors to reduce the number of investment choices available in their plans. In the past, many 401(k) plans, in an attempt to satisfy all potential needs, created such a variety of options, that people were overwhelmed. This resulted in many plans looking like a Chinese menu, without the helpful pictures!

Typically, plan sponsors encourage participants to diversify their portfolios, and avoid being overly conservative in their investment choices. Retirement plan experts argue that participants' who choose the safe, guaranteed option, may not realize that being too conservative with their retirement assets could leave them short of their retirement income needs. By offering many other options, it was hoped that people would be more likely to diversify their accounts.

Interestingly, even with all the additional choices, many participants chose to remain in the most conservative options. Simply increasing the number options did not motivate many people to make changes in their behavior. In fact, it may have actually backfired for some, by overwhelming them into decision paralysis.

When people request help in allocating their 401(k) assets, it is because they are overwhelmed by the number of choices are available. Sometimes, overwhelmed by the sheer number of options, they tend stick with what they know, refusing to change for years and sometimes decades.

There is a lesson in this for all investors. When faced with a large number of choices, it is possible that you may defer to your status quo bias, leading you to simply throw up your hands and do nothing.

Researching an overwhelming number of investment options for your portfolio may end up hurting your ability to make a decision. "I need to do more research before I can decide", may actually increase the odds of delaying a critical decision. Research often leads to even more research. And before you know it, you may have turned a relatively simple decision such as, "I need to fix this leaky faucet" into "let's replace all the plumbing in the house."

When faced with difficult decisions, we can be our own worst enemy. Occasionally, we can over complicate potential solutions and lose track of the original problem. At times we need to take a step back and ask ourselves, "what problem are we trying to solve." Investors can easily fall into the trap of over-expanding the original scope of the problem.

Take for example a person (let's call him Ed, the engineer) who is concerned that the stock market may soon decline, and feels he has too much of his portfolio in stocks. To help cushion his portfolio from a potential drop in the stock market he decides to immediately sell a portion of his stocks, and invest the proceeds into bonds. Doing his preliminary research, Ed comes up with a list of 12 highly rated bond funds from which to choose.*

The following week the market is still dropping, but Ed can't decide which bond fund to use. To make sure he is using the very best one, he decides to do some additional research. As he continues his search for the best bond fund, he comes up with another 11 funds to add to the list. As he sits in his dining room with the 23 funds spread out over the table, the confusion begins to set in. At this point they all seem to be blending together, and he is gets more confused. After a few hours of exhaustive research (he is an engineer!) he narrows it down to the final ten. Tired and frustrated, he decides to do the final analysis next weekend when he has more time.

Meanwhile, the market continues to slide. Ed is anxious and commits to making his final decision over the weekend. But, the decision becomes even more difficult because of slight differences between the funds. He finds that the average rate of return over the past 5 years between the best and worst of the ten funds is less than ½ % per year. After a few hours of intense study, he finally makes his final pick.

---

* Hypothetical examples are not intended to be indicative of any specific investment. Hypothetical results are for illustrative purposes only and are not intended to represent the past or future performance of any specific investment.

During the two weeks that he was making his decision, the market dropped an additional 6%. So in the end, his gut feeling was correct—the market did go down. Ed's quest to find the "best" bond fund distracted him from the real problem at hand—making his portfolio more conservative came at a real cost. In the short run, he would have been better off parking his money in a mediocre bond fund, for the time being.

Investor indecisiveness becomes even more difficult when one is under some sort of personal or financial stress. Juggling too many options under stress makes it even more difficult to make a crucial decision. In the end, it is important to focus on the critical task at hand, and not get distracted by other factors.

INVESTOR LESSONS:

- One way to head off paralysis analysis is to write down your primary and secondary objectives. Once established, determine the time frame in which those decisions must be made. In Ed's case, the primary objective was to reduce the risk in his portfolio by decreasing his stock holdings; the secondary issue was to find an appropriate bond fund. The first objective needed to be accomplished quickly. The secondary issue was less urgent. Prioritizing your objectives can help you stay focused on the important task at hand—in Ed's case, reducing his stock holdings, even if it meant temporarily going into an "average" bond fund. With his primary goal accomplished, he had the time to evaluate his options, rather than delay the initial action and suffer a loss.

- Set a realistic time frame to do your research. For example, researching five to ten highly rated bond funds may be reasonable—comparing 30 may be overkill. The key is to start with a list of highly rated funds. No need to create your own list, there is no shortage of *top ten* lists out there. At times, the situation may require a more extensive search, but most of the time this method can work. I have a rule of thumb, I'd rather be 90% right, than stuck at 0%. In other words, don't let the search for perfection be the enemy of solving your problem.

- Develop strategies to deal with various scenarios ahead of time. For example, determine in advance which one or two bond funds you would use if you needed to quickly shift your portfolio into a more cautious allocation. Or, determine which one or two stock funds you could use if you suddenly wanted to be more aggressive. It also makes sense to have what I affectionately refer to as my "Armageddon model."

This strategy is designed to deal with extreme situations, similar to the economic collapse of 2008. Make the time-consuming and difficult investment decisions ahead of time when you are calm, rather than when you feel rushed and anxious. Having a well-thought-out plan of action in advance, could help prevent making some very emotional and regrettable decisions. If done properly, the tough decisions will have already been made, and then the only thing left to decide is when to put it into action.

10. Know How Your Investments are Performing

A common investor mistake is failing to accurately measuring portfolio performance on a regular basis. To measure your portfolios performance, you first need to know its "net" rate of return. This is a simple task of calculating how much your investments went up or down from the last time you measured it. This should typically be done quarterly or annually.

Before you calculate your rate of return, you may need to make some of the following adjustments:

1. **Additions** – Did you add any money to the account during this period of time? If so, you need to subtract that from the total. Otherwise, you may overinflate the actual performance.

2. **Withdrawals** – Did you withdraw any money from the account? If so, you need to add that to the total. Otherwise, you may be under-reporting your performance.

3. **Fees & Expenses** – Make sure to subtract any fees you paid from the ending balance that did not come directly out of the account. If the fees were deducted from the account, no adjustment is necessary.

After making these adjustments, simply calculate the percent difference between the beginning balance and the ending balance. This is your portfolios "absolute net" rate of return.

The next step is to determine your portfolio's performance relative to existing economic and investment conditions. This is known as your "relative" rate of return. In this exercise you are comparing your portfolio performance against a specific benchmark, which could be an index, or some other measure. Regardless of the benchmark used, it is important confirm that the chosen benchmark accurately reflects the composition of your portfolio.

For example, if you had 100% of your investments in stocks, you would be very happy if your portfolio was up 20% while the stock market index was up only 10%, or if the market was down 20%, and your portfolio was only down 10%.

However, if you had 50% of your portfolio in stocks and 50% in bonds, you may be happy if the portfolio was up 10% when the stock market was up 10%, since half of your assets were in more conservative bonds.

Knowing the relative rate of return of your portfolio can be useful when measuring the performance of your portfolio, but it can also be a distraction. The relative performance of your portfolio may not have any bearing on whether or not you will meet your specific financial goals. As we discussed earlier in the book, you may beat the relative performance of your chosen benchmark, and still fall short of your goals.

For example, to meet your financial goals, let's assume you need to average a 7% return on your investments. And, let's suppose your portfolio's average relative rate of return beat the S&P 500 index by an impressive 3% from 2000 to 2012. From a relative point of view you should be very happy.

The S&P for those 12 years was basically flat, so your portfolio only averaged about 3% gain per year, when it needed to average 7% to meet your goals. Consequently, it's a small victory that your portfolio beat its relative benchmark, since you now have to work an additional 3 more years to meet your retirement goals!

Over the years I have heard people comment, "I was a little nervous coming in today because I was expecting some bad news." When asked why they would think that, they would answer, "well, with all the bad news I've been hearing, I figured my investments would be down as well." Or, "I haven't even opened my statements in the past few months because I figured they'd be down anyway."

This is another common mistake people make. This "illusory correlation" is simply our tendency to link together two unrelated things or events. In the example above, the person assumed that there was a direct relationship between the bad news they heard, and their investments' performance. While there are times when this may hold true, there are many times when it won't. The unfortunate consequence of illusory correlation is that a person may remain needlessly nervous simply because they have misinterpreted a situation.

You can easily alleviate your anxiety by simply reviewing your accounts on a regular basis. Most of your investments should be readily available to you online. If not, you should consider an alternative. Your current investment information should be available at your fingertips.

Another common investor mistake is failing to account for the effects taxes and fees have on your portfolios. These "deductions" from your investment results may not be apparent. The net rate of return on your portfolio is what counts, because that is what you get to keep. Regrettably, it is more difficult to calculate your portfolio's "real" rate of return.

For example, the tax consequences of an investment don't appear on your monthly portfolio statements. Your investment tax consequences may not occur until some later date, in some cases years or even decades later. Several things can trigger a taxable event for your investments, including: receiving taxable interest and dividends, selling an investment, a mutual fund declaration of a capital gain, or withdrawing money from a retirement account. With retirement accounts, taxes are deferred until you withdraw money from the account, so the tax consequences may be years or even decades away.

In any case, when you are designing your portfolio, keep in mind that in most cases, the return on your portfolio will be reduced by taxes. Uncle Sam is going to be there waiting for his unfair share!

Additionally, make sure you are taking into account all the fees associated with your investments. Some of the investments you own may have some fees and charges that you may not be aware of, so you may have to do some investigating. Keep in mind that some of your investment fees may be tax deductible. Check with your tax professional to see what fees are deductible.

INVESTOR LESSONS:

- Investors have some control over the taxes on your investments. There are several techniques to lower your investment tax burden, though they are becoming scarcer. The following are a few examples:

- If you have considerable taxable interest or dividends, consider using tax-free bonds or annuities.

- Take advantage of employer sponsored retirement plans such as: 401(k), 403(b), SEP, SARSEP and Simple IRA plans. The contributions may be tax deductible and the growth will be tax deferred.

- If allowable, consider contributing to a personal IRA or Roth IRA. Be aware that contributions may be limited by your earned income. Consult with an investment or tax professional for effective ways to reduce the taxes on your investments.

- Be aware of how long you have held an investment before selling it. Given the difference between short-term and long-term capital gains taxes, it's important to understand how your gain (or loss) will be treated for tax purposes. You want to do this BEFORE you sell an investment. Making frequent changes in your portfolio may also cause some of your capital gains to be taxed at the higher rate. If you were planning to sell an investment that you have owned for less than one year (a short-term capital gain), you may want to consider keeping it long enough to have it taxed at the lower, long-term capital gains rate. However, when you feel the investment is in imminent danger of dropping in value, don't wait!

- Tax consequences are just one consideration in investing, and should not control investment decisions. Keep in mind capital gains ONLY apply to taxable accounts, and not retirement accounts. (An exception may be company stock held in a 401(k) account, which MAY have some capital gains treatment.)

- In taxable accounts, you may also want to consider using "tax-efficient" funds. Basically, these types of funds employ a strategy designed to minimize taxable gains in the account. They accomplish this by minimizing their short-term trading in stocks, and possibly using tax-free bonds instead of taxable ones.

- Another investment tax strategy is to carefully time the distributions from your retirement accounts. All distributions from your retirement account are taxed at your marginal income tax rate. The U.S. tax code has a progressive tax rate which means that as your taxable income increases, so does your marginal tax bracket. State and local tax laws may also apply. Before making an additional withdrawal from your retirement account, you would want to know your current marginal tax bracket, and how close you were to the next higher bracket.

For example, let's say you are planning to take a $15,000 withdrawal from your IRA account to pay for a fabulous

European cruise. When you withdraw it from your IRA, the additional money can push you into the next higher tax bracket. Consequently you would not only have to pay taxes on the $15,000 distribution, but it may also be taxed at a HIGHER rate. In addition, by adding $15,000 to your taxable income, it may mean that a larger portion of your social security income will now become taxable, AND at that higher rate. That $15,000 vacation could end up costing you whole lot more than you bargained for!

A simple solution may be to take the $15,000 from a non-retirement account. If so, NONE of the distribution would be taxable (but be careful of capital gains), and the distribution would not affect the taxes on your Social Security benefits. Always check with your tax advisor before making large distributions from your retirement accounts, especially as you near the end of the year. And note that many states now do not tax Social Security benefits.

- Investment-related fees are another potential drag on your portfolio's return. All investments have fee's associated to them, even so-called no-load investments. There is no such thing as a benevolent organization on Wall Street! The key is to know what the fees are, and to judge whether they are worth it to you. Everyone deserves to get paid for their work. The question is, are you getting your money's worth.

11. Learn to Invest in "Shades"

> *"Take calculated risks. That is quite different from being rash."*
>
> General George S. Patton, Jr., *U.S. Army Commander*

Investing in shades doesn't mean wearing sunglasses when making your investment decisions (even though putting on a rosy pair may not hurt at times).

A common mistake is thinking in all-or-nothing terms. When contemplating a portfolio change, you don't need to be either all in, or all out. For example, I knew a GE executive who owned a considerable amount of GE stock. While he felt that the stock would probably continue to do well, he didn't feel comfortable having such a large portion of his total wealth in one company's stock. He knew the danger of having too much money tied up in one stock, but he didn't want to regret his decision to sell if it continued to go up.

Instead of trying to decide whether to keep or sell all his GE stock, a simple solution would be to sell only part of his GE holdings. This way if the stock kept going up, he would have been glad he kept half of it. If, on the other hand, the stock price dropped, he would have been glad he locked in the profits on the half he sold. It doesn't have to be all or nothing. Sometimes hedging your bets may make the most sense.

I know this may sound like an incredibly simple, but this is an example of how over-thinking a problem may cause you to lose sight of a simple solution (focus bias).

Typically it's wise to hedge your investment positions, and not make overly large allocations one way or another. Even though you have a strong feeling about an investment, you may still want to hedge your decision. As I said earlier, if you want to hear God laugh, make a plan!

This hedging technique is what I refer to as "investing in shades." When you make absolute bets on black or white, you simply change your shade of gray from darker to lighter. In addition, you may wish to hedge even further by changing the *shade* incrementally. For example, if you want to increase your stock holdings by 15%, instead of doing it all at one time, you may choose to buy in 5% increments over a period of time. By doing this you can avoid the temptation of trying to time the market. This may also help restrain any strong emotions you may be fighting at the time. By making incremental changes, you can satisfy the natural desire to do *something*, without jumping the whole way.

INVESTOR LESSONS:

- After deciding which portfolio changes to make, you need to determine when to make them. If you are not substantially changing the risk composition of the portfolio, (e.g. moving from one bond fund to another) you may decide to make the change all at once. However, if you are changing the risk composition (e.g. moving from bonds to stocks or visa-versa) you may want to consider making incremental changes.

- Pre-determine the desired ultimate allocation and the time frame over which to make these changes. If the situation or issue that is influencing the portfolio change is volatile, you may want to consider using a shorter time frame. If it's more of a general feeling, you may want to consider a longer time frame. The advantage of making incremental changes is you can always shorten or lengthen the time frame as the situation changes.

- Regardless of how confident you are about a decision, it rarely makes sense to make absolute bets. When investing in riskier assets, a good rule of thumb is to only invest an amount that you can afford to lose, or have tied up for ten years or more. We have seen several black swan events occur over the past decade or so. Given the current economic conditions, it probably makes sense to be a bit more cautious.

12. Just Because They Look Familiar, Doesn't Mean You Should Get Married

> *"I don't care what they say about me, as long as they keep talking about me."*
>
> Zsa Zsa Gabor, *actress*

At times investors may be prone to making decisions based on something familiar sounding. In these instances, the subconscious mind may be influencing their choice. The decision may not have been based on the investment's track record, its strategy, or the manager's acumen, but simply because the name sounded familiar.

Our human nature seems to find comfort in things that appear familiar to us, whether justified or not (familiarity bias). Investors want to be aware of this strong bias, especially when choosing between several alternatives. Left unchecked, we tend to migrate toward the familiar.

As discussed earlier, the best investment option may not be the one you recognize or that seems familiar. Frequently, some of the best-performing investments are hardly household names. In fact, some of the most popular investments may become victims of their own success, growing so fast that they outgrow their management resources. A fund can also grow so large that it may be difficult to implement a strategic or tactical change without disrupting the entire market for that particular investment.

For example, assume that ABC fund has $5 billion in assets, and 5% of its holdings are in XYZ stock. Due to disappointing earnings results, the managers want to sell all of the stock as soon as possible. If the ABC fund attempted to sell all $250 million worth of the stock at one time, it could cause the price to plunge temporarily. In addition, if the stock price is already under some selling pressures, trying to unload such a large amount could exacerbate the problem, possibly sending the stock price into free fall. By the time the allotment is sold, the fund may receive substantially less than the anticipated $250 million.

To reduce the risk of panicking the market, the fund may be forced to sell part of the stock over several days or even weeks (similar to trying to get out of the burning theater unnoticed). But, the price could continue to fall, so that the fund receives substantially less than the $250 million. The same is true when buying a large amount of a promising investment. Large purchases can send prices upward to the point where it may no longer seem attractive. In some instances, being a very large institutional manager can be a hindrance when implementing quick or substantial investment changes.

Be aware that certain investments may become ingrained in your subconscious for various reasons. You may have seen it as one of the options in your 401(k) plan, or because of the ads you have seen on television or in magazines. Just because the name is familiar doesn't necessarily make it a good investment.

- When deciding between investments, remind yourself that you may have a familiarity bias, and that your inclination may be to pick the one you recognize. By putting yourself on notice and becoming cognizant of this bias, you stand a much better chance of reducing its influence on your decision. Force yourself to look more closely at other options. If you did your screening properly, the other options should also be worthy contenders.

- Go out of your way to look for some lesser known investments. These funds may be smaller than their behemoth counterparts. This may allow them to be more nimble, and if necessary, to change directions more quickly. Don't make the mistake of dismissing a potentially good investment simply because you are not familiar it.

13. Judge Your Players Fairly

> *"Compared to some of the worst players I've seen, he's really not all that bad."*
>
> Yogi Berra, *Major League Baseball player and manager*

When first meeting with an investor, I find it helpful to have a discussion about their current investments and overall investment philosophy. Some investors may not even know what they own, or why they own it. At times they may not even know how it got into their portfolio. If you asked a good baseball manager, he would be able to tell you why every player was on the field, what he expects of them, and under what conditions he would substitute them. This is how an investor should fill the positions in their portfolio.

An investor should be able to identify the role every investment plays in their overall portfolio, how it would be expected to perform, and when economic conditions might suggest the need for a substitution. The role of some investments may be for growth, to generate income, or for tax benefits. Others may have been chosen asset preservation. Every investment should play a specific role in a portfolio.

Effectively diversifying your portfolio will mean that at any given time you may be disappointed in the performance of some of your investments. This does not mean that they were poor choices. They may not have been designed to perform well under those economic conditions. They may have been chosen to balance risk and benefits.

You wouldn't want all your flowers and plants blooming at the same time of the year, since that would leave your yard looking bare at other times. Similarly, you can't expect all your investments to perform well under all economic conditions. As with your plants, you would expect some of your investments to survive the bad-weather months, or at least until spring comes back around. As a downside, they may not do as well during the good weather months.

As with your garden or baseball team, it will be necessary to make occasional changes to your portfolio. Once a year you should look at your holdings and review their performance relative to their peer groups (not compared to the other investments in your portfolio). At times you may find an investment has underperformed its peers. There may be several reasons for this:

- The manager or management team may have changed. Management changes happen frequently. When managers change, it would be wise to evaluate the new manager's track record before deciding whether to keep or sell the investment. At times the new manager may be less experienced, and may not have a substantial track record to evaluate. This may suggest a change is warranted. There are plenty of excellent seasoned managers out there. Let the rookies practice on someone else's money!

- One common mistake is comparing an investment to an inappropriate peer group. This can happen with hybrid or "specialty" investments. Rating services will occasionally classify an investment with a unique strategy into a category that may not accurately reflect its actual investment holdings or objectives. There is a larger range of investment strategies than there are available categories. So occasionally you may find an investment that just doesn't fit into one of the general categories. An investor's challenge is to make sure the investment is compared to the appropriate peer group, one that closely reflects the strategies of investment. There is no easy way to accomplish this. Some rating agencies like Morningstar compares classes of investments by their objectives and ranking in the class, though not necessarily by how they achieve their objectives.

- At times a manager may simply make a change too early or late in an investment cycle, and consequently may temporarily lag behind his peers. This may be the case with "deep value" managers. This strategy tends to invest in "fallen angels," investments that other managers may have abandoned. A good manager may recognize the true value of these investments before the rest of the market. As a result, a deep value manager may lag behind his peers for a period of time, until the rest of the market catches on. This is one reason you may not want to pull an investment out of your portfolio too soon. If it is well managed, with a good long-term track record, you may want to give them some time before making a change. Every so often these deep value managers can come roaring back.

INVESTOR LESSONS:

At the beginning of each year make it a habit to review each investment in your entire portfolio. Most business and investment oriented publications tend to compile their own *top ten lists* in January, so the information is current and readily available. You may want to consider using the following process to review your investments:

Step 1 – Review the overall asset allocation of your portfolio, to make sure you are comfortable with it based on the current economic outlook. If not, determine what changes need to be made to meet your new overall allocation goals. At this point you are only allocating the different asset classes, such as: money markets, short-term bonds, high-quality bonds, high-yield bonds, balanced funds, large-cap stocks, mid-cap stocks, small-cap stocks, developed economies international bonds, emerging markets international bonds, developed economies stocks, emerging markets stocks, commodities, and precious metals. If you are uncomfortable doing this yourself, consult a financial advisor.

Step 2 – Determine the specific changes you need to make, based on each asset class. For example, you may decide to move 5% from high-quality bonds to high-yield bonds, 10% from small-cap stocks to mid-cap stocks, and 5% from emerging market stocks to developed economy stocks, etc. Once done, the percentages need to be translated into specific dollar amounts, rounding them as appropriate.

For example, if you wish to move 5% of a $100,000 portfolio from short-term bonds into large cap growth stocks, you will need to sell $5,000 of the bonds and buy that same amount in large cap stocks.

Step 3 – Update your peer funds list. One method is to start with your original list of funds, broken down by asset class. To keep the list current, review a few "best of" lists from financial publications such as *Forbes* or *Money Magazine*. Determine which top- tier funds you wish to use for your comparisons. Typically, you won't need more than three to five funds in each of your investment categories.

Step 4 – Evaluate your current funds against your updated peer group. Your current fund does not have to be at the top of the list. Since you are comparing it to the best-in-class, it only has to be competitive within the group. After doing this process for a few years you may notice that the funds tend take turns rotating between top, middle and bottom of your *best of* list. In some cases a fund may even fall off the list for a year or two, only to reappear at a later date. This may be due to a change in management.

The goal of this exercise is to review the performance of your current investments relative to the top performers *in their peer groups*. A change may not be necessary if they have held their own within the group. If an investment in the portfolio has substantially underperformed for the year, you may want to put it on your "watch" list. If the fund substantially underperforms much longer than a year, it may be time to consider a change. Even exceptional funds will have an occasional *off year,* so it may be unwise to pull the plug too soon. Experience shows that it often pays to be patient with investments that have exceptional track records.

In this section we covered some of the most common mistakes investors make, and how we may be influenced by our subconscious minds. We also provided some practical tools and techniques that may help you to overcome some of those powerful influences. Simply identifying and being aware of your subconscious mind can go a long way in mitigating its influence over your decisions. Hopefully you will be able to use some of these techniques to make better financial decisions in the future.

EPILOGUE

The Dark Side of Behavioral Finance

"You don't know the power of the dark side Luke!"

Darth Vader, *Star Wars, Episode VI, 1983*

My goal in writing this book is to share with you my observations of 30 years as a financial advisor, coupled with my newfound passion for better understanding human behavior, and how it affects our daily financial decisions. I wanted to reveal to you the power of the subconscious mind, its influence on investing behavior, and how to use that information to make better financial and investment decisions.

I have focused on the risk of making potentially catastrophic financial decisions based on incomplete information, nonexistent patterns or nothing more than our emotional whims. In other words, we are human, and at times we don't act logically.

My intention is to get you to pay attention to your emotions and understand how they and your subconscious mind affect your decisions. By becoming more aware of these powerful psychological tendencies and biases, my wish is that you can decrease their influence on your future financial decisions. Hopefully, this awareness will help you make more conscious and logical decisions. Much of the information I researched came from academia, and the perspective of better understanding WHY investors behave (or misbehave) the way they do. As this fascinating world began to unfold in front of me, I came to realize just how powerful this knowledge was. My objective is to bring to your attention the war that is being waged for your mind—both internally and externally. Internally it's the ongoing struggle between the impulsive and emotional **Oscar**, and the more logical **Felix**.

But, fighting the external battle for your mind may be just as important. This external battle is being waged by advertisers, the media, Wall Street, corporations, politicians, and others. Their goal is to shape and influence your opinions and behavior. Much of the time we are not fully aware of their powerful influences.

This struggle for your mind can be compared it to the classic movie "The Matrix." The movie is about humans who are unknowingly living in an illusionary world driven by a computer program called the Matrix. It's a grand computer simulation game that controls the lives of humans. The humans are unaware that The Matrix had taken over, and completely controls every aspect of their lives. In the movie there were a small group of rebels who were able to *unplug* from this illusionary world. Seeing the reality, their goal was to expose the deception. At the end of the movie, Neo, the main character played by Keanu Reeves, could actually see the computer code all around him in real time. Only then did he fully realized that what he thought was the real world, was actually an illusion created by the computer "matrix."

This is similar to the way your mind operates. Our subconscious has created our own personal Matrix. Many times we make decisions that have been heavily influenced by our subconscious. How often have you looked back on a decision and thought to yourself, "what in the world was I thinking?" The truth is you may NOT have been thinking, at least not consciously. Your decision may have been unknowingly influenced by the "program" in your subconscious.

What defines a person's subconscious program? As I've discussed in the book, it's a combination of personal experiences, learned information, heuristic shortcuts, numerous biases, vivid memories, our emotions and perceptions, and millions of years of survival-based evolution. In addition to these internal factors, it is also heavily influenced by *external* forces, such as advertisers, the media, and public relation campaigns. This combination of ingredients produces our own complex, often conflicting subconscious "Matrix."

Once you begin to better understand human behavior, it is truly an enlightening experience. You start looking at the world, the people around you, and even your own decisions in a very different light.

Some researchers suggest that over 90% of our decisions are made when we are in a "normal" operating status—meaning

Oscar and **Felix** are cooperating with each other. The other 10% may be more heavily influenced by the more impulsive and emotional **Oscar**. We could break it down even further, and assume that perhaps 1% of those decisions could be considered critical, ones that could potentially carry more serious longer-term benefits or consequences.

In the end, it's how we perform during that 10% of the time, and especially that 1%, that can mean the difference between success and failure. That 10% may also be more stressful and emotional, and as we've discovered, that's when our decisions may be more heavily influenced by our subconscious mind (**Oscar**'s domain).

Most of our daily decisions are trivial—scratch your head, change the channel, take a sip of your drink. Most of the time we may not even recall making them. They were just instinctive, born in our subconscious. Occasionally though, a decision can carry longer-term, and more serious consequences. It's during these times that you need to have a calm and rational mind.

Hopefully, this book will provide you the incentive and tools to become better equipped to make more rational and logical financial decisions during those critical times.

Better understanding human behavior has helped me immensely, especially when dealing with people who may be in a stressful or emotional frame of mind. This has helped me to better guide them through the difficult decisions they must make during that difficult period of time.

It may be the loss of a loved one, going through a divorce, the loss of a job or just trying to cope with all the frightening news we hear on a daily basis. I try to help them see how these issues may be influencing their subconscious decisions; often I can see a light go on in their minds. Helping someone come to their own "ah- ha" moment can be very gratifying. Assisting them to be aware of their possible vulnerabilities, and how to make more rational and less emotional decisions, is the right way to use the knowledge of behavioral finance.

There is also a dark side to this knowledge. As with any discipline, knowledge can also be used for self-serving purposes. As in all sciences, there is always pressure to exploit knowledge or technology for business, political or personal gain. All too often, new breakthroughs that begin with the best of intentions in academia and the sciences can move quickly to the exploitation stage.

For example, from the early days of understanding human behavior, it didn't take long for advertising firms to figure out how to exploit that new-found knowledge to subtly influence peoples' buying behavior. And they certainly have perfected those techniques! From there, it didn't take long for politicians and others to harness the science of persuasion for their own ends.

To be effective, you may only need to influence or nudge relatively few people to accomplish your specific goal. That goal may be to convince people to buy a specific car, vote for a certain candidate or agree with a specific cause. It can also be used to influence people to buy specific investment products, or in an attempt to influence the general direction of an investment or the economy (animal spirits).

Being a relatively newer discipline, behavioral finance is still in its awkward adolescent stage, not quite knowing what it wants to be when it grows up. Up until more recently, it has been primarily in the purview of academics, whose research focused on WHY investors may behave the way they do.

That got me thinking. Once you understand how and why people tend to behave in certain ways, and how they make financial and investment decisions, it's a short leap to use that knowledge in an attempt to influence behavior. It is certainly possible to use this knowledge in an attempt to influence people's financial and investing behavior.

The "opt out" policy many companies have in their 401(k) plans for new employees is an example of how this research is being utilized. Many companies now have an "opt out" policy for their new employees, where employees are automatically enrolled in the company's 401(k) plan, using a predetermined formula and "balanced" investment option. The employee can choose to *opt out* if they do not wish to participate, or to change the investment allocation.

Instead of an employee having to decide whether or not they wish to participate, they are automatically enrolled, and the only decision they have to make is if they wish to opt out. While on the surface this may look like a very subtle change, it has had some very dramatic effects. Many companies that have implemented this policy have seen the employee participation rate increase dramatically.

Saving enough money for retirement and having a well-diversified portfolio is important for most employees, and helping people make the right decisions should be applauded. However, this seemingly subtle change is an example of how you can influence people's behavior by simply leveraging some basic human tendencies. In this case, it may be utilizing several behavioral finance lessons. The first could be the *herding* effect. Many employees may think, "Gee, if this is what everyone else is doing..." You may also be helping them set up an additional *mental account*, or simply confirming something that they already felt (confirmation bias).

This is an example of how knowledge of human behavior can be used for a good purpose. Thanks to the research and assistance of some of the pioneers in the field, many more employees are on a path to a more secure retirement.

As I began this research, I ran across several articles by practitioners both in and out of academia, who have become concerned that some of the research is being used by companies for their own benefit. While initially much of this research may have been used to teach their salespeople about the basics of behavioral finance, the concern is how much of this effort is also being used to subtly frame and influence investors' buying decisions.

This brings to mind a story someone once shared with me about why he quit smoking. He told me that more than 20 years ago he was a "social" smoker. He rarely smoked during the week, and typically would only smoke on weekends when he was out with friends. One day he was driving home from work, when he suddenly realized that he had a lit cigarette in his mouth. He had no recollection of actually putting it in his mouth and lighting it. This really bothered him since he prided himself on being a disciplined person.

The next day as he was driving home, it hit him. While driving, he noticed a large billboard with a cowboy on horseback advertising Marlboro cigarettes. He realized that this image must have influenced him to light up a cigarette. Being a control freak, he was so upset with himself that someone could have so easily influenced him, he decided to quit right then and there. The purpose of advertising may be to subtly implant an image in your subconscious that may in turn influence your behavior at some later date. In advertising, this is called subliminal messaging and it is rampant.

My concern is that investors may be influenced to make certain financial decisions or purchases that may not be appropriate or suitable for them. Or in a more general way, they may be influenced to believe certain market or economic condition exists, that may not be accurate. The manipulation of economic data and the use of animal spirits have been used for a long time. A better understanding of behavioral finance has made it that much easier and more effective.

As you examine the financial world, both past and present, you can observe many examples of events that don't seem to make much logical sense—times when logic would suggest a certain response to an event, but the opposite happens. Situations when the reported economic data doesn't seem to support your real-life observations.

It's almost as if you were observing a magician levitating an object, seemingly having the ability to defy gravity. Since the laws of gravity haven't changed, some other outside force must be at work, such as magnets or invisible strings. I use this analogy to caution investors that at times things may not be as they seem, or as they are being explained.

When markets behave irrationally, it may be convenient to simply excuse it as an example of "investors acting irrationally." While investors certainly act irrationally at times, it is also possible to leverage that irrationality by further feeding those emotions to take it to the next level. This is similar to the martial arts, where you leverage the existing momentum of an opponent to defeat them.

For example, if investors are already beginning to become nervous (or greedy), how difficult would it be to ratchet it up to the next level—to further feed the panic or greed? Large amounts of misinformation are constantly being disseminated; or information may be released to manipulate trends. With the aid of the internet, the media and some well-placed sources, is it possible to influence enough people to get a story or viewpoint to the necessary "tipping point" to have it become widely accepted? Many politicians and political groups use this tactic very efficiently.

The same can be said of financial and economic data. Be wary of data and information that doesn't seem to support the facts you can easily observe (or your gut feeling). If it looks like a duck, walks like a duck, and quacks like a duck, be skeptical of someone trying to convince you it's a horse. There is nothing wrong with having a *healthy* dose of skepticism. Rely on your trusted sources, and at the end of the day, go with your gut instinct.

As I did the research for this book over the past few years, I occasionally discovered some information that I found quite interesting or disturbing, but which didn't fit into the context of this book. The fact that the information didn't fit usually didn't deter me enough from pursuing the information a bit deeper. One bit of information led to another, which usually led to yet another. Some of the information is very intriguing as well as disturbing on many levels. It has significantly altered my views on Wall Street, the banking system, government influence, and the media.

As I finish writing this final chapter, I am already beginning to draft the outline of a follow-up book. When I originally began writing this book, I had no idea it would ultimately lead me to the following conclusion: At times I feel that we investors, both large and small, are being played like a violin. I have come to the conclusion that "much of what we think we believe, we have been *led* to believe."

I decided to add these final thoughts, not as a shameless promotion of my next book (OK, maybe just a little), but rather to serve as an additional wake-up call to investors. Not only do we need to be aware of our own self-imposed psychological influences, but we must be equally vigilant of the external attempts to exploit those weaknesses.

The working title of the sequel is "What's Hiding in the Shadows", and as the name implies, will examine the potential "forces" and the techniques that are being used to influence the investment and financial world. My preliminary research on this topic is proving to be truly disturbing. There is no shortage of credible information that shows how pervasive and effective this manipulation may be.

This type of research tends to be fragmented, and many times it's difficult to see where the initial trail may eventually lead. Many of the things I'm discovering don't tend to operate in the light of day, but prefer to operate in the shadows. Frankly, there are times I don't even want to believe some of the research, and where it appears to lead. The thing about shadows though, if you shine enough light on them, they tend to lose their effectiveness.

In the meantime, make sure you keep your **Oscar** in check, and **Felix** gets invited to all of your important decisions! And above all, remember: **E**vents **+** Your **R**esponse **=** Your **O**utcome!

A "Mind Map" of Money Brain

T he following diagram is a visual outline, or "**mind map**" of Money Brain that my friend Chuck Sarka created after he finished reading the book. If you are not familiar with this technique, a mind map is a diagram used to visually outline information. It is often created around a single word or topic that is placed in the center, to which associated words representing various concepts and ideas are added. Major categories, or "branches", radiate from the center, while lesser categories branch out from larger ones. These sub-categories can represent additional key ideas, tasks, or other items related to the larger branch it extends from.

The idea of mind mapping is to take notes along the same lines that your brain stores information. By using visual cues along with key words, your mind may be better equipped to recall the information at a later date. It can be used for just about anything, including books, lectures, brain storming and reports. It is especially useful for tracking wide ranging or complicated topics, and as a problem-solving technique. Its effectiveness stems from its use of visual aids, which makes it easier from the brain to store and recall memories.

I included Chuck's mind map to help you remember some of the ideas you learned in the book. If you examine it closely, you will see many of the key concepts we covered, and how they interact. Consider it your visual "Cliffs notes" of the book.

You will also find a color version of this mind map at our website www.**moneybrainbook**.com, which you can download or print for future reference. As you review the diagram, you will be amazed at how quickly the information you learned will come streaming back into your mind. I hope you enjoy it and find it useful, and that you share it with a friend or loved one!

If you would like additional information on mind mapping, I would encourage you to visit Tony Buzan's website at www.**tonybuzan**.com. He is considered the godfather of mind mapping, and has written several excellent books on the topic.

ACKNOWLEDGEMENT

One of the things I realized after I finished writing this book was just how much of it was attributable to *other's* people knowledge. Most of the information contained in this book came from people who are experts in their own fields. Much like an orchestra conductor, you can't make music without talented musicians.

I would like to acknowledge some of the excellent resources that I used while researching and writing this book. The authors of these books were invaluable in sharing their knowledge and information that this book was based on, and I could not have completed this project without them. I offer my apologies for any oversight if any ideas or concepts were not specifically footnoted at the end of a chapter.

I would also like to thank my editor Debra Bash. I'm sure at the onset she didn't fully appreciate the magnitude of the work she was signing on to. At times she must have thought that English was *not* my first language! In fairness, I still think that it should be perfectly acceptable to write an entire book in bullet points.

In addition, I would like to extend a huge thank you to the people in our firm who worked extremely hard during this arduous process, and allowed me the time to finish this project. Your insights, input and encouragement where invaluable. Also I want to add a special thank you to Diana

Melenick, my client manager, who went way above and beyond the call of duty. Besides my wife, she is probably the most relieved that the book is finally finished!

And finally, a big thank you to Kelley Drumm, our firm's marketing director, who coached me through the whole process of writing and publishing a book, and who kept my feet to the fire when I started to stray (which was often!). Thank you for keeping me in line and being so patient.

RESOURCES USED IN WRITING THIS BOOK

"**Behavioural Investing: A Practitioners Guide to Applying Behavioural Finance**" (The Wiley Finance Series), James Montier, 2007

"**When Markets Collide: Investment Strategies for the Age of Global Economic Change,**" Mohamed El-Erian, 2008

"**Animal Spirits: How Human Psychology Drives the Economy and Why it Matters for Global Capitalism,**" George Akerlof and Robert Shiller, 2009

"**The Black Swan: The Impact of the Highly Improbable,**" Nassim Nicholas Taleb, 2007

"**Thinking, Fast and Slow,**" Daniel Kahneman, 2011

"**Currency Wars,**" James Rickards, 2012

"**Your Money & Your Brain,**" Jason Zweig, 2007

"**Mind Wide Open: Your Brain and the Neuroscience of Everyday Life,**" Steven Johnson, 2005

"**Influence: The Psychology of Persuasion,**" Robert B. Cialdini, Ph.D., 2007

"**The Ascent of Money,**" Niall Ferguson, 2008

"Crystalizing Public Opinion," Edward Barnays, 1923

"Confidence Men," Ron Suskind, 2011

"The (Mis)Behavior of Markets," Benoit Mandelbrot, 1995

"Manufacturing Consent: The Political Economy of the Mass Media," Edward S. Herman and Noam Chomsky, 2002

"Propaganda," Edward Barnays, 1928

"Brain Rules," John J. Medina, 2009

"Public Opinion," Walter Lippmann, 1923

"Bailout," Neil Barofsky, 2012

"Why We Make Mistakes," Joseph T. Hallinan, 2010

"The Tipping Point," Malcolm Gladwell, 2000

"Bull by the Horns," Sheila Bair, 2012

GLOSSARY OF FINANCIAL TERMS

Asset Allocation – An investment strategy that aims to balance risk and reward by apportioning a portfolio's assets according to an individual's goals, risk tolerance and investment horizon.

The three main asset classes—equities, fixed-income, and cash and equivalents—have different levels of risk and return, so each should behave differently over time.[1]

Bear Market – A market condition in which the prices of an investment are dropping, causing widespread pessimism and negative sentiment among investors. The pessimism may continue, as investors confidence continues to erode. Typically, a drop of more than 20% in values over a few month period can constitute an official "bear market". A bear market differs from a "correction" in that corrections typically last less than 2 months.

The terms "bull" and "bear" when used to describe to describe investment markets comes from the way the two animals tend to attack their opponents. A bull thrusts its horns up into the air (upward moving market), while a bear swipes its paws down (downward moving market).[2]

Black Swan Events – An event or occurrence that severely departs from what would normally been expected, and that would have been very difficult, if not impossible to predict ahead of time. These events are typically seen as random and unexpected. The term "black swan event" was popularized by Nassim Taleb in his book "Black Swan". Some examples of "black swan events" would be a magnitude 10 earthquake, The Black Plague, and world wars. These rare events are often unexpected because they fall outside of our view of what is perceived to be "normal" (Normalcy bias).

Bond – The generic name for a tradable loan security issued by governments and companies as a means of raising capital. The bond guarantees its holder both the repayment of capital at a future specified date (the maturity date) and a fixed rate of interest (also known as the coupon). Bonds offer a greater certainty of income, (some bond issuers might default on payments) but may fail to keep pace with inflation. You only know exactly how much your bond is worth if you plan to hold it to maturity (when you will be paid back the face value). But in the time between issue and maturity, a bond's value can be volatile, so if you plan to sell before maturity you run the risk of capital erosion. When a bond's price falls, the yield—the income expressed as a percentage of the capital value—rises, and vice versa. In general: bond prices fall when interest rates go up (because the interest rate rise attracts money out of bonds into cash) and when inflation rises (as investors worry that bonds will not bring enough income to keep pace with inflation). [1]

Bull Market – The term "bull market" is often used to refer to the stock market, but can be applied to any investment, such as bonds, currencies and commodities. Bull markets are characterized by optimism, investor confidence and expectations that strong results will continue. It's difficult to predict consistently when the trends in the market will change. Part of the difficulty is that psychological effects and speculation may sometimes play a large role in the markets. [2]

Chartist – An investor who plots information about share prices and trading volumes on a chart, looking for patterns. Chartists, or technical analysts, believe they can see recurring patterns on charts that enable them to predict future price movements.[1]

Collateral Debt Obligations (CDOs) – A CDO is an investment-grade security backed by a pool of various other securities. CDOs can be made up of any type of debt, in the form of bonds or loans. These obligations are then divided into slices that contain debts with various levels of. These different slices of risk are referred to as "tranches." Each individual tranche can receive its own credit rating.

CDOs are constructed as a way of separating the different aspects of an investment to investors. For example, some investors may be interested in the cash flow of an investment while others may desire the potential growth aspect. Many times high quality investments are packaged together with lower quality ones, to get higher ratings from rating agencies, thereby making them difficult to distinguishable one from another.[2]

Consumer Confidence – Often expressed in the form of a numerical index and the result of a survey, consumer confidence measures the optimism of consumers in an attempt to forecast their future spending, which is a major influence on an economy's well-being. Forecasts about consumer confidence feed through into stock market prices, as analysts make predictions about the volume of goods which retailers will sell, and the prices they can get for them.[1]

Devaluation – A formal reduction in the value of a currency with respect to another, often from a pegged level, and normally sanctioned by a government or monetary authority. It is the opposite of revaluation. It contrasts with the depreciation of a currency over time, which is generally a steady or more modest change in value of a freely traded currency. [1]

Derivatives – A derivative is a contract between two or more parties whose value is based on an agreed-upon underlying financial asset, index or security. Common underlying instruments include: stocks, bonds, commodities, currencies, interest rates, and stock market indexes.

Futures contracts, forward contracts, options, swaps and warrants are common derivatives. A futures contract, for example, is a derivative because its value is affected by the performance of the underlying contract. Similarly, a stock option is a derivative because its value is "derived" from that of the underlying stock.

Derivatives are used for either speculating or hedging purposes. Speculators seek to profit from changing prices in the underlying asset, index or security. For example, an investor may attempt to profit from an anticipated drop in an index's price by selling (or going "short") the related futures contract. Derivatives used as a hedge allow the risks associated with the underlying asset's price to be transferred between the parties involved in the contract.

For example, commodity derivatives are used by farmers and millers to provide a degree of "insurance." The farmer enters the contract to lock in an acceptable price for his crops; the miller enters the contract to lock in a guaranteed supply of the commodity. Although both the farmer and the miller have reduced risk by hedging, both remain exposed to the risks that prices will change. For example, while the farmer locks in a specified price for the commodity, prices could rise (due to, for instance, reduced supply because of weather-related events) and the farmer will end up losing any additional income that could have been earned. Likewise, prices for the commodity could drop and the miller will have to pay more for the commodity than he otherwise would have.

Derivatives can also be used to either managing risk in an investment portfolio, or in an attempt to enhance the returns. When using it for defensive purposes, a derivative contract can act as a "hedge" by providing compensation in the event an unexpected or undesired event occurs. [2]

Dollar Cost Averaging – A plan which enables investors to accumulate shares in stock or a mutual fund by purchasing on a regular basis (for example monthly) with a fixed dollar amount. When the price is low, more shares will be purchased and fewer when the price is high. Also known as a constant dollar plan. [1]

Dow Jones Industrial Average – One of the main USA share indices which monitors the movement of 30 industrial companies traded on the New York Stock Exchange. The Dow Jones Industrial Average has just been joined by a new index, the Dow Jones Total Market Index, which covers a much broader range of companies.[1]

Earnings Per Share (EPS) – Total earnings divided by the number of shares in issue. EPS is a key ratio used in share valuations. It shows how much of the company's profits, after tax, each shareholder owns. For example, if a company makes a post-tax profit of $1.2 million and there are 20 million shares in issue, the EPS would be $0.6, or 60 cents. Earnings are normally shown for the previous year, based on actual data, but can be estimated for the current year or a future year. What is theoretically an easy calculation becomes complicated because the rules on what constitute earnings are fuzzy, especially when it comes to "extraordinary" items. Often when newspapers report EPS they use "adjusted" EPS (also known as "headline earnings") which strip out all profits/losses attributable to non-core activities.[1]

Efficient Frontier – A set of optimal portfolios that offers the highest expected return for a defined level of risk or the lowest risk for a given level of expected return. Portfolios that lie below the efficient frontier are sub-optimal, because they do not provide enough return for the level of risk. Portfolios that cluster to the right of the efficient frontier are also sub-optimal, because they have a higher level of risk for the defined rate of return. Since the efficient frontier is curved, rather than linear, a key finding of the concept was the benefit of diversification. Optimal portfolios that comprise the efficient frontier tend to have a higher degree of diversification than the sub-optimal ones, which are typically less diversified. The efficient frontier concept was introduced by Harry Markowitz in 1952 and is a cornerstone of Modern Portfolio Theory.[2]

Efficient Market Theory – The theory that claims that the current price of a share reflects everything that is known about the company and its future earnings potential, and that is it impossible to beat the market consistently. Efficient market theory suggests that active portfolio management is a futile exercise because everything they find out is rapidly transmitted around the market, and share prices instantly reflect the common knowledge. In other words, no one can get one up on anyone else.[1]

Fed Funds – Funds deposited by commercial banks at the Federal Reserve banks. To allow those organizations temporarily short of reserve requirements to borrow from those that have excess reserves. The rate of interest on fed funds, influenced though not set by the Fed, is a key short-term interest rate, changing daily.[1]

Federal Reserve System – The American central banking system which comprises 12 regional Federal Reserve Banks, their branches and all national and state banks within the system. The Federal Reserve sets monetary policy, regulating the flow of money and credit, in the US and regulates the banking system. Established in 1913.[1]

Financial Contagion – Financial contagion refers to a scenario in which small shocks, which initially affect only a few or a particular region of an economy, spread to the rest of and other countries whose economies were previously healthy, in a manner similar to the transmission of a medical disease.

Financial contagion happens at both the domestic and international level.

At the domestic level, usually the failure of a domestic bank or financial intermediary triggers transmission when it defaults on interbank liabilities and sells assets in a fire sale, thereby undermining confidence in similar banks. An example of this phenomenon is the failure of Lehman Brothers and the subsequent turmoil in the United States financial markets. International financial contagion, which happens in both advanced economies and developing economies, is the transmission of financial crisis across financial markets for direct or indirect economies.[2]

Financial Repression – A term that describes the means by which governments redirect funds to themselves to deal with excessive debt and the interest payments required to fund them. This concept was first used by Stanford economists Edward S. Shaw and Ronald I. McKinnon in 1971. Financial repression can include the following measures:

- Caps or ceilings on interest rates
- Government ownership or influence over domestic banks, insurance companies and other financial institutions
- Creation or expanding the purchases of government debt
- Restricting the entry to the financial industry
- Credit availability to selected industries[2]

Fundamental Analysis – A method of evaluating an investment that attempts to measure its intrinsic value by examining related economic, financial and other qualitative and quantitative factors. Fundamental analysts attempt to study everything that can affect the security's value, including macroeconomic factors (such as the overall economy and industry conditions) and company-specific factors (such as financial condition and management). Although primarily used to value stocks, this methodology can be used for a wide variety of investments.

The purpose of fundamental analysis is to compare an investments intrinsic value to its current price. Armed with that information, an investor can better determine whether the investment is underpriced (therefore buy it) or overpriced (therefore sell it). [2]

Gross Domestic Product (GDP) – The value of all goods and services created within an economy in a given year, equal to total consumer and government spending, and investment plus the value of exports, minus the value of imports. It equals gross national product minus income from abroad. In most countries GDP figures are released quarterly. The figures can be in nominal or real, inflation adjusted, terms.[1]

Initial Public Offering (IPO) – The first offering of a company's shares to the public known in the U.K. as a flotation. IPO was originally an American term but is now used across all world markets. The shares offered may be existing ones held privately, or the company may issue new shares to offer to the public. Companies choose to offer shares to the public to raise new capital for the company; to widen the shareholder base of the company; to give the shareholders a liquid market in which to trade their shares; achieve the publicity that a public listing brings.[1]

Internal Rate of Return – A measure of the return on investment taking into account both the size and timing of cash flows; alternatively, the interest rate which, when used as the discount rate for a series of cash flows, gives a net present value of zero. To understand this, remember that $1 received in ten years time is not worth as much as $1 received now because $1 received now can be invested for ten years and compound into a higher amount.[1]

Investment "Bubble" – A situation where the prices of an investment far exceed their intrinsic value. It could also be described as a situation in which the prices appear to be based on improbable expectations of the future. In an economic bubble, prices can fluctuate erratically, and become very difficult to predict simply by using fundamental analysis. Since it is often difficult to ascertain the true intrinsic values of investments in real-time, bubbles are typically identified only in retrospect, after a sudden drop in prices occur. These drops are known as a *crash* or a *bubble burst*. Both the boom and the burst phases of the bubble tend to be heavily influenced by psychological forces such as herding effect, group think, confirmation bias, recency bias, and overconfidence.

Junk Bonds – Bonds which offer high rates of interest but with correspondingly higher risk attached to the capital. In the U.S. they carry a credit rating of BB and below. Junk bonds fell into disrepute in the late 1980s, and are now termed 'high yield bonds'. [1]

Margin Account – An account with a broker where a client is able to purchase securities on credit after other securities have been deposited as collateral. The amount that can be borrowed depends on the type of security that has been put up as collateral.

Market Timing – Buying or selling securities in order to take advantage of the market's short-term movements. Decisions are often based on expected economic news or upcoming corporate announcements. It is regarded as the opposite of the "buy and hold" startegy[1]

Mid Cap – One of a trio of terms in common use to describe the relative size of a corporation. The others being small cap and large cap. The terms refer to market capitalization, but there are no fixed thresholds distinguishing one from the other, so the descriptions can be vauge.[1]

Modern Portfolio Theory (MPT) – An investment theory that asserts that investors can construct portfolios to maximize the expected return based on a given level of market risk, emphasizing that risk is an inherent part of an expected higher rate of return.

According to MPT, it's possible to construct an "efficient frontier" of optimal portfolios offering the maximum possible expected return for a given level of risk, by varying the proportions of the assets in the portfolio. This theory was pioneered by Harry Markowitz in 1952.

There are four basic steps involved in portfolio construction:

- Security valuation
- Asset allocation
- Portfolio optimization
- Performance measurement[2]

Monte Carlo Simulation – A problem solving technique used to approximate the probability of certain outcomes by running multiple trial runs, called simulations, using random variables. Monte Carlo simulation is named after the city in Monaco, where the primary attractions are casinos that have games of chance. Gambling games, like roulette, dice, and slot machines, exhibit random behavior.[2]

Mortgage Backed Security (MBS) – A security, backed or secured by one or, more typically, a pool of mortgage loans. Interest payments from the mortgage loans are passed on to the bond holders.[1]

Municipal Bond – In the U.S., a bond issued by a state, city or local government to raise money sometimes for day-to-day activities but often to pay for special projects such as infrastructure development of road, hospitals or sewerage systems. In certain cases, interest is tax exempt.[1]

National Debt – The sum indebtedness of a country's public sector (government debt) following cumulative annual budget deficits and surpluses. The debt is normally financed through the issue of government bonds, Treasury bills and Treasury notes. The government has to pay interest on its borrowings, and this obligation is one of the major budget items for many governments.[1]

NASDAQ – The first electronic stock market, which uses computers and telecommunications to trade shares rather than a traditional trading floor. NASDAQ is owned and operated by the National Association of Securities Dealers (NASD). It is the fastest growing major stock market in the world with well over 5,000 companies listed. Market makers compete to buy and sell NASDAQ-listed stocks of US and non-US-based companies via a worldwide computer network for large and small investors.[1]

"Negative Real Rate of Return" – When the interest rates paid on "safe" investments, such as Money Markets, CD's and short-term U.S. Treasuries, are paying less than the current level of inflation. For example, if the yield on a money market is 1%, and inflation is 3%, your real rate of return is negative 2%.

New York Stock Exchange – The world's largest stock exchange, based in New York and with a history traced back to 1792, with 2,700 companies, closed-end funds and exchange traded funds listed and a market capitalization of trillions of dollars. The NYSE is an international exchange, with many non-American companies listed. [1]

Oligopoly – The situation where a small number of firms control the supply, and strongly influence the price, of a good or service.[1]

Ponzi Scheme – A fraudulent investment scheme that promises high returns that are achieved only by using the inflow of new money rather than wise investment decisions. It is also known as a pyramid scheme. Charles Ponzi was an

Italian immigrant to the US who, in 1919, promised to double investor's money in 90 days. [1]

Price Earnings Ratio – The P/E equals the current share price of a company divided by its earnings per share in the latest reported period. For example, a company with a share price of 100 and earnings per share (EPS) of 5 has a P/E ratio of 100/5 = 20. A company's P/E (also known as its multiple) shows how high its shares are priced in relation to its historic earnings, and it is one of the most commonly used tests of market value. Although mathematically it relates share price to past performance, the reality is that P/E's are more about forward expectations than the past. A high P/E indicates that markets expect the company's earnings to grow rapidly in the future.[1]

Prime Rate – The interest rate which banks offer to their prime customers, that is, those with the most creditworthy records. [1]

Prudent Man Rule – An investment standard. In some U.S. states, the law requires that a fiduciary, such as a trustee, may invest the funds money only in a list of securities designated by the state, the so-called legal list. In other states, the trustee may invest in a security if it is one that would be bought by a prudent man of discretion and intelligence, who is seeking a reasonable income and preservation of capital. [1]

Put/call Ratio – The number of puts traded in a market in relation to the number of calls. Used as an indicator of market sentiment. [1]

Quantitative Analysis – A business or financial analysis technique that seeks to understand behavior by using complex mathematical and statistical modeling, measurement and research. By assigning a numerical value to variables, quantitative analysts try to replicate reality mathematically.

Quantitative analysis can be done for a number of reasons such as measurement, performance evaluation or valuation of a financial instrument. It can also be used to predict real world events such as changes in a share price. In broad terms, quantitative analysis is simply a way of measuring things. Examples of quantitative analysis include everything from simple financial ratios such as earnings per share, to something as complicated as discounted cash flow, or option pricing. [2]

Rate of Return – The measure of profitability of an investment. For a security, it measures the income obtained from an investment compared with its purchase or market price. For a company, it would be expressed as net profits divided by the capital employed. [1]

Real Return – The return provided by an investment after inflation has been taken into account. [1]

Regression Analysis – Statistical analysis that examines the correlation between two or more variables in a mathematical model and attempts to indicate whether the past relationships will be the same in the future. Regression analysis is used in the Black-Scholes option pricing model, portfolio theory and the capital asset pricing model. [1]

Reserve Requirements – The percentage of deposits that commercial lenders must by law have available as liquid assets or keep with the central bank. An increase in reserves forces lending to be reduced. [1]

Risk – The possible downside on an investment can take many forms including, for example, currency risk, country risk, inflation risk, market risk, political or settlement risk. [1]

Risk Premium – The expected additional return for investing in a riskier asset class over a less risky asset class. As an example, equities and corporate bonds have a risk premium over government bonds or inter-bank rates. [1]

Risk/Reward – Comparison of the returns that can be earned from different types of financial instrument (bank deposits, bonds, shares, unit trusts, investment trusts, property) and the risks that are attached to them. Government bonds are the safest investment as a government is most unlikely to default but the interest payable is relatively low. In contrast, investment in equities will normally give greater returns over the long-term but the risk is much higher as in the short-term they could easily fall in value. [1]

Rule of 72 – An arithmetic equation used to calculate how many years it would take for an investment to double in value, given knowledge of its annual rate of return and reinvestment (compounding) of income. The rule says that if you divide the compound growth rate of any investment into 72, you get the approximate number of years it takes to double your money. A return of 12% would double the investment in 6 years, while a return of 2% would double the money in 36 years. [1]

Secular Trend – A persistent or underlying trend in any direction of a longer-term nature than a temporary, cyclical or seasonal movement. [1]

Secondary Market – The trading of shares amongst investors which does not involve the company itself. When people talk about trading on the stock market, they are generally referring to the secondary market, which involves brokers, market makers and an exchange providing a technical platform for trades to take place. The companies and its shares are the subject of the trading, but they are not directly involved as participant's. The primary market refers to the situation in which a company sells newly issued shares to investors, possibly in an IPO, or places them with institutions. [1]

Securitization – The creation of financial assets by combining other similar assets, ranging from mortgages to royalties, and selling them in the new, tradable form to investors. [1]

Sell Side – A financial institution that sells expertise in research, order execution or any other service to an individual or institution. It has trading as its primary business in contrast to a buy-side organization that makes investments for itself or on behalf of others. [1]

Short Selling – A strategy that involves selling borrowed shares in the expectation that the price will fall and they can be bought back at a lower price later (thus making a profit). [1]

Small Cap – One of a trio of terms commonly used to rank companies according to their size, the others being mid cap and large cap. Cap is short for market capitalization, which is calculated by multiplying the number of a company's shares in issue by the market price. So a company with 500 million shares in issue and a share price of $50 has a market cap of $250 million. There are no fixed rules about where the thresholds lie. [1]

Stagflation – Economic stagnation (very slow growth, rising unemployment or recession) combined with high rates of inflation. [1]

S&P 500 Stock Index – The S&P 500, or the Standard & Poor's 500, is based on 500 leading companies in the U.S. stock market, as determined by Standard & Poor's. It differs from the (DJIA) due to its much larger and diverse base (the Dow consists of 30 stocks) and it's weighting methodology. It is the most commonly followed equity indices by professionals and many consider it the best representation of the overall stock market.

Stock – There are two commonly used meanings; first, it is the term for shares, i.e. the ownership stake in a company that represents a proportional claim on the profits of the company. The two main types of stock are common stock and preferred stock. Secondly, in accounting terms, stock refers to inventory Ð that is, goods that a company has produced but not yet sold. [1]

Stop Loss – A stop loss is a simple concept designed to limit losses on shares of stock. The investor sets a limit that when a share price falls to a certain level, the shares will be sold. The stop loss could be specified in percentage terms, being triggered by a price fall to, say, 90% of the purchase price or of its highest value. It does not however guarantee that the stop loss price will be achieved. [1]

Stop-limit Order – An order to buy or sell that goes into force as soon as there is a trade at the specified price. The order, however, can be filled only at the limit price or better.[1.]

Technical Analysis – A method of pricing publically traded stocks by examining their historical chart patterns and trends. Technical analysis uses tools such as bar or candlestick charts and trading volumes to determine the possible future behavior of a stock's price. Technical analysis involves examining the overall trend line of a stock's movement, and not necessarily the underlying fundamentals of a specific company or the economy at large. It is one of the two key methods of analyzing stock prices, along with fundamental analysis. And while the two disciplines are very different, they are often used in tandem as a way to double check the accuracy of the other.[2]

Thin Market – A market in which there are few bids and offers and few transactions occur, characterized by high spreads and volatility. This may apply to the shares of a specific company or the market as a whole. Sometimes also called a narrow market. [1]

Ticker Symbol – An abbreviation used to identify securities on the exchange floor, a screen, and a newspaper page or media outlet. The symbols were originally developed in the U.S. in the 1800s by telegraph operators to save bandwidth. One-letter symbols were therefore assigned to the most active stocks. Railroads were the dominant issues at the time, so they retain a majority of the one-letter designations. Each exchange allocates symbols for companies within its purview, working closely to avoid duplication. [1]

Total Return – The gain or loss on an investment that is made up of two components: income (dividends or interest) and capital growth (increase in the share price or bond price) and usually expressed as an annualized percentage in relation to the amount invested. [1]

Treasury Bill – A domestic government security usually with a life of 3 months but also up to one year maturity and considered to be a money market instrument. Such bills are issued at a discount and redeemable at par with no interest payable. They provide a principle way of financing borrowing. Other methods of government borrowing include the issuing of bonds, usually fixed interest, with a variety of redemption dates.[1]

Treasury Notes – Medium-term U.S. government negotiable securities with maturities of one to ten years.[1]

Treasury Bonds – Long-term securities with minimum denominations of $1,000 and maturities of ten years or more. [1]

Trend – A trend in a share price, whether upwards or downwards, which indicates an imbalance in the supply and demand for the share. When there are more sellers than buyers the trend will be downwards. When there are more buyers than sellers the trend will be upwards. If the number of buyers and sellers is roughly equal, the market will move sideways and the share price will stay within a 'trading range'

Once a trend comes to an end, it is usually reversed. So, if a downward trend is broken then it usually means the beginning of an upwards trend and for technical analysts this is a signal to buy. Similarly, if an upwards trend is broken, it is a signal to sell because the price is due to move downwards. If this is not obvious to you, try to think of it in terms of buyers and sellers: a downwards trend is caused by there being more sellers than buyers. If that trend comes to an end, the inference is that there is no longer a surplus of sellers and demand is beginning to outstrip supply. With fewer sellers compared to buyers, the price will be expected to rise.

As well as being classified by direction (upwards, downwards), trends are also classified by duration: Minor trends – last from a few days to several weeks. Intermediate trends—last from several weeks to several months. Major trends—lasts for anything from several months to several years. [1]

Uptrend – An uptrend line or rising trend is defined by successively higher prices for a share. There will be dips in the price throughout the uptrend, but each time the price drops, due to a small correction such as profit taking, the 'bottom' will be higher than the previous bottom. On a chart of price against time, you can draw a line connecting the successive bottoms. [1]

Valuation – The value or worth of a portfolio of investments (or an asset or company) recorded on a statement. A valuation will normally be partially subjective in the absence of perfect data. [1]

Volatility – A measure of a security's propensity, compared to other securities, to go up and down in price. A volatile share is one that has a tendency to move sharply through a wide share price range. Mathematically, this is expressed as the average standard deviation of daily price change from the average. In general, high volatility means high unpredictability, and

434 | MONEY BRAIN

therefore greater risk Đ but also greater opportunity to make money. Generally speaking, the higher the volatility of a share, the higher the price of option/warrants on the share will be. Historical volatility is a measure based on past performance while implied volatility is derived from the price of an option.[1]

Volume – The number of shares, bonds or contracts traded for a security or on a whole exchange for a given period, also known as market turnover. Low volume is sometimes referred to as thin trading. One significance of volume, particularly for technical traders, is that the higher it is, the more reliable the closing price is as a barometer of market sentiment. Conversely, when the volume is low the price may not be totally representative of the true value.[1]

Whipsaw – When a share price moves in one direction and then abruptly reverses direction. Whipsaws are dangerous to traders because the first movement may throw up a buy signal, completely wrong-footing the trader when the price subsequently tumbles.[1]

Yield Curve – A graphical representation that plots current yields of a set of bonds or fixed interest securities against their times to redemption (maturity). Yield is plotted on the vertical axis and time on the horizontal. This enables investors to compare the yields of short, medium and long-term securities at a given time. A normal yield curve is upward sloping, with yields rising as maturity increases. An inverted curve is the reverse.[1]

Yield Spread – The difference between yields on different types of bonds reflecting factors such as creditworthiness and supply and demand.[2]

---

[1] Source: FinancialGlossary

[2] Investopedia

GLOSSARY OF PSYCHOLOGICAL TERMS

Availability Bias – Describes the tendency to draw a conclusion about the probability of an event occurring based on the recollection of a similar past event. (Also referred to as "**availability heuristic**")

Anchoring – Describes the tendency of people to focus on a single factor as the primary reason for a decision or central explanation of an event. (Also referred to as "**insufficient adjustment**")

Bandwagon Effect – Describes the phenomenon of a group of people following a crowd, with an emphasis on social consensus rather than analysis. (Also referred to as "**herding**")

Confirmation Bias – Describes the tendency of people to seek and overweight information that confirms their views while avoiding or underweighting what is contradictory, albeit often inadvertent.

Disposition Effect – Describes the tendency of selling assets that are performing well and holding assets that are losing value. It can be characteristic of loss-averse investors.

Familiarity Bias – Describes the tendency of people to favor things they know over things they don't know.

Framing Effect – Describes the tendency of people to react differently to a particular choice depending on how it is presented.

Gamblers Fallacy – Describes the belief that if deviations from expected behavior are observed in repeated, independent trials of some random event or process, future deviations in the opposite direction are then more likely to occur.

Groupthink – Describes the tendency of individuals of a group to yield to the desire for consensus or unanimity at the cost of considering alternative options.

Heuristic – Describes the cognitive process of finding an acceptable solution by means of mental shortcuts to ease the cognitive load of making a decision.

Hindsight Bias – Describes the tendency to see events that have already occurred as being more predictable than they were before they took place. This allows investors to believe that they predicted a poor outcome all along when they had not. It reduces the probability they'll learn from their mistakes.

Illusion of Control Bias – Describes when people believe they can influence the outcome of events despite the fact that their actions actually have no effect on said outcome.

Immediate Gratification – Describes the tendency of short-term aims and wanting the rewards immediately rather than waiting to receive them in the future.

Loss Aversion – Describes the tendency to prefer avoiding losses to acquiring gains.

Mental Accounting – Describes the practice of separating assets and treating each asset as a discrete entity dedicated to a specific use rather than as an integral part of a total portfolio. (Also referred to as "**narrow framing**")

Optimism Bias – Describes the tendency of some people to believe that they are less at risk of experiencing a negative event compared to others.

Overconfidence Effect – Describes the tendency of someone's subjective confidence in their judgments is greater than their objective accuracy, especially when confidence is relatively high.

Pattern-seeking Heuristic – Describes the tendency of people to seek out patterns in an effort quickly decipher large amounts of information.

Pseudo-certainty Effect – Describes the tendency to overemphasize a risk-free solution and to miscalculate the relative probability of alternative outcomes when all the choices involve risk. Often the resulting choice is not the best choice available.

Recency Bias – Describes the tendency to weigh recent events as more likely or important than past events.

Representativeness Heuristic – Describes the mental shortcut that people take as they draw conclusions. These include making judgments about the probability of an uncertain event based on similar experiences.

Snake-bite Bias – Describes the tendency of people to avoid investment opportunities in sectors where they have previously suffered significant loss, even when that sector offers the potential for strong positive returns.

Made in the USA
Charleston, SC
25 May 2014